Organisational Behaviour
FOR
DUMMIES®

Organisational Behaviour FOR DUMMIES®

by Cary L. Cooper, PhD,
Lynn Holdsworth, PhD,
and Sheena Johnson, PhD

A John Wiley and Sons, Ltd, Publication

Organisational Behaviour For Dummies®

Published by
John Wiley & Sons, Ltd
The Atrium
Southern Gate
Chichester
West Sussex
PO19 8SQ
England
www.wiley.com

About the Authors

Cary L Cooper is Distinguished Professor of Organisational Psychology & Health at Lancaster University Management School. He is also Chair of the Academy of Social Sciences and President of the British Association of Counselling & Psychotherapy. Cary is Editor of the journal *Stress & Health* and the author or editor of many books and articles in the areas of organisational behaviour, stress, and wellbeing at work. He received a CBE from the Queen in 2001 for his contribution to organisational health.

Lynn Holdsworth, PhD, is a Chartered Psychologist. She lectures in work psychology and organisational behavior to undergraduate and postgraduate students at Manchester Business School (MBS) at the University of Manchester, and is a visiting researcher at MBS and Lancaster University. Prior to her academic career, she worked in human resources and in management positions in media and advertising.

Lynn is a qualified Life Coach and advises organisations and individuals in the areas of stress, empowerment, job satisfaction, and leadership development.

Sheena Johnson, PhD, is an Occupational and Chartered Psychologist. She lectures at Manchester Business School at the University of Manchester. She teaches work psychology and organisational behavior topics to undergraduate, postgraduate, professional, and international students. She is an active researcher into the topics of stress and health, and training.

Sheena is the author of numerous journal articles and book chapters on organisational behavior topics and regularly presents her work at national and international conferences.

Authors' Acknowledgements

From Cary: I would like to dedicate this book to all my postgraduate students who educated and stimulated me.

From Lynn: Thanks to my co-authors, work colleagues, and friends for your invaluable help and wise advice. To my husband, Phil; parents, Rita and Eric; boys, Kris and Lee; and parents-in-law, Dorothy and John. Many thanks for your support during the writing of this book.

From Sheena: Thanks to my co-authors and work colleagues for being so great to work with. Thanks to my family and friends for your continued and much-appreciated support and encouragement. Special thanks and love to my mother Elva, father Gwyn, and my two wonderful daughters, Keely and Bethan.

Publisher's Acknowledgements

We're proud of this book; please send us your comments at http://dummies.custhelp.com. For other comments, please contact our Customer Care Department within the U.S. at 877-762-2974, outside the U.S. at 317-572-3993, or fax 317-572-4002.

Some of the people who helped bring this book to market include the following:

Acquisitions, Editorial, and Vertical Websites

Project Editor: Steve Edwards

Commissioning Editor: Claire Ruston

Assistant Editor: Ben Kemble

Development Editor: Charlie Wilson

Copy Editor: Kelly Ewing

Technical Editor: Ashley Weinberg

Proofreader: Kim Vernon

Production Manager: Daniel Mersey

Publisher: David Palmer

Cover Photos: © iStock/Don Bayley

Cartoons: Rich Tennant (www.the5thwave.com)

Composition Services

Senior Project Coordinator: Kristie Rees

Layout and Graphics: Jennifer Creasey, Sennet Vaughan Johnson, Laura Westhuis, Erin Zeltner

Proofreader: John Greenough

Indexer: Christine Karpeles

Special Help

Brand Reviewer: Carrie Burchfield

Publishing and Editorial for Consumer Dummies

 Kathleen Nebenhaus, Vice President and Executive Publisher

 Kristin Ferguson-Wagstaffe, Product Development Director

 Ensley Eikenburg, Associate Publisher, Travel

 Kelly Regan, Editorial Director, Travel

Publishing for Technology Dummies

 Andy Cummings, Vice President and Publisher

Composition Services

 Debbie Stailey, Director of Composition Services

Contents at a Glance

Table of Contents

Introduction

Welcome to Organisational Behaviour For Dummies! We already know that this book is of interest to you – not just because you're reading this bit (although that does rather give it away), but because organisational behaviour is all about people at work. If you answer yes to the questions 'Are you a person?' and 'Do you work or plan to work?' then you can benefit from an understanding of organisational behaviour.

Organisational Behaviour For Dummies is meant to be fun to read, informative, and useful to you. We've bunched topics roughly into those that relate to employees, employers, and organisations, and you can dip into any topic you like without reading earlier chapters. Whether you're studying organisation behaviour or just interested because of what you see happening in your workplace, we're confident you'll find information of interest in this book.

About This Book

We authors have many years' experience (far too many to count and admit to) of teaching and training organisational behaviour topics. Our aim in this book is to introduce you to the key ideas and concepts that you'll find both interesting and relevant to your studies.

We introduce you to the main organisational behaviour topics and explain why applying organisational behaviour principles at work can help make organisations more effective. We cover lots of relevant research and theories as we explain, but we also give lots of examples and descriptions so that the book is as much practical as theoretical.

We introduce you to the ideas and theories underpinning organisational behaviour and look at how to apply them in the workplace. You can therefore easily find out about the things you can do based on the theory we describe. We have as many years experience of applying psychology at work and working directly with organisations as we do of teaching the theory. This extensive experience is important because it means that we know the issues that are relevant to organisations, and we've worked with *real people* as opposed to just knowing the theory. We tell you theory throughout the book, but we also give practical advice about what this theory means to you as a manager.

For each topic, we cover the key points in the area, which can mean covering well-known theory and old research. You may have already heard of some of this information, but much of it is probably new to you. We include theory where we think doing so helps you understand the topic now. If ideas and practice have changed over time, we talk about those changes, too.

As well as covering essential background, we bring the topics right up to date and consider what they mean to the organisations of today, and what you can do with the information.

Conventions Used in This Book

To help you navigate through this book, we set up a few conventions:

- *Italics* are used for emphasis and to highlight new words or defined terms.
- **Bold faced** text indicates the key concept in a list.
- `Monofont` is used for web and email addresses.

We try not to use jargon in this book, and when we do, we explain what we mean. We also restrict technical terms to those we think you need to know about. We're more interested in *why* things happen than using fancy words to describe them.

We have a lot of experience working directly with organisations using organisational behaviour techniques. So, where relevant, we use stories from our own experience to illustrate points we're making. Sometimes we adapt these examples to make sure that we don't breach confidentiality, but we leave the relevant points in.

Foolish Assumptions

We assume that you're reading this book because

- You're studying organisational behaviour and want an easy introduction to the topic.
- You're a manager who wants to better understand your own, and your employee's, behaviour at work and how this impacts other people and the organisation as a whole.
- You're simply interested in the topic.

We don't assume that you've work experience, and you don't need experience of organisations in order to gain an understanding of organisational behaviour. Having said that, we do use a lot of examples set in the workplace when we explain topics, so you may find it easier to understand some of the things we cover if you do have work experience.

How This Book Is Organised

We include theory and real-life examples in this book and give lots of practical advice and suggestions about the topics we cover. We divided the book into five parts, and each part contains two or more chapters. The following sections outline each part in turn.

Part 1: Getting to Grips with Organisational Behaviour

Before you look at the individual topics we discuss in later parts, check out Part I to get to grips with what organisational behaviour is and how an understanding of psychology and behaviour can help organisations.

This part gives you a good idea about the general topics that fall under the umbrella heading of 'organisational behaviour' and how people gather information on such topics (for example, through using workplace questionnaires or conducting face-to-face interviews with employees or managers). You find out here about changes that are happening in workplaces and how psychology can inform on these changes. You also start to discover how to best manage change (something we go into more detail about in Chapter 14).

Part II: All About the Employee

In Part II, we look at topics that relate to individuals and cover some of the ways in which people differ and how work can affect people.

Here, you find out about things like work attitudes, personality, and intelligence, and how they differ between people and what this means in the workplace. You explore the links between these things and behaviour at work and consider what this means for you as an employee or as a manager. You also find out how organisational behaviour can help you understand teams and groups, gain insight into why teams may fail and discover how to make your teams high performing.

Also within this part is a look at some of the negative things employees can experience at work, such as the costs and causes of stress, and how using your emotions in the workplace can negatively affect you. Throughout, we provide tips on how to manage stress.

Part III: All About the Employer

In Part III, we explore those organisational behaviour topics that we think are primarily under the control of *employers*.

Here, you find out about how different leadership styles influence people in the workplace and the different ways in which people can be motivated at work. You get to grips with some newer organisational behaviour topics such as the *psychological contract,* which is an unwritten agreement between employer and employee that can have negative consequences for both sides if broken or violated. This part also considers the importance of feeling fairly treated at work, and what can go wrong in a workplace if people feel they've been unfairly treated.

Part IV: All About the Organisation

In this part, we look at more general topics that affect organisations. You find out about the importance of job design, and how paying attention to job design issues can lead to more productive workplaces. You find out about *organisational culture* (the shared understanding in a workplace) and how important culture is, especially during times of change, and organisational change. You consider how people react to change and how to manage change.

Part IV also takes a look at the impact of an increasingly global workplace, and especially at how an understanding of different cultural values is becoming ever more important as organisations become more global. And in case that's not enough, technology also gets a look in here – how it has changed, and is continuing to change, and what impact this change has on organisations and work.

Part V: All About Hiring and Developing People

How can organisations hire, and retain, the best people? Part V takes a look at an organisation's key assets, people, from recruitment and assessment through to building the managers of tomorrow.

Part V delves into the variety of selection methods that are available to you and considers which of them work well and which work less well, providing advice on how you can put together a good selection process. In a similar manner, this part looks at assessment and appraisal issues and considers how you can successfully assess performance at work. Employee training and development, a consideration of the different types of training available to you and a look at how to best ensure that training transfers back to the workplace, wrap up this part.

Part VI: The Part of Tens

No *For Dummies* book is complete without the Part of Tens – a part full of handy chapters containing ten top topics or tips apiece. Here we offer a collection of interesting and helpful lists about hot organisational topics such as employee relations, stressed occupations, ways of managing your manager, up-and-coming organisational behaviour issues, and employee engagement.

Icons Used in This Book

Throughout this book, we use helpful icons to draw your attention to different information:

When you see this icon, we're highlighting a key point in relation to the topic. This icon flags information we think is worth remembering.

We use this symbol to represent practical tips and ideas in relation to organisational behaviour that you may find handy.

This icon signifies something you can't or shouldn't do, or something you should take particular care with.

The example icon highlights a real or made-up story that illustrates the topic we're discussing.

We use this icon sparingly, but when you see it, you find extra background or a detailed description of the topic.

Where to Go from Here

This book is an introduction to organisational behaviour. If you're a student, you can use it to find out about the basic principles of organisational behaviour and, if you're a manager, you'll benefit from the helpful tips throughout on how to get the best out of your employees. Throughout the book, we introduce key organisational behaviour concepts and theories and give practical advice and tips for how to put these into practice in the workplace.

You don't have to read this book from beginning to end (unless you really want to). We've organised it so that you look at employee, employer, and organisational perspectives, but each chapter also stands alone so that you can read the material in any order you like. If you're interested in team building, head on over to Chapter 5. Likewise, if you want the lowdown on motivation, jump straight to Chapter 9 and look no further! Just use the table of contents and index to help you find exactly what you need.

We hope you enjoy finding out about organisation behaviour.

Part I

Getting to Grips with Organisational Behaviour

The 5th Wave
By Rich Tennant

"I assume everyone on your team is on board with the proposed changes to the office layout."

In this part . . .

In Part I, we introduce organisational behaviour and work psychology and explain how an understanding of psychology and behaviour can help organisations. We briefly look at the variety of topics the book covers and consider how to gather information about such topics; for example, through using workplace questionnaires or conducting face-to-face interviews with employees or managers. We also think about what's going on in today's workplace and why applying psychology in workplaces can help organisations to be successful.

Chapter 1

Introducing Organisational Behaviour

*T*he three of us writing this book (Cary, Sheena, and Lynn) are all *work psychologists*, which means that we use some of the principles of psychology to study people and behaviour in organisations.

When asked, we tend to describe ourselves as work psychologists rather than organisational behaviourists. Why is that? Well, introducing yourself as a psychologist is bad enough with the questions that follow (for example, can you read my mind?). Imagine calling yourself an organisational behaviourist at a party – not the best opening line! At least people have heard of psychology, and it doesn't take too much thought to figure out that work psychology is basically psychology applied to the workplace.

You may be wondering, then, why this book isn't called *Work Psychology For Dummies* as opposed to *Organisational Behaviour For Dummies*? Well, organisational behaviour and work psychology look at similar ideas and have similar aims. Both involve looking at the ways in which people behave at work and what this behaviour means for organisations. However, the term 'work psychology' can imply a more focused look at individuals. Organisational behaviour, on the other hand, is a broader term because the name implies an *overall look at behaviour* (that is, from the perspective of people, groups, and the overall organisation), and that is our approach in this book.

We look at organisational behaviour in more detail throughout this chapter and focus on the application of organisational behaviour/psychology at work in Chapter 2. Reading these chapters gives you a good understanding of what organisational behaviour is and, perhaps more importantly, why it's relevant to you and your workplace.

Describing Organisational Behaviour

We define organisation behaviour for you in full in this section, but first take a look at the following questions. These questions are the sort that organisational behaviourists consider when looking at people at work. Having an idea of what questions are of interest in organisational behaviour gives you an understanding of what it is and why it's relevant to you and your studies or workplace. We provide answers to all these questions in different parts of this book.

Typical questions that an understanding of organisational behaviour can begin to answer for you are:

- What do you think about work?
- Why do you behave in certain ways at work?
- How do you react to the things that happen to you at work?
- What impact can your reactions have on the wider workplace?
- How does work affect you?
- What does your manager need to know about managing and motivating you at work?

If you're a manager, here are some more questions that organisational behaviour can begin to answer that you're sure to be interested in:

- What can I do to ensure that I recruit the best person for a job?
- How can I best motivate my employees?
- What is the best way to identify training needs in my employees?
- How can I instigate change without risking losing employee trust?

Offering a helpful definition

You can probably come up with an explanation of what *organisational behaviour* is without looking in a dictionary or searching on the Internet. It's how organisations behave, yes? And because you know that organisations aren't living things, then organisational behaviour has got to be about how the people and groups within organisations behave.

To elaborate a bit, here are some basic themes that cover what organisational behaviour is all about:

✔ Appreciating how people affect each other at work

✔ Applying knowledge at work based on what we know about how people act at work

✔ Understanding how people are affected by work

✔ Studying how people, individuals, and groups act at work

✔ Using organisation behaviour principles to improve an organisation's effectiveness and productivity

What organisational behaviour isn't

Organisational behaviour isn't about reading minds or reading body language. Organisational behaviour helps you understand how people behave at work and what's important to them and their organisations. But organisational behaviour doesn't give you amazing powers of insight so that you suddenly just have to look at people to know what their attitudes are toward things.

Organisational behaviour doesn't enable you to perfectly predict what will happen at any given time at work. Having an understanding of some general rules about the types of behaviours you may see at work doesn't mean that you can predict exactly how someone will behave!

Who Needs to Know about Organisational Behaviour?

Anyone who's ever worked, or who'll work in the future, can benefit from finding out about organisational behaviour – in other words, pretty much everyone needs to know about organisational behaviour! Organisational behaviour is all about people and work, so if you're a person who works or has worked, then this topic is relevant to you.

Understanding the ideas underpinning organisational behaviour not only gives you insight into past events but enables you to better predict what may happen at work in the future.

Understanding and using organisational behaviour principles in the workplace can help you keep yourself and others happier at work.

You may be reading this book because you're studying organisational behaviour (or work psychology). Indeed, this area of study is now more popular than ever. This growing interest is unsurprising because people now generally accept that looking at issues relating to staff in the workplace is an effective way of improving organisational efficiency and of supporting and encouraging employees.

Most organisational behaviour students are within the university sector, which has vast numbers of undergraduates, postgraduates, and professional training individuals. Many of these students go on to apply the principles directly at work either in their capacity as managers or as professional advisors with expert knowledge into organisational behaviour or work psychology.

Having work experience isn't essential, but it does make understanding some of the things that organisational behaviour covers easier.

You may already be in a managerial or advisory role, in which case this book is also aimed at you. Perhaps you want to better understand how to manage your people, in which case you need to know about organisational behaviour, too.

Organisational Behaviour in Action

People use organisational behaviour theories all the time in the workplace in a number of diverse ways. For example, managers can use these theories to attract and recruit the best candidates to a job position and also to handle downsizing and retirement issues so as not to lose the goodwill of remaining employees. We explore a wide range of organisational behaviour topics throughout the book and split them into three main areas:

- ✔ **Individuals:** Covers things such as what we know about the differences between people and how these differences affect behaviour in the workplace.
- ✔ **Employers:** Looks at things like how different leadership and motivational styles affect employees.
- ✔ **Organisations:** Includes things like looking at the culture of an organisation and considering how change can best be implemented.

Helping individuals at work

People differ in many ways. (In fact, Part II of this book is all about the individual at work.) Consider your closest friend. Clearly, you like that person, or she wouldn't be your friend. You probably don't agree on everything, though, which means you've different attitudes toward some things. You also have different personalities.

Take a minute to think about how you and your friend act (or would act) at work. Not always in the same way, right? Now think about what this means to an employer. Because people are different, they act in different ways at work. Understanding these differences can help you understand what happens at work and allow you to better manage situations.

Organisational behaviour research has taught us a lot about how people differ and also offers advice on how to understand and manage these differences to your advantage. For example, if you're hiring a new employee, then fitting the person to the job in terms of her personality and job requirements can lead to better performance and there being less likelihood of her leaving because she doesn't fit in. A lot is also understood about how attitudes affect behaviour at work. As an example, paying attention to keeping job satisfaction and employee commitment levels high should pay off in terms of good performance and employee willingness to help the organisation meet its aims and goals.

Topics we include under *individual* organisational behaviour are

- ✔ Personality and individual differences (see Chapter 3)
- ✔ Work attitudes (see Chapter 4)
- ✔ Working in teams and groups (see Chapter 5)
- ✔ Health and wellbeing at work (see Chapter 6)
- ✔ Emotion work: working with people (see Chapter 7)

Affecting the employer

Almost all organisational behaviour topics are of interest to employers, but in this area, we specifically focus on those topics that are mostly under the control of the employer. As an example, different leadership styles affects employees, and perceived unfairness from employers affects performance at work.

Understanding these issues and appreciating the influence an employer can have on the reactions of employees can help employers get the best out of their workforce and prevent them making expensive mistakes with how they manage people at work. (Part III of this book is all about the employer at work.)

In addition to looking at the key organisational behaviour topics such as leadership styles and motivation theories, we introduce newer topics, such as the *dark side* of leadership, which is where leaders behave in a manner that is destructive, and the importance of creating fairness at work if you want to get the best out of your employees.

Topics we include under *employer* organisational behaviour are

- ✔ Leadership at work (see Chapter 8)
- ✔ How to motivate your workforce (see Chapter 9)
- ✔ The *psychological contract* – the unwritten agreement between employer and employee (see Chapter 10)
- ✔ The importance of fairness at work (see Chapter 11)

Aiding organisations

Organisational behaviour doesn't just look at individual employees and employers; it also considers the organisation as a whole, looking at things such as how organisations can design jobs to achieve high performance and what advice exists for organisations that face major change events. Issues such as the culture of an organisation, why culture is important to employees and how employees behave at work are covered under the umbrella of organisational behaviour.

Organisations are facing times of great change. In addition to change as a result of the economic downturn, other changes are evident in the world of work, such as the increasingly global market that organisations now have to work within and the technology explosion that has occurred over the last few decades. Having knowledge of organisational behaviour can help you to understand and decide how to best manage these changes.

Here are the topics we include under *organisational behaviour*:

- ✔ Job design (see Chapter 12)
- ✔ Organisational culture and climate (see Chapter 13)
- ✔ Organisations and change (see Chapter 14)
- ✔ The global workplace (see Chapter 15)
- ✔ The impact of new technology (see Chapter 16)

Some areas affect all organisations that have employees. We include these topics in the *organisation* section because they're under the control of the organisation (even though they do relate to employees). These three topics are

- ✔ Hiring new employees (see Chapter 17)
- ✔ Assessing and appraising employees (see Chapter 18)
- ✔ Training and developing employees (see Chapter 19)

Studying People in Organisations

Organisational behaviourists go about studying people at work in a number of ways, including *testing* people and theories, *talking and listening* to people, and *watching* what happens in a workplace. We discuss each of these methods in more detail in the following sections.

The theories and studies we discuss throughout the book are based on information and data collected using these methods. We also have direct experience of using each of the methods in workplaces.

Testing

Organisations commonly use *psychometric tests*, which measure psychological attributes, such as knowledge, ability, intelligence, and personality. Individuals are often tested during recruitment, which we focus on in Chapter 17.

Looking more generally, testing is evident throughout organisational behaviour research in the form of *theory testing*. The term *theory* usually denotes something that's been tested or proven. Usually, when a study is designed to look at a specific issue, such as stress at work, researchers form *hypotheses* (ideas) about the likely links, such as increased exposure to stress at work causing poorer health. Researchers can then test these hypotheses through a study where both stress and health are measured and the relationship between the two examined. Studies and accumulating evidence that supports the links between stress and health then support the general theory that stress affects health.

Questions about organisational behaviour topics are developed into *hypotheses* that workplace studies can prove or disprove. Organisational behaviourists and work psychologists use the evidence that comes from such studies to develop theories about organisational behaviour topics.

An idea or thought that's not based on evidence can be wrong or misleading.

Asking and listening

Probably the most popular methods of researching organisational behaviour come under the broad heading of asking people things (either by talking to them or asking them to complete written questions) and then listening to what they have to say. This approach makes sense really. If you want to find out about what people think about work and how they behave, then you can't go far wrong by talking to the people involved.

Comparing people's responses to see whether they match can be an interesting endeavour. For example, we've talked to managers who state that their employees are happy, and yet the employees are quick to tell us they're not! Looking at misunderstandings between people and groups of people can be important to understanding organisational behaviour.

In Table 1-1, we outline key methods that fit under the heading of asking and listening.

Table 1-1	Asking and Listening Methods	
Method	*Advantages*	*Disadvantages*
Questionnaires	Cheap to use Can be completed by many people, so you can get information across an organisation fairly quickly	Made up of fixed questions, so you're unlikely to discover unexpected information Can be completed dishonestly or without much care, meaning that answers are of limited use
Interviews	Can give more detailed information than questionnaires Allow for information outside the remit of the questionnaire because you're not restricted by fixed questions	Are time-consuming Usually involve smaller numbers of people than a questionnaire study
Focus groups (usually between six and eight people)	Gives you perspectives on an issue from different people People can respond to each other's comments, which can open up interesting discussions that you may otherwise not uncover	People may not be as honest in a focus group as they can be reluctant to say things in front of others, particularly if they're people they work with and they've opinions that they think other people will disagree with or be unhappy about

Watching

You can find out a lot about people and workplaces just by watching what happens at work, such as through direct observation studies where you physically visit a workplace and observe behaviours directly.

Be careful with observation studies because you can affect how people behave because they know that you're watching. (For more on this subject, check out the Hawthorne studies that we discuss in Chapter 9.)

In addition to direct observation, organisational behaviourists also look at more general workplace information to try to understand work behaviours such as

> ✔ The type of work being done and the type of people in work (see Chapter 2 for more on this topic and how it is changing)
>
> ✔ Work laws, rules, and regulations, along with the changes that occur with them and the reasons for the changes
>
> ✔ Other indicators of work attitudes and behaviours, such as discrimination claims and the reasons cited

This kind of information can help you understand work attitudes and work behaviour, but you're limited on how sure you can be about the causes and reactions without directly researching the people involved.

Observing work behaviour indicators can give you ideas of areas you may want to investigate further.

What's in Store for Organisational Behaviour?

In the future, organisational behaviour studies will continue to investigate and understand workplace behaviours. Workplaces are constantly changing, meaning that we need to keep looking at new issues and recognise when organisations need to change to allow successful adaptation to new and changing situations. At the moment, you can see the most obvious example in almost all workplaces as organisations struggle to survive in difficult economic conditions.

Chapter 23 takes a look at up-and-coming issues in organisational behaviour and offers detail on what we believe are the key contemporary issues:

✔ Changing jobs and career development

✔ Happiness at work

✔ Health and wellbeing

✔ Managing constant change

✔ Managing post-recession

✔ The ageing workforce

✔ The new industrial relations

✔ Understanding management style

✔ Workforce engagement

✔ Work–life balance

Chapter 2

Working Nine to Five: Understanding Psychology and Behaviour in the Workplace

*A*s the business world becomes increasingly competitive, with profits more difficult to make, organisations are looking for new ways to be more effective and productive. In addition, the traditional workplace is changing with less focus on making things (manufacturing) and more on doing things for other people (service jobs). How jobs and the workplace are evolving changes employees' expectations and needs and, ultimately, impacts on how they behave.

The study of work psychology and organisational behaviour can help employers make the changes that they need, such as improving productivity and the quality of working life. Psychologists and organisational behaviourists develop theories, test them, and use this knowledge to meet the changing needs of the workplace.

In this chapter, we consider what changes to jobs mean to employees and employers and explain how psychology and organisational behaviour is useful in today's workplace. Understanding the changes to the makeup of the workforce and being aware of how they can affect employee needs are important parts of understanding organisational behaviour.

We talk about organisational behaviourists predominantly in this chapter, but don't forget that work psychologists do much the same job.

Figuring Out the Changing World of Work

The late twentieth century witnessed sweeping changes to the nature of work. Economic trends and technological advances, such as improved communications and the ability to work virtually, were at the root of many of these changes. (We look at the impact of these changes at work in Chapter 16.) One enduring trend is the movement of manufacturing jobs from developed countries to developing countries – a result of which is that job opportunities in the USA and UK are increasing in service industries but becoming scarcer in manufacturing. These changes impact on the type of leaders organisations require (see Chapter 8) and on employee expectations.

In the UK, USA and other developed countries, changes have also taken place in the working population, due to demographic patterns, legislation, and growth in higher education opportunities. For example, the average age of the working population and increasing life expectancy suggests an increase in the number of older workers and resulting challenges for organisations in terms of employee health; and an increase in the number of female workers can create a greater need for fairer selection processes (see Chapter 11) or more flexible working practices. Investigating the consequences of these, and many other, changes to the world at work are a large part of organisational behaviourists' roles.

Decreasing manufacturing, increasing services

Jobs are evolving, and change affects how you behave at work. For example, the development of machinery and technology means fewer people need to work in jobs with natural resources, such as mining and farming (the *primary* sector). Next time you see a farmer gathering crops using farm machinery, think about how many people would have been needed if crop gathering was still manual! A farmer working alone in a tractor behaves differently from a farmer working with a team of farm hands.

Over the last few decades, some countries have seen a large rise in the number of people working in the service sector – for example, in jobs within financial, business and information services, in hospitality, retail, insurance, and real estate. In countries like the USA and the UK, the majority of people work in the service sector (the *tertiary* sector), and manufacturing has decreased. In comparison, in poorer countries, most people still need to work in the primary sector – for example, in fishing, mining, and forestry. So, in the USA and the UK, around three quarters of people are tertiary workers, whereas in Nepal, over 80 per cent of people work in the primary sector.

China, meanwhile, has seen a drop in the percentage of people working in manufacturing, and the service sector is growing.

The worldwide trend is generally toward more service work. Managing an increasing service sector workforce successfully is paramount across much of the industrialised world. The study of organisational behaviour recognises the different challenges facing managers in the service sector compared to the manufacturing sector.

For example, in the service sector, satisfying customers is the key to an organisation's success, so employees need support to cope with the demands of difficult customers. If employees don't get the support they need, it has a knock-on effect: The employees feel under too much pressure, the stress may affect their health, and levels of customer satisfaction may get worse. This example demonstrates how an understanding of organisational behaviour can help employers. You can read more about issues specific to the service sector in Chapter 7.

Growing the female labour force

A large part of the changing face of the workforce is that women now make up half of the total workforce in the UK and USA and, in some regions, even outnumber men. Increasingly, women are becoming more and more important to the economy. Using established knowledge from psychology, we can predict the consequences. If employees are juggling a full-time job while rearing children, or caring for ageing relatives, their work–life balance can fall apart, and daily stress levels rise. (We discuss stress in Chapter 6.) The problem of managing family schedules and household chores can also put pressure on relationships at home in dual-income families, because deciding who does what around the house can become a bit of a battleground.

Considering different job roles

One challenge of understanding behaviour in organisations is the vast differences in job roles (and, of course, the differences between people – see Chapter 3). Understanding different work sectors and types of jobs can help you to appreciate aspects of employee behaviour. For example, the experience of someone working in manufacturing making things is different than the experience of working in retail selling things. Also, if you consider specific jobs, how different is working in nursing compared to working in investment banking? Have a look at Chapter 7 on 'Handling emotionally demanding jobs' to get an idea of what we mean.

Think about whether different types of people are likely to be attracted to different types of jobs. Jobs have a variety of motivations, rewards, and day-to-day tasks, meaning that the job your best friend loves may be one you hate. Just fitting the right person to the right job is important for the employee, in terms of health and wellbeing, and to the organisation in view of wasting money. (See Chapter 17.)

All these differences make the role of an organisational behaviourist challenging!

Organisational behaviourists look at how to redesign jobs so that employees can fit in family responsibilities without calling in sick or leaving their jobs. Proposing that employers offer options, such as *tele-working* (working from home – see Chapter 16), flexible working, job sharing, and part-time working (see the following section), for example, are possible responses to the increase of women in the work force that can benefit employees and organisations.

Increasing part-time work

Part-time work has become popular over the past 20 years because it can offer more flexibility for workers and employers. Being part-time basically means that you're not working as many hours as a full-time worker. As it presents a solution to combining family and work (see the previous section), the increasing availability of part-time work is helping the female workforce to grow, although the opportunity to take part-time work tends to be concentrated in lower-skilled, low-pay sectors.

Organisational behaviourists can help employers redesign work to be suitable for part-time workers, and as a result, these employers can reach out to a more diverse pool of workers. For example, you can attract more people to part-time work if you pay attention to these sorts of issues:

- Fitting work around family commitments
- Combining work with studies
- Returning to work after having children

But offering part-time work to employees isn't always straightforward for the employer. For a start, the employer has to pay to recruit and train more workers and the jobs themselves may offer limited career opportunities. How many part-time chief executive officers of organisations are there? Organisational behaviourists can apply their knowledge to guide employers around the pitfalls. For example, to get the most out of part-time workers, employers need to ask are people working part-time to maintain their work–life balance, or are they trapped in this type of work due to lack of choice? And if they feel trapped, how does this feeling affect their motivation to work? You can read more about employee motivation in Chapter 9.

Expanding graduate labour force

Higher education available for all and *up-skilling* the population is a growing trend. Is this trend a good thing? Is it changing the world of work? Can the labour market absorb this increase in the number of graduates? So many questions!

Organisational behaviourists can help employers understand the needs of graduates in the changing workforce. For example, you probably know someone who gained a degree and is now working in a fast-food restaurant. Organisational behaviourists call this *skill-mismatch*, *under-employment,* or *over-qualification,* and this problem is more likely to happen as a result of the recession. If an organisation is not prepared to find opportunities to utilise the graduate's abilities and skills, the graduate is likely to become demotivated and dissatisfied, which can lead to low productivity (bad for the organisation!) and poor psychological and physical health (bad for the employee!).

One of the many ways organisational behaviourists suggest that employers can get the best out of graduate trainees is to appreciate them and support them along their career path so that their investment in the new talent won't be wasted. Organisational behaviourists know that graduate career paths aren't clear-cut. Studies show that career paths evolve slowly, and it can take more than five years to settle into a career. This journey may involve further study, a number of false starts, and a few rethinks about initial career choices.

This type of knowledge can be useful for organisations to understand. For example, managers often look at a job applicant's résumé and dismiss it if the applicant left a number of previous jobs. A typical response is, 'What's the point of taking them on because they'll only leave?' But by knowing that some degree of job-hopping in a person's twenties is normal, the employer gains confidence in hiring the graduate.

In Chapter 19, we discuss general training and development principles that can provide support to your employees as they progress through their careers.

Changing age range

Following the Second World War, the UK saw an increase in babies born. This *baby boom generation,* born between 1945 and 1965, is now entering the older worker age range. By 2016, in the UK, the number of workers below 50 years old is likely to fall by 2 per cent, and those aged 50 to 69 are likely to increase by 17 per cent. And this trend is the same in the US and other developed countries.

Did you know that that if you're over 50, getting a job is a lot more difficult?

An understanding of organisational behaviour is useful here because we can help employers to appreciate that they need to do things differently:

✔ **Overcome prejudices within the organisation.** Despite anti-age discrimination regulations, some managers believe that you can't teach old dogs new tricks, particularly tricks that involve technology.

✔ **Change how they advertise and recruit employees.** Not all over 50s are up to speed with Internet job searching.

- ✔ **Look at existing training methods.** Something as simple as how you train employees can turn people off if you use inappropriate methods. For example, take into account older employees' existing experience and knowledge, as sitting through hours listening to what they already know may turn them off learning.

- ✔ **Understand how to keep an ageing workforce engaged.** Ensure that older employees feel valued through communication and feedback. Continue to revaluate career objectives, and be flexible over working hours (for example, by offering flexible working or phased retirement packages) and compensation packages (such as health insurance).

We carried out a series of interviews with staff in a large retail organisation. The aim was to find out what the employees thought about the continuous training and development on offer. (You can read more about training and development in Chapter 19.) The extra skills training was voluntary and consisted of working alone through manuals and filling in the exercises as you go along. The younger employees felt comfortable with learning this way, but few of the older employees bothered to pick up the manuals and learn the extra skills. The organisation presumed that the older employees couldn't be bothered to develop their skills and justified this opinion on the basis that they were too old to acquire new skills. Through interviews, we realised it wasn't that the older employees didn't want to progress; it was that they wanted to be shown how to do something by a real person and not a book. The organisation has now set up a mentoring scheme where the younger employees demonstrate their new skills to older employees.

You can find out more about how organisational behaviour can help alleviate age discrimination in Chapter 11.

Recognise that people respond differently to different opportunities and that they need different types of support.

Applying Psychology in the Workplace

Organisations can apply the principles of psychology in many ways in the workplace. For example, organisations can

- ✔ Update the design of jobs so that workplaces can function efficiently

- ✔ Understand what motivates people in the workplace to work harder

- ✔ Improve morale and job satisfaction, both of which are likely to lead to better performance

- ✔ Change employee behaviour, for example to meet legal requirements in areas such as health and safety and to prevent discrimination

In the following sections, we look in detail at how organisations can use psychology to increase productivity, improve morale, raise profits at work, and meet legal requirements.

Understanding and using psychology principles at work can help directly increase profits and reduce other things, such as turnover and absenteeism that negatively impact on profits.

Increasing productivity through better job design

You may be wondering how exactly psychology can impact productivity. Well, one famous example is the Hawthorne Studies (see Chapter 9), where employees were motivated to increase their productivity as a reaction to the attention given to them. It's not a huge leap from this study to realise that if you make sure that jobs are well designed, it can also affect productivity and efficiency in a good way.

How well you do your job can boil down to something as basic as how the job is designed. The strategy behind most job redesigns is part of an over- all plan by employers to get the workforce to work harder with fewer people and less money. However, based on knowledge of psychology, organisational behaviourists look at job design from a different approach and focus on how the redesign improves the quality of people's working life. For example, some people are satisfied by doing the same thing at work every day; they want to follow instructions and have no decisions to make. But other people are motivated by doing a job with variety that offers a challenge, gives responsibility, and allows them to do it the best way they can.

The basic approach to job redesign involves some, or all, of the following principles:

✔ Creating a meaningful job (that has a relevance to the organisation as a whole)

✔ Giving more control over how the job is done

✔ Varying the types of tasks or skills used

A few years ago, we went into a call centre. The customer service representatives didn't like the job and kept leaving. The job was simple: Answer the phone, follow a scripted conversation, pass the query to the correct department, and finish the call in no more than 2.35 minutes, and start the process all over again by answering the next call . . . Can you see the problem here?

The job was monotonous. Sometimes monotony is good – a chance to think about where to go for your summer holiday is handy – but not every day. The customer service representatives had no control over what they said, and even if they were able to solve the problem, they had to pass the customer on to the 'right department'.

We made some simple suggestions for redesigning the job following the principles we mention earlier in this section:

- ✔ Create a meaningful job by providing training to solve the customer's problems first time.
- ✔ Give some control over the conversations with less emphasis on scripts.
- ✔ Vary the tasks by allowing time to answer customers' emails as a break from the phones.

In other words, there was some variety, the staff had more control, and the employees had the satisfaction of making the customer happy. Before you run off and redesign some jobs, though, be aware that doing so is not always this simple – at least read Chapter 12 first!

You can change jobs in many ways:

- ✔ Get people to swap and change jobs with each other.
- ✔ Leave people to get on to do they job as they want to.
- ✔ Make the job more difficult – sorry, we mean more challenging.
- ✔ Put staff in a team and tell members that the job is all their responsibility.

Basically, the idea is that a person who's involved in their job views their role as important, feels good about what they do, feels satisfied, and as a result works harder towards organisational goals.

If a person is satisfied, they're more likely to have a positive attitude, experience high levels of morale, and be motivated to work harder for the organisation.

Improving morale

Morale and productivity are linked. So when you improve morale in the workplace, you improve productivity. In this section, we talk about the importance of getting motivation right. We also introduce other important areas, such as fairness and job satisfaction. These three areas are key to employee morale.

Motivation

Motivation is a driving force; what propels you to act. Understanding the psychology of why people are motivated to behave in certain ways at work is extremely useful.

The most basic example is that pay is often what motivates people to get up out of bed in a morning and go to work. Imagine that you were told tomorrow that you'd no longer get paid for the work you do! Would you set your alarm and get up early the next morning to head to work? Most people would probably decide that staying in bed was better than working for nothing.

Of course, people are motivated to work in a number of ways. Pay isn't the only motivating factor (although often the most important). Other motivators may be the opportunity to socialise with other people (a social motivator); the longer-term opportunities that a job may offer (such as gaining experience that helps you to further your career); or you may actually just want to do that particular job.

How organisational behaviourists look at motivating people at work is related to some of the changes in the workforce that we talk about in the earlier section 'Figuring Out the Changing World of Work'. For example, differences exist between what motivates younger compared to older employees, or women compared to men. Chapter 9 looks at motivation in detail.

Fairness

Fairness may seem an odd topic for organisational behaviourists to get involved with, but just stop for a moment and think about why fairness is so important at work. If you think about a time when you felt unfairly treated at work and remember how that made you feel, you can imagine how people may respond to unfairness. Not well! Fairness is one of the areas where psychology has a lot to offer the workplace.

Psychological research shows that people make changes to their work to make their situation fairer, even in some extreme cases to the extent of people stealing from work in order to redress the balance.

For example, imagine how you'd feel if the people you work with were paid more than you for doing the same job. You'd think it was unfair! The discrepancy may make you angry, and you may want to redress the balance in some way to make things more equal. One of the easiest ways to achieve this goal is to simply do less work. By doing less work, even though your pay is still lower than your colleagues, you can console yourself that at least you do less work than they do. The unequal levels of pay are then fairer. Although this solution may seem easy, morally, most people believe that working less hard is not the right thing to do.

You can read more about fairness in Chapter 11.

Demonstrating to organisations that employees may behave differently if they treat them fairly is important. If employees feel that they're being fairly treated, they're more likely to be motivated to do good work and to not take time off sick or leave the company – all of which is positive for both the organisation and the employee!

Job satisfaction

Job satisfaction is a useful psychological concept that organisational behaviourists draw on when explaining and changing employee behaviour. Employee satisfaction is often linked to employee health, and the productivity and profitability of organisations. Job satisfaction has an impact on organisations because dissatisfaction can result in people taking less care in their job or leaving; for employees, dissatisfaction affects stress levels and wellbeing. This area is one where psychology really focuses on making a difference in organisations.

By surveying the workforce, organisational behaviourists can find out what really satisfies and dissatisfies an organisation's employees. We can then make suggestions to increase employee satisfaction, including proposals such as

- ✔ Improving two-way communication
- ✔ Making work more fun
- ✔ Proposing different ways to reward or recognise employee performance
- ✔ Redesigning jobs

Job satisfaction is a work attitude, which we explore in Chapter 4.

Raising profits

Much evidence shows that paying attention to the areas we discuss in the previous sections on job design and morale can have a direct impact on profits. Quite simply, people are more likely to work hard for a company that treats them well – it makes sense when you think about it.

Organisations can also use psychology to positively affect aspects of work that influence profits, such as reducing absenteeism and improving employee wellbeing.

And what about employing the right person for a job? Psychology has a long tradition of developing selection and recruitment methods that can predict how well people are going to perform on the job. You can easily see how hiring people who are able to successfully do the work is far preferable to hiring people who are going to struggle.

Hiring the wrong person means that the new employee is likely to leave the job, and you have to hire again and hope to find a more suitable replacement. The cost of recruiting for that particular post is therefore at least double what it could have been!

We explore recruitment in more detail in Chapter 17.

Following legal requirements

Organisations have to comply with many legal requirements in order to operate successfully and safely, and psychology can help here. Some of the main areas that come to mind are

- ✔ **Discrimination:** Laws are designed to prevent discrimination. One example of where psychology informs the legal requirement of being non-discriminatory in the workplace is in the development of selection methods that aren't biased towards or against particular groups of individuals. We discuss selection in Chapter 17, and in Chapter 11 we explore discrimination in more detail.

- ✔ **Health and safety:** Psychological research shows how health and safety issues can be presented to a workforce to try to encourage safe working. It also helps to inform how high-risk organisations (like the oil industry) can manage in terms of creating a safety culture that helps reduce the number of accidents and injuries. Chapter 13 examines culture at work.

- ✔ **Stress management:** Organisations are increasingly looking at employee health and wellbeing at work in recognition of the links between health and wellbeing and organisational performance. Plenty of evidence shows that stressed employees perform less well and are likely to become ill, especially with prolonged and intense stress. The knock-on cost to organisations is substantial. We go into a lot more detail about this topic in Chapter 6.

Increasing the Relevance of Psychology

As the Western world slowly emerges from recession, the nature of work is unlikely to be exactly the same again. Consider a situation that many people now face: the organisation you work for is cutting costs to survive the downturn in business, or as a response to public spending cuts, and as a result jobs are being lost or changing. How do you feel, and will you behave differently at work?

Thinking from an organisational behaviourist perspective, here's a likely negative scenario. You're feeling insecure, so you make sure that you're present in the workplace and work longer hours. You're feeling more stressed, overloaded with your redundant colleagues' work, and less inclined to be cooperative with your remaining work colleagues. You're looking after number one. The more information you share, the less valuable you are, and the more vulnerable you become. And tactical meeting attendance becomes the game. Meetings are a great way to find out what's happening, to increase visibility, and be seen to work hard – but they're a waste of time unless they're short and focused.

And what are the consequences? From an individual perspective, consistently working long hours eventually damages your health, as well as your private and family life. From an organisational perspective, spending longer hours at work (we call this *presenteeism*), and as a result becoming less effective, increases organisational costs and reduces profits. And as we explain in Chapter 6, presenteeism actually costs an organisation more money than absenteeism.

From experience of organisations and employee **behaviour**, organisational behaviourists can advise managers what to do to survive: and flourish in the long run. For example, managers can

- ✔ **Appreciate the importance of team work.** Managers can cut down on the growth of the self-interest agenda, which makes teams less effective and productive. Organisations need to focus on team directives, not individual directives. Managers need to think about incentivising teams and not individuals.

- ✔ **Increase employee resilience.** Understanding employee wellbeing offers numerous effective interventions to help people be more resilient when they get to work.

- ✔ **Get support.** Being a manager is easier in good times, but in bad times (with fewer resources and demotivated employees), good management is more of a challenge. Managers need support and relevant training to cope.

Part II

All About the Employee

The 5th Wave — By Rich Tennant

...and finally, do you feel well connected to the other members of your department?

In this part . . .

In Part II, we focus on those aspects of organisational behaviour that relate to individuals, thinking about the ways in which people are different and the different reactions to work that people can have. We cover personality, intelligence, and attitudes, and how each influences behaviour at work. We also take a look at how individuals work when they come together in teams and groups. Finally, we discuss how work can take a toll on people in terms of stress and emotional reactions.

Chapter 3

Getting to Know People: Personality and Intelligence Differences

In This Chapter

▶ Exploring personality theories

▶ Using personality at work

▶ Predicting behaviour through personality

▶ Seeing how intelligence plays a part at work

*P*art II of this book looks at employees; we can think of no better way to start Part II than by exploring how individuals differ, and how these differences impact the workplace. People have different hopes, fears, talents, experiences, beliefs, attitudes, and ways of thinking. You explore some of these differences in later chapters. But a lot of the differences between people can be said to boil down to personality, so in this chapter, you take a look at different theories of personality, at how personality is used in the workplace and how personality is linked to behaviour. We also discuss intelligence as another key difference between people and consider how intelligence is measured and used in the workplace.

So why look at individual differences like personality and intelligence? Well, understanding and measuring the ways in which people differ from one other enables you to see whether they act and perform in different ways at work because of those differences. Researchers have conducted many studies in these areas, which means that a lot is known about personality and intelligence. So, for example, knowing what type of personality is likely to be best suited to certain jobs and how levels of intelligence can affect job performance. This information is useful if a manager wants to hire somebody to work in his business.

Defining Personality: Type Versus Trait

Personality is people's tendency to act and think in certain ways. If you were asked what type of personality you have, you may reply with something like outgoing or adventurous, or perhaps reserved or quiet. In fact, how you decide to describe yourself reveals a bit about the person you are and the things you're likely to enjoy doing (assuming that you're telling the truth, of course; we discuss lying in the later 'Matching personality to the job' section). Of course, even a person who has an outgoing personality sometimes acts in a reserved and quiet way – for example, when he's attending a funeral. The situation a person is in affects his behaviour just as much as the type of personality he has.

Psychologists have proposed a lot of different ways of looking at personality over the years, which isn't surprising given people's interest in understanding why they and others act the way they do. This section gives you a whistle-stop tour of the main personality theories and then looks at the two most popular personality theories that psychologists use in the workplace to predict and explain behaviour, that is the type theory of personality and the trait theory of personality.

Reviewing personality theories

Psychologists have proposed several theories to try to explain and understand personality and how it affects behaviour. Different people agree with different theories and no *definite* agreement of personality exists – just suggestions for what it may be. The following list gives you an overview of the main theories.

- **Biological theory:** *Biological theories* of personality are based on the premise that personality and behaviour are related to purely biological factors (nature). Any difference between people is therefore based on biological differences and not differences in upbringing or experiences. Most people now accept that biology alone can't explain all personality differences.

- **Environmental theory:** *Environmental theories* go to the other extreme and propose that personality differences are all due to environment (nurture) rather than biology. In other words, your family and friends influence your personality. Of course, this theory is too simple a picture, too! Most theorists now agree that *both* biology and environment – both nature and nurture – are important to personality and behaviour.

- **Social learning theory:** *Social learning theory* is environmentally based but has been so influential, it deserves a bullet point of its own. This theory proposes that personality develops through socialisation with other people and that you find out how to behave by watching what other people do. In the most famous experiment of social learning theory, researchers found that if children watch adults being violent when they play with a doll and then see this behaviour approved of by another adult, then the children are more likely to be violent to the doll when they're given the chance to play with it. If, however, the children see an adult disapproving of the violent behaviour, then they were less likely to show aggression.

✔ **Psychoanalytic theory:** Psychoanalysts place a lot of emphasis on the unconscious mind and on how thoughts and motivations we are not aware of influence behaviour. The most famous psychoanalyst was Sigmund Freud, who, as well as talking about the unconscious mind a lot, also said that personality comprises three facets:

- **Id:** Controls instincts and looks to bring you pleasure.

- **Superego:** Provides you with a conscience and morals.

- **Ego:** Strives to meet the desire of the Id without compromising the superego's moral stance.

For example, say that you see a fantastic-looking slice of lovely, gooey, chocolate cake. Your id says, 'Eat it now'. Your superego says, 'But you're on a diet. You'll feel bad if you eat it, so leave it on the plate.' Your ego then mediates between these two and decides on your actual course of action. (To be honest, we'd probably have eaten the cake by now . . . .)

✔ **Humanistic theory:** *Humanistic theory* suggests that your personality is driven by the desire for self-development. You want to grow as a person and acquire new knowledge, and this desire influences the way you behave. Organisational behaviourists use humanistic theory in workplaces to try to understand and predict work behaviours, but mainly as a way of explaining motivation rather than as a true personality theory. Abraham Maslow and his hierarchy of needs is the most famous humanistic theory, and we discuss this more in Chapter 9.

✔ **Type theory:** *Type theory* sees personality as belonging to distinct groups (so you must be 'this' or 'that' type of personality).

✔ **Trait theory:** *Trait theory* sees traits as being on a continuum, so you can be anxious, a little anxious, or not at all anxious, for example, rather than being just one way or the other (as type theory would suggest).

Work psychologists measure personality and use the information they obtain to try to predict behaviour (check out the later section 'Assessing Personality to Predict Behaviour' to find out more) and their studies have revealed that personality is linked to performance at work. The two theories from the preceding list that they use most in the workplace when doing so are type theory and trait theory. The following sections provide more detail on type and trait theories.

Seeing personality as black and white with type theory

Type personality theory splits people into two main types when describing personalities. For example, in type theory, you describe yourself as introverted or extroverted, pessimistic or optimistic, disorganised or organised.

Take a look at Figure 3-1, which shows the personality types pessimistic and optimistic for four people: Alan, Becky, Colin, and David. If we accept that people can have different degrees of optimism and pessimism, then the curve shows how some people are low on optimism or pessimism, some people high and most people are around the middle. Type theory, though, forces people to be described as one thing or the other (here, pessimistic or optimistic). Under type theory, Alan and Becky are both described as pessimistic people, whereas Colin and David are seen as optimistic people. So far, so good. But an obvious problem exists. Look at the positioning of Becky and Colin. Despite being seen as having different personality types, they're actually the closest of all the people to each other, and so are the most similar of the four people. How does that similarity happen?

Type theory can be useful when making clear distinctions between people and is commonly used in the workplace in personality type questionnaires based on the Myers-Briggs Type Inventory (MBTI). The MBTI splits personality into four key areas, with two main personality types in each area, as shown in Table 3-1. Sixteen potential combinations derive from these personality types. How easy would you find it to place yourself in one of these types? Are you a thinker or a feeler? An extrovert or introvert? Looking at personality in this way can help to explain similarities and differences between people, but using distinct types means that you lose some detail.

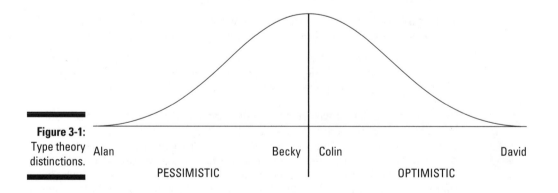

Figure 3-1:
Type theory distinctions.

Alan   Becky | Colin   David

PESSIMISTIC   OPTIMISTIC

Table 3-1	MBTI Personality Types
MBTI Personality Type	*Description*
Extroversion/introversion	Extroverts enjoy interaction with other people, whereas introverts prefer to be alone. Extroverts like to work in teams, whereas introverts are more reflective and reserved.
Sensing/intuiting	Sensors have a preference of gathering information using their senses, so they enjoy working with facts and information. Intuitors, on the other hand, are good at working with possibilities and the abstract and theoretical.
Thinking/feeling	Thinkers like to make decisions in a logical, objective way, whereas a feeling person makes decisions in a more personal way.
Judging/perceiving	Judging people like structure and are decisive and time oriented. They like to be organised. In comparison, perceivers like flexibility and spontaneity. They prefer things to be open ended rather than rigid and organised.

One of the advantages of type theory is its simplicity. The theory is easy to understand and easy to communicate and use in the workplace. However, the simplicity of type theory is also the source of its major criticism: Can you really distinguish between people in such a simplistic way? Is everyone optimistic or pessimistic? Surely you could describe two people as optimistic, and yet they could be optimistic to different degrees? Another criticism is that by forcing people into distinct categories, type theory ignores some of the similarities between people. So, type theory can be limiting.

Taking the broader view with trait theory

The trait approach to personality has been influential in work psychology and has allowed work psychologists to make a lot of links between personality and work behaviours. (See the section 'Predicting Behaviour Using Personality,' later in this chapter.)

Trait theory is different from type theory (see the previous section) in that it sees personality characteristics as on a *normally distributed continuum.* This term sounds highly technical but it simply means that some people are low on a trait and some people are high, but most people are around the middle. Figure 3-2 illustrates this point, focusing once more on extroversion. (You may recognise this curve from Figure 3-1.)

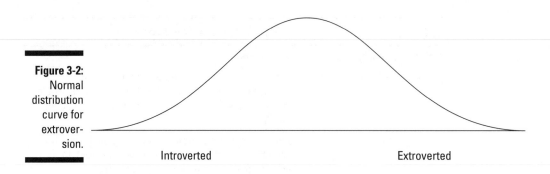

Figure 3-2:
Normal
distribution
curve for
extrover-
sion.

Introverted   Extroverted

Trait theory proposes that people can be at the extremes of a personality trait, but they can also be anywhere between the two. So unlike type theory, which allows you to compare people only in categories, trait theory gives you more detail. This additional detail makes comparisons easier and allows a better understanding of which personality traits are linked to which behaviours.

Trait theory proposes that personality traits influence the way people act and behave and that although behaviour differs depending on the situation, the underlying personality trait is still important in explaining why people behave the way they do. Trait theorists believe that traits are stable in adulthood, so although your personality may change a bit as you get older you're pretty much the same person in your 60s as you were in your 20s, 30s, 40s, and 50s.

If you've taken a personality test during a job interview, you may well have come across a personality questionnaire based on the work of Raymond Bernard Cattell, a famous personality trait researcher. The 16PT is a personality questionnaire that provides information on Cattell's 16 personality traits. (Can you guess where they got the name from?) You can see these 16 traits in Table 3-2.

Compare Table 3-2 to Table 3-1 on the MBTI from the previous section and consider the amount of information provided by the two. Clearly, you discover a lot more about a person using trait theory rather than type theory. Remember also that type theory only tells you that a person is in one category or another, whereas trait theory tells you where a person sits on a continuum for each trait.

Trait theory is more useful than type theory in the workplace because it gives more detail about personality. However, some people disagree and argue that type theory is the one they feel more comfortable using.

Both type and trait theories are used at work but remember the limitations of type theory if you decide to use it.

Table 3-2	Cattell's 16 Personality Traits
Personality Trait	**Brief Description**
Cool/warm	From cool and reserved to warm and outgoing
Concrete thinking / abstract thinking	From *lower intelligence* (thinking based on facts and descriptions) to *higher intelligence* (thinking involving abstract mental processes)
Affected by feelings/ emotionally stable	From less stable and easily upset to emotionally stable and calm
Submissive/dominant	From co-operative and conflict-avoiding to forceful and assertive
Sober/enthusiastic	From serious and restrained to lively and enthusiastic
Expedient/conscientious	From a disregard to rules and self-indulgent to dutiful and conscientious
Shy/bold	From shy and easily intimidated to bold and thick-skinned
Tough-minded/ tender-minded	From unsentimental and tough to sentimental and sensitive
Trusting/suspicious	From trusting and not suspicious to sceptical and distrustful
Practical/imaginative	From practical and solution-focused to impractical and absent-minded
Forthright/shrewd	From open and forthright to discreet and diplomatic
Self-assured/apprehensive	From confident and secure to worried and insecure
Conservative/experimenting	From traditional and conservative to liberal and open to change
Group-oriented/ self-sufficient	From affiliative to individualistic
Undisciplined/controlled	From impulsive and careless to self-disciplined and a perfectionist
Relaxed/tense	From relaxed and patient to tense and impatient

Using Personality in the Workplace

In the previous section, we outline some popular theories for exploring personality. The next questions, of course, are, 'So what? Why examine personality? What does personality tell you?' Well, different personality theories explain quite a bit about behaviour. This section introduces three influential personality theories – Type A and Type B, locus of control, and the Big 5 – and describes what they reveal about behaviour and how they're used in the workplace.

Type A and Type B, locus of control, and the Big 5 are all based on trait theory, so they see personality as being on a continuum.

Considering Type A and Type B personalities

Are you a Type A or Type B person? If you've already come across these terms, you may already know. If you haven't yet heard these terms, you can do a personality test that tells you. Having said that, we reckon you'll have a good idea which type you are if you read this section.

Type A or Type B personality descriptors come under trait theory. (For more on trait theory, see the earlier section 'Taking the broader view with trait theory.') Traits are on a continuum, so, for example, you can be highly Type A or slightly Type B. Here's a basic overview of Type A and Type B personalities:

- ✔ **Type A:** High Type A means that you're competitive, high achieving, aggressive, hasty, impatient, time conscious, and hard driving. Type A people tend to be workaholics.
- ✔ **Type B:** High Type B is the opposite to Type A. Type B people are less competitive and tend to be more relaxed and fun loving.

The work attitudes and behaviours of Type A and Type B people differ, and both have their strengths and weaknesses, as outlined in Table 3-3.

What type of jobs suit Type A and Type B people? Well, Type B people may be more team or person-based and well-suited to jobs in which they can use their skills of empathy and patience. Type A people are well-suited to jobs in which they've a lot of control and are constantly faced with challenges they can throw themselves into. Type As can thrive in these kind of conditions and are commonly high achievers.

But health risks are associated with being Type A, especially if you've a high need for control in your job and you don't have it or it's taken away from you. In fact, in the 1950s cardiologists identified the Type A and Type B patterns of behaviour and discovered that in a study of more than 3,000 employees, Type A men had more than twice the rate of coronary heart disease than Type B men. (For more on stress, see Chapter 6.)

Table 3-3 Comparing Type A and B Personalities in the Workplace

Type A Personality	*Type B Personality*
Tend to work long hours	Tend to be productive under stress
Are constantly under deadlines and overload conditions	Are relaxed and patient and have a lot of self-control
Take their work home with them	Do not get irritated, angry, or frustrated easily
Find it hard to relax	Aren't particularly competitive
Have a habit of not taking vacations or cutting them short	May be tolerant and flexible and can change in order to adapt to situations
Like to compete with themselves and others	Tend not to overreact and do not mind waiting to get work done
Often drive themselves to meet high (and sometimes unrealistic) standards	Like to plan things in advance and keep aware of time available and deadlines
Can feel frustrated at work	Rarely complain or worry
May be irritated by the work efforts of subordinates	Do not constantly wish to lead or be in control
May feel misunderstood by superiors	Are emotional and not indifferent toward other people

Think about whether you'd rather be managed by a Type A or a Type B person? You may choose Type B because that person's likely to be the easiest to work with. But will a Type B manager keep the business going? Perhaps a Type A person who's hard driving and ambitious would be best for this role? Probably the best manager is someone who isn't too far in either extreme!

Looking at locus of control

How much control do you have over your life and the things that happen to you? If you believe that you're in control and can influence what's going on around you, you've what's called an *internal locus of control*. If, however, you think that events are out of control and things just happen to you, you've an *external locus of control*. Your belief about the amount of control you have over your life is an aspect of your personality and influence how you see your life.

People with an internal locus of control put good performance at work down to their abilities and effort and believe that they did well because they tried hard.

An internal locus of control means that you feel you can influence events around you, so if you work hard, you perform well. Compare this attitude to people with an external locus of control. If they perform well, then they believe it's because of luck or chance and that nothing they did influenced the outcome in any way.

Here are a few locus of control facts:

- People with an internal locus of control enjoy better health and greater job satisfaction, even more so for women than for men.
- People tend to get more internal as they age.
- People in management and leadership positions tend to be more internal.
- Internals tend to be better off financially (possibly due to being higher achievers and having better jobs).
- Some people believe that locus of control is linked to the situation and is not just a personality trait.

Generally, you're probably better off having an internal locus of control rather than an external. For example, imagine that you're the manager of someone with an external locus of control. How would you motivate the employee to work hard if he believes he can't influence the outcome and that doing well just boils down to luck and not effort? However, in some instances, having an external locus of control is useful. For example, if major work changes occur that are out of your control, having an internal locus of control can be more stressful than having an external locus of control. Overall, though, internals tend to fare better than externals.

The Big 5 personality traits

Probably the most famous and most commonly used personality theory in the workplace (and elsewhere) is the Big 5. Unsurprisingly, this theory has five personality traits. An easy way to remember the traits is to use the acronym OCEAN:

Openness

Conscientiousness

Extroversion

Agreeableness

Neuroticism

As trait theory (see the earlier section 'Taking the broader view with trait theory') dictates, the traits are on a continuum. Table 3-4 outlines the five traits of the Big 5.

Table 3-4	The Big 5 Personality Traits
Personality Trait	*Brief Description*
Open to experience/closed to experience	From open to new experiences and imaginative to less open to new experiences, narrow-minded, and unimaginative
Conscientious/disorganised	From well-organised, focused on targets, goals, and deadlines, dependable and good at paying attention to detail to impulsive, disorganised, and less detail-focused
Extroverted/introverted	From outgoing and good at dealing with people (managers tend to be above average on extroversion) to less outgoing, comfortable in own company or that of their close friends
Agreeable/tough-minded	From usually good natured, keen to co-operate with others, takes care to avoid conflict, easy to get on with, and not argumentative to unfriendly, strong-willed, and not averse to conflict
Neurotic/stable	From a tendency to experience negative states, such as anger, anxiety, and guilt, to stable, rarely upset, and typically calm

You can probably see how you may describe yourself in relation to these traits and recognise traits in friends and colleagues. You've no doubt got a tough-minded pal who tells the truth about something even if you don't like it and extroverted friends you'd invite out to the pub. You may also recognise the neurotic friend who panics over everything and blows the smallest problems into huge issues. Is this description ringing any bells?

Finding the Big 5: The lexical approach

Early personality researchers had the bright idea of looking at language to see the different ways in which people are described and created huge long lists of different terms that relate to personality. They argued that any important differences between people would have been recorded in language at some point, so where better to look when trying to find out about personality? As you can imagine, lot of words describe people – one of the surveys done discovered over 17,000 different words!

When investigated, though, these words all related to five basic personality factors, and the Big 5 was discovered. And the Big 5 exists across nationalities, such as American, British, Chinese, Czech, Dutch, German, Hebrew, Hungarian, Japanese, Korean, Polish, Portuguese, and Turkish. What is really impressive about this list is that researchers compiled it before computers were available, so all the analysis was done by hand.

What's really interesting about the Big 5 theory is that it can incorporate all other theories of personality. Research has shown that even where personality theories propose more than five factors (for example, Cattell's 16 factors; see the section 'Taking the broader view with trait theory'), they can all fit into the five-factor theory of personality.

The Big 5 is an excellent theory to use to predict behaviour in settings such as in the workplace. Take a look at the 'Assessing Personality to Predict Performance' section below where you'll find more on how the Big 5 is linked to work performance.

Assessing Personality to Predict Behaviour

The previous sections in this chapter demonstrate ways to measure and use personality theories, such as the Big 5 at work, to describe and compare people. So what? Is it at all useful to be able to say that one person is more extroverted than another? Well, yes, when knowing that someone's personality traits help you predict their behaviour.

Researchers have conducted lots of studies and have discovered that individual or combinations of personality traits predict:

- Job performance
- Academic success
- Mortality
- Divorce
- Alcoholism
- Health behaviours
- Drug use

Personality relates to academic success and job performance. As a result, you can use personality questionnaires in the workplace to look at what types of personalities are likely to perform best at different types of jobs. Employers commonly do this kind of thing when selecting employees.

This application of personalities makes sense when you think about it. Say that you want to employ a sales manager. Would you want an introverted person who isn't hugely outgoing or an extroverted person who's outgoing and good at dealing with people? Now, unless you've an odd idea of what a sales manager does all day, you've probably decided that an extrovert would suit the job best.

Some people are clearly better suited to certain jobs than others. Looking at personality and job characteristics allows you to match up people to jobs in a logical manner.

Performing and personality

A recent study of the Big 5 personality traits (see the earlier section 'The Big 5 personality traits') showed that four of the five factors were related to job performance:

- ✔ Conscientiousness predicts performance across most jobs and organisational settings.
- ✔ Openness to experience predicts training performance.
- ✔ Emotional stability predicts job performance.
- ✔ Extroversion predicts performance for some jobs (for example, sales).

As well as overall job performance, personality traits relate to detailed aspects of work, such as how dedicated people are to their jobs and how likely people are to be absent from work. Table 3-5 shows areas in which researchers have found links between personality and work behaviour.

Table 3-5	Work Behaviours Linked to Personality
Overall Job Performance	*Counterproductive Work Behaviour*
Getting ahead	Procrastination
Task performance	Absenteeism
Training performance	Team performance and teamwork
Learning and skill acquisition	Job and career satisfaction
Organisational citizenship	Subjective wellbeing
Altruism	Innovation
Job dedication	Creativity
Overall managerial effectiveness	Goal setting
Promotion	Managerial level
Turnover	

Matching personality to the job

EXAMPLE

When interviewing for a job, organisations commonly ask candidates to complete a personality questionnaire. But what does a personality test look for?

Take the following example ad:

> **DATA PROCESSOR REQUIRED.** *CLS Ltd. Hours of work 9–5. You will be required to manage incoming data, check for duplications and errors, mail merge data, and produce weekly reports. Good IT skills are essential.*

Just by reading the advertisement, you can identify some of the qualities a person who would do well in the job would possess. For example, he needs to be happy working on his own because he'll likely spend most of his time working with data rather than people. He also needs to have good attention to detail because he'll be required to check for errors and mistakes and produce reports. What personality traits would you look for in the applicants then? Probably a more introverted than extroverted person and somebody who's conscientious rather than disorganised.

Of course, personality assessment isn't as crude as this example, and you wouldn't just guess at the personality factors that would fit the job. Loads of research in this area can tell you what to look for and how to go about it – flick to Chapter 17 for more on using personality tests in selection.

You may be thinking at this point that personality testing is all very well, but what's to stop somebody lying when he fills out his questionnaire? For example, an applicant may pretend he's extroverted to get a well-paid bar manager job he wants rather than staying in work as a data processor. Well, for one thing, why would somebody want a job that he's obviously not going to be suited to and may hate? More seriously, though, most personality measures have lie scales built into them that assess whether or not people are providing the answers that they think people want to hear rather than telling the truth. An example of a lie scale is a simple question like, 'Have you ever told a lie?'. The assumption is that nobody can really say 'no' to this question, so if you do you must be lying!

Measuring Intelligence

The previous sections look at how people differ in terms of their personality, but that's not the only difference between people. Another important difference between people, often used in the workplace during selection as a way of identifying the best candidate, is that of intelligence.

Intelligence – also known as general intelligence (g), cognitive ability and general mental ability – is a person's general mental ability to understand things around him. You use your intelligence to try to figure out solutions to the problems you're faced with. Researchers believe that intelligence is inherited, to a point; some researchers say up to 80 per cent of intelligence is inherited whereas others suggest environmental factors can contribute up to 50 per cent.

Intelligence has a normal distribution curve (see the earlier section 'Taking the broader view with trait theory'), so some people have low intelligence, some people have high intelligence, but the majority of people are around the middle and have average intelligence.

Researchers also believe that in addition to general intelligence, you can measure different types of intelligence, such as

- ✔ **Visual/spatial:** Being able to make sense of visual images, such as reading a map (if you struggle with map reading, you're probably low on visual/spatial intelligence).
- ✔ **Perceptual speed:** Being able to identify and understand objects quickly.
- ✔ **Reasoning:** Being able to solve complex problems.
- ✔ **Numerical skills:** Having good mathematical ability.
- ✔ **Learning and memory:** Having the ability to recall knowledge.

Looking at intelligence in more detail allows you to assess how well people are likely to perform in different tasks. This assessment is especially useful in the workplace. Some jobs, such as being a pilot, require good visual perception, whereas others, such as acting, call for good memory skills. Measuring intelligence can therefore help you match people to job requirements.

Having higher-than-average levels of general intelligence is thought to increase the chances of being successful at work and in life in general. Intelligence has been linked to educational achievement, better finances, social status, and – most important for this discussion – work performance. People with higher general intelligence are more likely to be effective at work, especially in complex or difficult jobs. They're able to pick up jobs quicker and are more likely to acquire knowledge and succeed in training.

To best predict success at work, you can look at specific types of intelligence that are relevant to the job. For example, an accountant will probably perform better if he has high numerical skills and may have less need for visual/spatial skills.

Testing intelligence

You can assess somebody's intelligence by how well he performs at problem solving. You can probably think of somebody you believe to be low on intelligence because of his poor problem solving. (We won't ask you to name names, of course.)

Many intelligence tests exist that are designed to measure general intelligence or the subscales of intelligence. Most people have at some point completed an intelligence test for fun (you can find plenty of intelligence tests online if you fancy a go) or as part of a career interview (to see what your skills are) or job application (to see whether your skills match the ones needed to do the job).

Intelligence tests often standardise the scores and results, so the test reviewer can compare people easily. When standardised, the midpoint of the normal distribution curve (that is, the average intelligence level) is set at 100. About two-thirds of people have scores between 85 and 115. Any score below 100 is seen as below average intelligence, and any score over 100 is seen as above average intelligence.

One study looking at predicting job performance compared many different assessments of new recruits, such as interviews, references, personality tests, intelligence tests, and work sample tests. Intelligence was the best predictor of performance of all the different assessments except the work sample test. A work sample test, where the candidate spends time completing work similar to that he would do on the job, can be expensive and time consuming to set up. An intelligence test, in comparison, is quick, cheap, and reliable. No wonder they're used so much in the workplace to identify good candidates for a job! (To find out more about intelligence assessments and other tests, see Chapter 17.)

Intelligence tests have issues, so you need to use tests that don't discriminate and are fair. See Chapter 11 for more on fairness at work.

Valuing emotional intelligence

Emotional intelligence is often seen as a new concept, mainly due to the popular success of psychologist Daniel Goleman's book *Emotional Intelligence: Why It Can Matter More Than IQ* in 1995 (Bloomsbury Publishing Plc). The idea that people have emotional intelligence isn't really that new, though. Researchers have been discussing emotional intelligence since the 1930s.

Emotional intelligence is the ability to

✔ Perceive emotion

✔ Reason using emotion

✔ Understand emotion

✔ Manage emotion

Studies looking at performance and emotional intelligence have reported links between the two, suggesting that the higher your emotional intelligence levels, the better your performance (for some tasks at least). Emotional intelligence has been shown to predict

- ✔ Classroom performance of managers
- ✔ Sales performance
- ✔ Performance on group tasks
- ✔ Potential leadership ability
- ✔ Good customer interaction
- ✔ Leaders ability to manage employee job satisfaction
- ✔ Supervisory ratings of work performance

Emotional intelligence is important when you're working with other people. If a job involves working with colleagues, employees, or customers, then having good emotional intelligence is likely to make the job easier to do for many reasons:

- ✔ **Customers respond better to emotionally intelligent staff.** Think about being faced with an angry or upset customer. Understanding why the customer is angry and controlling your own emotions during the customer interaction are both really important to how well you perform your job and how happy the customer is. (We discuss these emotional demands of jobs in Chapter 7.)

- ✔ **Managers with higher levels of emotional intelligence are better able to understand the feelings of their employees and can use this information to better manage the workplace.** If a manager giving a performance review understands that an employee may be disappointed or upset by negative feedback, he may take care to handle feedback sensitively and ensure that the employee has the opportunity to ask any questions. If the manager doesn't realise the possible emotional reaction of the employee (because he has low emotional intelligence, for example), he may be too blunt with his comments and leave the employee feeling demoralised and upset.

Dispute exists as to whether emotional intelligence is an ability you're born with or something you can develop and improve. However, some organisations and business schools train people in emotional intelligence and they report success, so it seems that emotional intelligence can be taught to some extent. The development of emotional intelligence training proves that a demand exists for these types of skills in the workplace.

How emotional intelligence benefits organisations

The following examples illustrate the impact of emotional intelligence in the workplace.

- Salespeople selected partly on the basis of their emotional abilities outsold sales people selected using 'normal' methods. They were also less likely to leave the organisation.

- In an insurance company, salespeople high in emotional abilities sold more than double the policies of those salespeople who had lower emotional abilities.

- Executives who were low in emotional ability encountered problems with handling change and working in teams and also had poor interpersonal relationships.

- Following supervisor training in emotional skills at a manufacturing plant, accidents and complaints plummeted. Similar training in another plant led to increased profits.

- High-performing debt collectors were found to have better emotional skills than lower performing debt collectors.

Chapter 4

Having the Right Attitude at Work

*A*ttitudes are important when you're at work: fact. The way you think about your organisation and your employers influences the way you behave at work, so things like the quality of the work you do, customer satisfaction and whether or not you remain in your job are all affected by your work attitudes.

This chapter describes what attitudes are and why they're important in the workplace. We discuss how you can predict some work behaviours based on the attitudes that people hold. As well as general attitudes at work, you explore two areas where attitudes have a huge impact: job satisfaction and work commitment. You look at these relationships in terms of what they mean in the workplace and explain why organisational behaviourists are so interested in them. Finally, we offer practical information about measuring attitudes and trying to change attitudes in the workplace.

Understanding Attitudes

Attitudes are settled ways of thinking or feeling that range along a continuum from positive to negative. When asked, most people can explain what their attitude is toward something. For example, if someone asked you what you thought of capital punishment, you'd probably find it easy to get into a discussion about what you believe is right or wrong about the death penalty. Of course, people also hold attitudes toward less important (in our opinion) issues such as whether or not drugs should be legalised and how important it is to attend church each week. People have a multitude of attitudes toward the beings and things that surround them.

So in the workplace, you've attitudes toward different aspects of your job and the people you work with, and these attitudes affect your behaviour.

Breaking down attitudes

Attitude theory views attitudes as comprising three elements, a view that is known as the *tripartite view of attitudes*:

- ✔ **Cognitive (what you know):** Thoughts, ideas, and beliefs
- ✔ **Affective (what you feel):** Feelings and emotions
- ✔ **Behavioural (what you do):** Behaviours and actions

Usually, when people talk about attitudes, they're referring to the cognitive and affective elements, so attitudes are based on what you know and what you feel. The way in which you behave is often seen as an *outcome* of attitude rather than a component of it.

Often the cognitive, affective, and behavioural elements of attitudes are consistent with each other, but they can be inconsistent. This inconsistency is partly why making the distinction between the different aspects of attitude is useful.

For example, imagine that you're a student supplementing your income by working while going to school. The job you're doing isn't something you want to do with your career, but the pay isn't bad and the hours suit you. What attitude do you have toward that job? Well, you may feel that the job is boring, and you just want to get your shift over with each time you go to work (affective attitude). However, you may also realise that this job is the best way to earn the money you need for your studies, and so believe the job is worth showing up at and doing well (cognitive attitude). These two elements aren't matched: one attitude is a negative view, and the other is positive. Both these attitudes affect your behaviour at work and depend on what's most driving you at a given time. If you're focusing on your future career and studies, you probably continue to work hard. If, however, you focus on how you feel day to day, you may party a little more and work less. Ideally, you want to work in a job that you both think and feel positive about – a good reason, then, to study hard to get the job you really want . . .

Here are other points to ponder. Attitudes are

- ✔ **Internal:** You can't look at a person and know what her attitude is toward something, although you can (and do) look at the way in which somebody is behaving and try to figure out what her attitude is likely to be. However, you can't be sure that you interpret behaviour correctly. For example, if you see someone drop coins into a charity collecting tin, you may believe that she has a positive attitude toward that charity.

You may be right, but not necessarily. The individual may be donating the money in order to impress the sexy charity collector holding the tin and not even have noticed which charity she's donating to!

✔ **Unstable:** Attitudes are more changeable than personality. You can probably identify with this point and think of ways in which your own attitudes have changed over the years. For example, when you were little, you probably believed that all adults were old, dull, and boring, and yet hopefully as an adult, you've now changed this attitude somewhat.

✔ **Formed by experiences:** Evidence suggests that attitudes are linked to genetics. Some studies show that identical twins hold similar attitudes, whereas fraternal twins' attitudes differ more. However, although a genetic link may exist, most people agree that attitudes form as a result of experiences (the classic nature/nurture debate – see Chapter 3 for more information). So, we mean here the things that happen to you influence your attitudes. Say, for example, that someone walked into the room where you're reading this book and started to yell at you for being lazy and not reading fast enough. You'd (quite rightly) form the attitude that this unreasonable person likes to shout at complete strangers. That scenario has nothing to do with genetics, but everything to do with the context of the situation.

Having an attitude at work

Needless to say, people have numerous attitudes about their jobs, their workplaces, and the people they work with. You may love your job and like the people you spend your days with at work, or you may be unlucky and hate your job and have nothing in common with your colleagues. In the first case, you may have a positive work attitude, while in the latter situation, you may have a negative work attitude.

You can have an attitude toward many things at work. Some common workplace attitudes are toward

✔ The organisation you work for

✔ The work environment (the physical place where you spend your time)

✔ The tasks you do day to day

✔ The amount of pay you receive

✔ The type of supervision you have at work

✔ The people you work with – colleagues, managers, supervisors

✔ Your customers (if you have them)

Understanding what work attitudes people hold can help you to understand some of the behaviours that you see in the workplace. For example, if you see a workplace where people generally try to avoid the boss and rarely approach her with a problem, you may wonder why a negative attitude exists toward that boss. Perhaps the manager has a bullying leadership style (see Chapter 8) that makes her employees want to avoid her. In other cases, certain groups of people may have different attitudes about the same situation. For example, older employees may feel that their boss discriminates against them, while younger employees feel that the same boss treats them well. Looking at the different attitudes of individuals and groups can reveal quite a lot about a workplace.

Because workplace attitudes are linked to behaviour, they can have significant implications for organisations. Many organisations understand this impact and take the time to look at employee attitudes so they can understand what their employees think about work.

Measuring Attitudes with Surveys

Managers and organisational behaviourists have used attitude surveys in workplaces for many years to gather information on employee thoughts, feelings, and behaviours at work. Not only can attitude surveys help you find out about general work attitudes, but they also provide insight into more specific parts of the job or workplace.

Many people regard self-completed questionnaires as a reliable method of assessing attitudes. But using this tool to measure attitudes doesn't come without problems. Table 4-1 reveals the pros and cons of measuring attitudes with attitude questionnaires.

Table 4-1 Advantages and Disadvantages of Attitude Questionnaires

Advantages	*Disadvantages*
Cheap to administer	People may answer the way they think that they are expected to rather than being honest, known as giving *socially desirable answers*
Can include everyone in a workplace	Time-consuming to design and administer
Provide good detail on workplace attitudes	You must be careful with the wording of questions to ensure that the questions are valid (that is, that they measure what they are supposed to measure)
Allow comparison of different groups at work (for example, men versus women, or two teams managed by different people)	Measuring attitudes can lead people to expect change, and if this change doesn't happen, more negative attitudes may form

As Table 4-1 illustrates, a big problem with attitude questionnaires is the honesty of responses. So why would people not tell the truth when answering the questions? Well, imagine that your boss asks you to complete an attitude questionnaire, and some questions relate to your boss and your attitudes toward her – for example, Is she a good boss? Does she encourage you to discuss problems? If you don't trust your boss and you believe that she'll hold any negative comments against you, then you may be wary of answering these questions honestly.

Organisational behaviourists are aware of the problems of honest question-naire completion and take care to design questions so they're unambiguous and relevant.

If you want people to answer honestly, then you should reassure them that their answers will be kept confidential. In fact, attitude questionnaires are often completed anonymously so that people can be completely confident that they can't be identified and punished for giving a negative report.

Poorly designed attitude surveys don't give an accurate picture of attitudes in a workplace and may even give a distorted positive view. This mistake can be costly for organisations because they're paying for an attitude survey that isn't working properly. These poor attitude surveys also fail to uncover any problems at work that the organisation could take action to improve.

In addition to attitude questionnaires, you can use other tools to try to understand attitudes at work:

- ✔ **Observation:** Looking at the way people behave can tell you a lot about their attitudes. However, you need to take care because sometimes people exhibit behaviour that doesn't match their attitude. For example, don't assume that people show up for work because they like their jobs; in fact, they may actually hate the job but need the money they earn.

- ✔ **Interviews:** You can directly ask people about their attitudes. Interviews can be useful if you want to gain a detailed understanding of an issue. However, conducting interviews is a more time-consuming process than using questionnaires, and it restricts the number of employees who can realistically be involved.

Relating Attitudes to Behaviour

You may be wondering why you'd even want to measure attitudes in a work-place. The reason is that attitudes influence behaviour, so what happens at work directly correlates to employee attitudes.

How positive employees pay off

An interesting study by Dr Greenberg, a professor at Ohio State University, in the 1990s showed that employee theft rates were affected by negative attitudes toward work. Greenberg studied different manufacturing plants where pay was being temporarily cut by 15 per cent. Theft rates rose in those plants after the pay cuts occurred. This increase was linked to the negative attitudes the pay cuts provoked in employees and was seen as a way of them trying to redress the balance after what they saw as an unfair drop in pay. This reaction is known as *equity theory* (see Chapter 11 for more details).

Greenberg discovered that when the management of the plants took the time to explain to employees the reasons behind the pay cuts and how long they would last, the theft rates reduced. So paying attention to keeping employee attitudes positive (or as positive as they can be when people are losing pay) paid off.

Connecting behaviour and attitude

Attitudes at work affect the way people behave at work. Think about working in a job where you've a positive attitude, you like the work, and you get along well with your boss. You can see yourself working at this place for many years to come. If you're asked to help the boss out by covering for a sick colleague when it was meant to be your weekend off, you may say yes – partly because you like the boss and want to help her; partly because you like your customers and don't want to let them down; and, of course, partly because you want to progress in the job and helping out looks good on your record!

Now consider working in a job you dislike and where your boss is always complaining about the work you do, even when your performance is good. You may have a pretty negative attitude toward work. Imagine the same scenario where the boss asks you to help out. Would you say yes? Your negative work attitude would suggest not, because you wouldn't want to help the boss and are probably already looking for another job. Of course, you may help out if your other attitudes override these negative work attitudes – for example, if you really needed the money. Or, more worryingly, you may agree to help because you were worried what the boss may say or do if you refused. (We talk about this type of workplace bullying in Chapter 11.)

Attitudes influence behaviour in the following areas:

- ✔ **Motivation:** The different attitudes people hold about work influences how motivated they are to work and also which aspects of the job motivate them. Flip to Chapter 9 for more on motivation.

- ✔ **Morale:** Positive attitudes at work usually lead to fairly high employee morale. Conversely, negative attitudes can reduce morale.

✔ **Performance:** Attitudes influence performance. For example, if you've a positive attitude, you're likely to work harder than if you've a negative attitude.

✔ **Safety:** Positive attitudes about working safely and following safety procedures decrease the risk of accidents. (See Chapter 13 for more detail on safety.)

✔ **Commitment:** Attitudes influence how committed you are to your work and the organisation you work for. (See the section 'Looking at commitment', later in this chapter, for more information.)

✔ **Job satisfaction:** Attitudes also influence job satisfaction. (See the section on 'Fostering job satisfaction', later in this chapter, for more information.)

Motivating behaviour by understanding attitudes

Different attitudes at work reveal different ways of thinking about work. The way in which people feel about their job and the behaviour they exhibit as a result of these thoughts and feelings varies across people because people have different thoughts, feelings, and overall attitudes depending on their lives outside work.

Consider the following examples.

Holly is 53 and has grown-up children who've left home. She holds a full-time senior position in a library. She says:

> *I love my job! I've always enjoyed working, although I was only able to work part-time when my children were young. Now, though, I'm able to work full-time and love feeling part of the team. I get on very well with my colleagues, many of whom I have known for years. Now that my children have left home, I don't know what I'd do if I wasn't working.*

Daniel is a 21-year-old with no childcare responsibilities who works part-time in a burger bar. He says:

> *I work to earn money so that I can travel and go to gigs. I'm a college student and have just formed a band with my friends. I only work part-time because I spend a lot of time either in lectures or playing with the band. I don't have time for any more work! The job isn't hard, but it's also not very interesting. I spend most of my time working on my own in the kitchen so it's pretty monotonous. I don't even get to chat to the customers much. The pay isn't too bad for part-time work, though, and I need the money.*

Holly and Daniel clearly have different work attitudes. Holly is quite positive about her job, while Daniel is fairly negative about his. Their motivation to work is also different. Holly is motivated by the social aspect of her job and puts a lot of emphasis on her colleagues and feeling that she is part of a team. Daniel, however, is motivated by the money instead of the job itself, which he finds rather dull.

Imagine that you're Holly and Daniel's manager (yes, you manage a library and a burger bar, an interesting combination, we know). You want to ask these employees to work late in order to meet an important deadline – say, making all the book orders at the library and keeping the burger bar open late into the night for a birthday party. How would you choose to motivate these people? Well, you may ask Holly to work toward a team target of achieving all orders with the reward of a staff night out, thus focusing on the social motivator. Daniel would probably be most motivated by the extra pay he can receive, so offering him overtime pay may provide motivation for him to work extra hours. Would it work the other way round? Possibly not. For example, Daniel isn't likely to be motivated by a night out with work colleagues when he wants to earn money to spend time with his new band or travel.

Of course, not just lives outside work influence work attitudes but also the things that go on inside work. The work conditions and the way people are treated at work influence their attitudes and the behaviour they show in the workplace. Chapter 12 explores how jobs can be designed to influence employee attitudes and behaviour.

Predicting behaviour

Predicting behaviour from attitudes isn't simple, not least because of the many attitudes people hold; some attitudes are conflicting, such as someone working in a disliked job simply because he needs the money.

To predict likely behaviour from attitudes, you need to gather information on specific attitudes. The more specific the attitude, the more likely it is to be linked to how people behave.

For example, if you want to investigate the links between attitudes and accidents in the workplace, you'll be more successful in your quest if you ask people directly about their attitudes about safety instead of their general work attitudes. If an employee has a positive attitude about safety, she probably follows safety rules, whereas if she has a negative attitude about safety, she probably breaks safety rules, which makes an accident more likely to occur. So positive safety attitudes lead to safe behaviour and negative safety attitudes lead to unsafe behaviour (although, as we explain below, the relationship between attitudes and behaviour is not definite as other things influence the relationship).

If you ask about work attitudes, you may discover that a person has a positive attitude about work in general, but not realise that she has a negative attitude about workplace safety. So even though she likes the job, she doesn't like following all the safety procedures; asking about general attitudes won't show you this link between attitudes and accident rates. Asking about safety attitudes, though, tells you much more about the risk of an accident at work. In fact, many studies demonstrate the links between safety attitudes and accidents (see Chapter 13).

 Psychologists use a theory that predicts behaviour in a range of settings, not necessarily work-related. Interestingly enough, research has shown that the theory works. The theory of planned behaviour, proposed by Ajzen and Fishbein, suggests an indirect link between

- ✔ **Attitudes:** What you think and feel about something
- ✔ **Subjective norms:** How other people may view your behaviour and how much you care about this viewpoint
- ✔ **Intention to act:** Whether or not you intend to display a behaviour

For example, say that you hold an attitude that customers are annoying, and you want to shout at them. You don't shout at customers, though, because your intention to act is influenced by subjective norms – how other people will view your actions. In this example, your employer influences these subjective norms because she won't be happy if you start shouting at customers. The importance of keeping a job and not upsetting the employer overrides the negative attitude toward the customer, so you don't start shouting. So, the importance of attitudes and subjective norms to an individual influences her intention to act.

Sharing attitudes

In addition to individual attitudes (see preceding sections), the attitudes of groups are also important in workplaces. The culture or climate of an organ-isation affects *group attitudes,* or the tendency for a group of people to hold shared opinions and attitudes toward things (and people) in the workplace. Looking at shared attitudes and organisational culture and climate can help with the prediction of group behaviours in the workplace.

So when should you look at shared attitudes? Well, a good example is during times of change in organisations, such as when the company is going through a merger. Research has shown that many mergers fail because of cultural issues, and the attitudes of workers in the two merging companies are often mismatched. Paying attention to employee attitudes and culture during a merger can increase the chances of the merger being successful. (See Chapter 13 for more on culture, climate, and mergers.)

You can easily see how shared attitudes evolve in an organisation. If you think about a job you've had (or a class you've been in), you know that people talk to each other. You start to share ideas and thoughts about the place you're in, the things that you do, and the people who are there with you. So, for example, if a person is treated unfairly by her boss, she's highly likely to share that fact with her colleagues. Her anecdotes may invoke a general feeling that the boss is an unfair person, and her coworkers' attitudes toward the boss will be influenced by what they hear. A shared negative attitude about the boss therefore develops.

Attitudes are influenced by the things that happen around you. The people around you (referred to as *salient others* by attitude theorists, if you want to impress your friends with the technical term) have a significant amount of influence on your attitudes and subsequent behaviour. You think about how the people around you will react to the things you do, and these thoughts guide your behaviour. (For example, you conform to subjective norms; see the previous section.)

People who may affect your attitudes at work include

- Your boss
- Your colleagues
- Your employees (if you're the boss)
- Your customers
- People from other organisations you interact with
- People in your home life (they may have attitudes about your work, particularly if work is affecting your home life; see Chapter 6 for more on work–life balance issues)

People tend to go along with what others think. Why? Well, people usually want to feel that they belong in a group, and so they willingly conform to group attitudes and behaviours. Imagine that you start a new job, and on your first day, you dress in your best suit and head to the office. When you arrive, you realise that everybody is dressed far more casually than you. Now, in all your previous jobs, you've been expected to dress smart; it's what you're used to doing, and you're happy to do so. However, because everyone else in your new job dresses casually, you're likely to begin to dress down a bit in order to fit in. After all, showing up in a suit every day will get you pegged as unusual and not like the other employees. So you alter your attitudes and behaviour about appropriate dress for work to match those of the group you're with.

Of course, the amount that people are willing to change their attitudes has limits. If people hold dramatically different attitudes than you have about things you care about, you're less likely to alter your own attitudes. As an extreme example, imagine that you start a new job and discover that your colleagues are stealing from the company. Would you also steal in order to fit in? Or would that be an attitude change that's gone too far?

Being a good citizen

Organisational citizenship behaviour (OCB) can result from holding positive attitudes toward work. OCBs:

- **Are discretionary:** They're behaviours that you can choose to do or not do – for example, working during your lunch break to help out when people are off sick.

- **Aren't part of your job description:** These behaviours go beyond your core work tasks – for example, volunteering to help colleagues complete a task in order to meet a target.

- **Contribute positively to the organisation:** For example, you work long hours in order to ensure that the accounts are up to date at the end of the financial year.

OCBs may also lead to personal reward. The reward may be indirect – for example, you work into your lunch break not because you get paid for it (a direct reward) but in order to be helpful, make a good impression on the boss, or receive a later promotion.

Attitudes influence OCB because you're more likely to be helpful if you've a positive work attitude. Other antecedents of OCB, such as job satisfaction and commitment, also link to attitudes.

Encouraging and fostering positive attitudes from your employees (that is, trying to ensure that they feel positive about work) can increase OCB, which will be good for your organisation. Some of the positive results OCB can lead to are:

- Good organisational performance
- Organisational success
- Lower turnover
- Customer satisfaction

Fostering Job Satisfaction

Job satisfaction is a positive emotional state that can result from having positive attitudes and beliefs about work. If you're satisfied at work, then you're probably enjoying your job and feel that your needs are being met through work. Generally, if you've high levels of job satisfaction, you're happy at work. If you've low levels of job satisfaction, you're unhappy at work.

You can look at overall job satisfaction by asking people how they feel generally about their job. You can also look at specific aspects of job satisfaction by asking about different parts of the job, such as

- Pay
- The job itself
- Workload
- The amount of control people have over decision-making
- Promotion opportunities
- Supervisors and managers
- Colleagues

Thousands of studies measure job satisfaction, which means that we have a pretty good understanding of job satisfaction.

What does job satisfaction lead to?

No direct link proves that job satisfaction and performance are related, so being happy with a job doesn't automatically make people perform well in it. However, researchers have linked job satisfaction and organisational citizenship behaviour. (See the earlier section 'Being a good citizen' for more on OCB.) In other words, being happy at work (job satisfaction) is likely to lead to OCB, which is likely to in turn positively influence performance.

Employees with high levels of job satisfaction are likely to be committed to work, be content to stay with the organisation, take less sick time, and have lower stress levels. Conversely, low job satisfaction can lead to high stress levels, low work commitment, unplanned time off, and a desire to leave the organisation. Clearly, having satisfied employees is much better than having dissatisfied employees.

The older you get, the happier you get

Interestingly, job satisfaction seems to increase with age. So as people get older, they typically become more satisfied with work. Exceptions exist, of course, and you can probably think of some dissatisfied older workers. Nevertheless, as people get older, they're more likely to move into jobs and roles that they enjoy. Older workers tend to have more control over work and are often better rewarded for it. All these factors positively influence job satisfaction. (Of course, you may look at the increase in job satisfaction as people age as being caused by lowering expectations in older people; but we prefer to think that people aren't settling for less in their twilight years.)

How can managers ensure that employees are satisfied at work?

Managers aren't helpless when it comes to fostering job satisfaction. For starters, they can

- ✔ Ensure that they communicate well with employees so that people know what's going on in the workplace (especially important with things that directly affect the workforce)
- ✔ Treat people fairly
- ✔ Support employee development
- ✔ Consistently reward good performance
- ✔ Arrange flexible working if appropriate (flexible working influences employee health and wellbeing – see Chapter 6)
- ✔ Ask about, and address, any concerns employees have about work

Although this list isn't definitive about what influences job satisfaction (factors are numerous and often job specific), paying attention to these areas fosters positive employee attitudes and increases their job satisfaction. (For more on motivating employees, take a look at Chapter 9.)

Looking at Commitment

Organisational commitment means the degree to which a person feels involved with an organisation and how much she identifies with it. High levels of organisational commitment indicate that employees feel good about their organisation and have a positive attitude toward it. They want to perform well both for their own benefit and to help the organisation. Conversely, low levels of commitment may mean that employees don't much care for their organisation, and they may not feel motivated to work hard.

Organisations that want to understand more about the commitment of their employees can look at commitment attitudes using organisational commitment questionnaires. Remember that attitudes influence behaviour, so the attitudes that underpin feelings of commitment to an organisation influence how people behave at work. For example, do they follow rules, perform well and exhibit organisational citizenship behaviours?

If an organisation finds that employees aren't committed and discovers why, then it can take steps to improve organisational commitment. For example, commitment may drop in an organisation because a new manager makes changes to the shifts, and people end up working hours they aren't happy with. Finding out the cause of this drop in commitment may lead the new manager to discuss the shifts with employees in an attempt to reach a mutual agreement. If the employees feel that their concerns are being listened to, their commitment should rise.

Although we focus on organisational commitment in this section, people can be committed to their professions as well as to their organisations. A good example is a teacher who's disillusioned and unhappy about the school she works in but who's also committed to teaching and wants to provide the students with a good education. When thinking about how committed a person is to her organisation, consider whether the commitment is an actual organisational commitment or a professional commitment. Having high professional commitment doesn't mean that a person has positive attitudes about their job.

Recognising the three types of commitment

People can be committed to an organisation in different ways. Psychologists split commitment into three types:

- ✔ **Affective:** How emotionally attached are you to an organisation? A person with high affective commitment identifies with the organisation and wants to remain with the organisation as an employee. This positive feeling of commitment means that people work for an organisation because they want to and not because they have to.

- ✔ **Continuance:** What is your perceived cost of leaving the organisation? For example, if a person believes that she wouldn't be able to find another job, she may remain with the current organisation because she needs to rather than because she wants to. The person is committed to stay but only because she can't risk leaving. An employee who has only a continuance commitment won't do as much for the organisation as an employee who has an affective commitment.

- ✔ **Normative:** What sense of responsibility/loyalty do you feel for an organisation? You can describe this type of commitment as the *moral dimension*. For example, say that an organisation pays for an employee to complete training, and the employee then believes that she should stay with that organisation because it supported her. With normative commitment, the employee stays with an organisation because of obligation, not because she wants to (affective commitment) or needs to (continuance commitment).

These three different types of commitment reveal that people can be committed to work in different ways. Someone can have a low level of affective commitment and a negative attitude about her organisation, and still have a high level of continuance commitment because she can't afford to change jobs.

Strengthening commitment

So how can organisations ensure that employees are committed at work?

Here are some basic tips:

- ✔ Have good communication with employees.
- ✔ Treat people fairly.
- ✔ Reward good performance with consistent rewards.
- ✔ Support employee development.
- ✔ Ask people whether they have concerns about work, and if they do, address these concerns.

These points are almost identical to the ones identified in the earlier section on job satisfaction section. That's because job satisfaction and organisational commitment are linked, and employees who have high levels of job satisfaction are also likely to have high levels of organisational commitment.

Changing Attitudes

Every organisation, at one time or another, has to work on changing attitudes. For example, say that a manager wants to introduce performance-related pay into her workplace. More than likely, she'll encounter some hostile attitudes. People can be quite resistant to change, and often employees prefer to stick with a system they know rather than trust a new way of working. So how can this manager convince her employees that performance-related pay is a good rather than a bad thing?

She can start by paying attention to issues that can reduce the chances of employees forming negative attitudes toward work as a result of the change. Here are some pointers for managers trying to change attitudes:

- ✔ **Recognise the point of view of the employees.** Even if you don't agree with it, show that you understand the employee point of view.
- ✔ **Be prepared for some hard work.** The more opposed to the change people are, the more extreme the attitude change, and the harder it will be to successfully change attitudes.
- ✔ **Give it time.** You can't change attitudes overnight.
- ✔ **Be consistent with the message.** If you want to convince people that your argument is right, then you need to show that you believe in it and won't be persuaded to change your mind.

In addition, as we outline in the following sections, both the message and the messenger are important when trying to change attitudes.

Trusting the messenger

The characteristics of the messenger are important with regards to attitude change. In general, people are more likely to be influenced to change their attitudes by somebody they believe to

- ✔ Be trustworthy
- ✔ Have expertise on the topic
- ✔ Be attractive (not in a physical sense necessarily, although that can help; attractive in this sense means more that you like the person)

So when you're trying to convince people to change their attitude, it helps to ensure that these characteristics are evident in the person who sends the message. If people trust their boss, get along with her, and believe that she knows what she's talking about, then they're more likely to be persuaded by the argument presented to them. If, however, people don't like or trust the boss, they're unlikely to be convinced by her arguments for change.

Having negative opinions of the messenger can even influence good news not being received well because people have so little faith in the person telling it to them.

Sending the right message

Pay attention to the both the content of the message and the way this message is communicated to people. For example, when providing information about proposed changes, ensure that people actually understand the message. Sending everyone a detailed email and assuming they carefully read it isn't enough. If the change is important, then time should be made for it.

Managers can demonstrate that they understand how important the issue is by holding meetings about it and talking to people. Basically, managers should use all the channels of communication they have available. That way, they can be sure that the information is being received by their employees.

Attitude change is more likely to be successful if people are actively involved in the changes and not just passively told what is happening.

For example, if you're introducing performance-related pay, people are likely to be scared that they're going to lose pay under the new system. Managers should make sure that people receive the message that less money doesn't have to be the case. For example, perhaps the manager should pay particular attention to the increase in pay employees may receive if they're high performers.

Repeat the message to both ensure that the message is getting through and increase the influence of the message. People are more likely to remember bad news (the risk that pay will drop under the new system) than good news (that pay will rise for high performers). Repeating the message can help to ensure that people are hearing the good news.

Chapter 5

Working Together: Teams and Groups

*H*ave you ever tried to carry out an important project at work without consulting anyone? Or organise a celebratory party for a large group of friends or work department all alone? If the answer is yes (or even no), we're sure you agree that these aren't easy jobs to do alone. You can imagine how much easier, and more enjoyable, it is to organise these events with others. Organisations also realise that teamwork is critical to their success. Effective teamwork enables organisations to get the most out of their employees, such as achieving targets on time. Business leaders (particularly in the UK and US) view teamwork as so important that they look for the ability as one of the core skills of graduate employability.

In this chapter, we explore why understanding teams and groups is essential for a successful organisation. We describe the benefits of teamwork and explain how you can avoid potential pitfalls to become a high-performance team member or leader.

Understanding Work Teams and Groups

People need to work together in a variety of ways, whether it be collaborating on a specific project task or working within functional groups, such as the marketing or finance department. In the workplace, you come across terms like *cross-organisational*, *multidisciplinary* and *interdisciplinary* groupings, *autonomous work groups* and *self-managing teams*. But what it all comes down to is you need to be able to contribute effectively to group working, as a team member, a team leader, or a manager in an organisation.

A *team leader* isn't necessarily a manager. Often, a manager establishes a work team, but he doesn't take on the day-to-day responsibility for allocating the tasks or making the decisions. A manager, though, can help guide the team and provide relevant technical advice.

Defining teams and groups

You notice that we use the words *team* and *group* throughout this chapter. Many people use these terms interchangeably, but psychologists argue that the words have different meanings, as Table 5-1 reveals.

Table 5-1	Difference between Groups and Teams
Groups	**Teams**
You work independently of each other.	You work by supporting each other.
You've individual goals.	You collaborate and work together toward goals.
The leader gives direction and deals with conflicts.	Everyone is equally responsible.

For psychologists, a team is much more than a group. Although you've never heard of *groupbuilding*, *teambuilding* is probably something you're familiar with, particularly in relation to leadership training (see Chapter 8). Some organisations have working groups that call themselves teams, but their work is produced by a combination of individual and independent contributions. Team members, on the contrary, are more dependent on each other and produce work that's based on collaboration and collective effort. Throughout this chapter, our recommendations and observations are applicable to both teams and groups.

An example of a work group is waiters in a restaurant. Each waiter has similar individual objectives (take orders and serve the food), but no small-group common goal exists. The waiters do co-ordinate and collaborate (they decide which tables they cover), but they don't really share any responsibility – if a waiter gets a customer's order wrong, the mistake is unlikely to affect the other waiters. By comparison, if an emergency room trauma team doesn't function as a team, the results are serious: They must work together and help each other to save the patient's life.

Working with teams and groups

Most people tend to seek out the company of others. You may choose to belong to a team or group for a number of reasons, such as safety, self-esteem, similar interests, or shared goals. But just because you're in a team setting doesn't mean that you automatically work well together. An effective work team has

- **A common approach to working together:** Teams need to agree on how they work together. For example, members can take roles like devil's advocate (challenging the team's thought processes) or timekeeper to keep the project on time. (See the section 'Creating a balanced team', later in this chapter.)

- **A shared purpose or goal:** Teams must have a purpose that means something to everyone and is something they all feel responsible for. That purpose may be something as important as finding a cure for cancer or, as the author Lynn is doing at the moment, walking around the world with a pedometer (figuratively speaking!) as part of a team competition at work to get healthier.

- **A task to complete in a certain time:** Specifying the goals and evaluating them regularly helps. (Chapter 9 covers goal setting.)

- **Complementary skills:** Members need to bring together different ideas and multiple skills. If everyone thinks in the same way, they're unlikely to be as creative (and you can encounter the problematic groupthink – see the later section, 'Thinking as a group').

- **More than two members, but ideally less than nine:** Five to nine members is most effective. When a team has more than nine members, people struggle to get an opportunity to speak to each other, conflicts are more likely, and sub-groups may form. Fewer than five members may mean an insufficient skill, knowledge, and experience base.

- **Shared understanding:** More important than the size of the team, though, is that all the team are aware of the reality of the task it faces.

- **Mutual accountability:** Members need to feel shared responsibility for the team's outcomes – whether success or failure.

Norming to performing

Effective teamwork is essential in the workplace today, but as you may know from your own experience, teamwork doesn't happen instantly. Teams and groups go through certain stages (how long each takes is impossible to say) as they develop from a group of strangers to a cohesive team with a common purpose.

Educational psychologist Bruce Tuckman described the stages a team goes through in an easy-to-remember phrase: *Forming, storming, norming, and performing.* Tuckman suggested that teams progress through these stages.

He later added a fifth stage, *adjourning*, which some experts have renamed *deforming* or *mourning* because it rhymes better!

If you join a temporary team or a new permanent team, understanding what happens during these stages helps you get the team productive as quickly, and painlessly, as possible.

Exploring the five stages of the Tuckman model

Here are the five stages:

- ✔ **Forming:** This stage is fairly short, rather like a first date, where you're getting to know each other and gathering information. You tend to hold back from strong views, and you're polite to each other. Some members are anxious and others excited, and the roles and responsibilities are unclear for all apart from the leader. You feel comfortable at this stage, but the avoidance of conflict and threat means that the team doesn't actually accomplish much, which can be frustrating to some members.

  Teams that experience frequent comings and goings of members (particularly if the team is small) can often find themselves back at the forming stage.

- ✔ **Storming:** Reality sets in at this stage, and your emotions can be a bit up and down. People can be nice to each other only for so long! You're likely to experience conflict and disagreements over basic issues, such as how to do the task or the roles the members want to play. Some members withdraw from the tension, while others make a power play for roles and responsibilities. The team needs to avoid becoming distracted by emotional and relational issues and move forward by focusing on the goals. If a team fails, it usually does so at this stage.

  Anticipating, and then managing, conflict at the storming stage leads to a more productive team.

- ✔ **Norming:** Having had your disagreements during the storming stage, you understand each other better and value each other's abilities and experience. You may even socialise together and feel comfortable enough to offer constructive criticism. The team develops a stronger commitment to the team goal, and you feel part of a cohesive and effective team.

  Storming and norming stages can overlap for a drawn out time. If new tasks are introduced, the team may slip back into classic storming behaviour, but eventually this turmoil disappears. Some work teams like the comfort of the norming stage and are afraid of moving back into storming or forward into performing. This fear affects their attitude toward each other and their response to change.

- ✔ **Performing:** By this stage, the team knows why it's doing what it's doing, although not all teams make it to this stage. You trust each other and can cope confidently with any relational or process issues that may crop up. You may easily slip into different roles and take on other responsibilities, and everyone is focused on achieving the task and supporting the team.

✓ **Adjourning:** This stage marks the end of the team. Some work teams are established just for a specific task and have a short life span, like a project team set up within an organisation to look at a specific issue. For example, in a manufacturing organisation, a team may be set up to reduce the number of defects from one production line. When the issue is resolved, the team is disbanded. Other more permanent teams may be dismantled as a response to organisational restructuring and downsizing. If the task is completed, you can usually move on to new challenges, feeling good about what you've achieved. Sometimes, however, the breakup of a team can be hard, particularly if the task was unsuccessful or incomplete. You may also experience feelings of insecurity, particularly if you've got on really well with other team members, or your future role looks uncertain.

The Tuckman model deals with human behaviour, which can be unpredictable, so the characteristics of each stage aren't necessarily fixed. Sometimes a team may overlap stages or be unsure when the team's moved on to the next stage.

Becoming more productive at each stage

Both team leaders and team members can use the tips in the section for the next time you're in a newly formed team or you're a manager putting a team together. To be more productive at each stage, here are some pointers:

1. **Forming:** Encourage the team to establish the objectives clearly. For example, suggest creating a team charter where you state the purpose and the objectives (see Chapter 9); analyse the skill sets of the team members and identify any missing skills; scope the task; and agree on rules about meetings, communication, and expectations, and determine how to evaluate your progress.

2. **Storming:** Be prepared to deal with conflict and support team members who seem less confident. Remind the team about the process and rules in the charter to prevent conflict from continuing. Explaining the forming, storming, norming, and performing concept may help others understand why arguments are happening.

3. **Norming:** Suggest a social get-together to build on the growing positive relationships.

4. **Performing:** Remind others of progress against the targets to show that what you're doing is worthwhile. Relax a bit more and enjoy your achievements!

5. **Adjourning:** Be sensitive to the feelings of other members who may feel threatened by the change or loss of close friendships. Suggest a special celebration (any excuse!) and encourage team members to keep in touch, which can help you go forward into your next team more positively.

Organisations use work teams because they can achieve more than individual members on their own. But getting to the level of a high-performing team takes time and experience. You can reduce the chance of teething problems and speed up the process, if you understand the stages a team goes through.

Troubling Teams: When Things Go Wrong

When teams and groups work well, they can do great things for an organisation. But when teams and groups don't pull together, the consequences can be disastrous for productivity and effectiveness.

Poor performance can result from what psychologist Ivan Steiner called *process loss,* where teams become unproductive because members can't be bothered (*motivation loss*) or a team fails to co-ordinate or combine the contributions of individual members (*co-ordination loss*). In addition, individual behaviour, personality factors (see Chapter 3), and status issues may also spoil the effectiveness of the team.

Take a small team with four members, Alec, Ben, Charlotte, and Debbie.

- ✔ Charlotte has what you call a dominant and loud personality – very vocal and dismissive of other people's ideas.
- ✔ Ben is shy, hesitant to offer his opinion and his knowledge.
- ✔ Alec states his points confidently and seems knowledgeable about everything.
- ✔ Debbie is their manager.

Who do you think is most likely to influence the team's opinion? Well, Ben doesn't stand a chance! Charlotte has a strong personality, Alec has good communication skills (despite the fact that he may not be the expert in everything!), and Debbie has status – all factors that can influence a team's performance. The risk to the team is that Ben may have the solutions to the problems they face, but he's less likely than the others to take the opportunity to share his knowledge because he's shy.

As a team member, you need to realise that any contribution you make to team decision-making is unique and very important, however insignificant you think it is. Without your contribution, your team functions less efficiently and effectively.

As a team leader, or manager, take care to ensure that all team members have the chance to contribute their ideas.

The following sections help you identify and alleviate common problems that occur in work teams and groups.

Loafing around

One of the many ways process loss can happen is through a phenomenon called *social loafing*. Yes, social loafing is exactly what you're thinking! Under the cover of team work, you can become unmotivated and have a tendency to slack off, thinking that other team members are probably doing the same. You assume that others will take on the responsibility, so you think that you can get away with hiding in the crowd and doing less work.

For example, if you're in a team of eight and you've been tasked to come up with five potential names for a new biscuit launch, you think that it doesn't matter if you can't be bothered to think of many ideas because you're sure that one of your seven colleagues will! Social loafing is human nature. It's all very well when only biscuits are involved, but in a crisis situation, assuming that another team member will make the right decision can be dangerous.

Social loafing tends to happen as a team gets larger, and members find it harder to see what each other member is contributing. Members have less incentive to contribute because they feel that they're less likely to be noticed or praised for working hard (or blamed for not working enough) as the team increases in size.

TECHNICAL STUFF

Experimenting with social loafing

As a professor of Agricultural Engineering, Max Ringelmann first demonstrated social loafing in 1913 while investigating the relative efficiency of men, animals, and machines. Ringelmann had men pull horizontally on ropes, by themselves and in teams of various sizes. He found that the larger the team, the less work each man did. For example, someone pulling the rope alone would average 85 kilograms (187 pounds), but in teams of seven, the total would be 450 kilograms (992 pounds), only an average of 64.3 kilograms (141.7 pounds) each; in teams of 14, the average weight pulled reduced further to 61.4 kilograms (135.4 pounds).

Other studies show similar results. For example, Latané, a psychologist, measured students cheering and clapping as loud as they could. The clapping and cheering grew louder with larger teams, but not in proportion to the number of people. Two-person teams performed at 71 per cent of the sum of their individual capacity, teams of four at 51 per cent, and teams of six at only 40 per cent.

This decline in productivity is quite worrying for organisations, particularly for *additive tasks*, such as when managers bring in more workers to finish a job to meet a deadline. Think how many times you've been held up in traffic queues due to overrunning road repairs! Social loafing has been found in many different cultures, but more so in individualistic Western cultures (like the UK and United States) than collectivist countries, such as China and other Asian countries. (You can read more about cultural differences in Chapters 13 and 15.)

If you're a manager, you can do some things to ensure that less loafing around occurs:

- ✔ Sell the task as being important to the organisation.
- ✔ Give the team status and identity to make it important to its members (for example, by wearing different overalls or name badges).
- ✔ Ensure that you openly identify every team member's contribution and give praise to each individual accordingly.

Thinking as a group

Every day in governments and boardrooms across the world, people come together in groups and teams to make decisions. On many occasions, these decisions turn out to be wrong, and sometimes even disastrous.

For example:

- ✔ **The Challenger Space Shuttle disaster:** Engineers of the space shuttle knew about some faulty parts months before take-off, but they didn't want any negative press, so they pushed ahead with the launch anyway.
- ✔ **The US decision to invade Iraq:** The decision by the Bush administration and Congress to rush to invade, without waiting to build a broad-based coalition of allies, placed the US in a difficult military situation with high costs in terms of military deaths and casualties, as well as economics, and increased anti-American feelings around the world.
- ✔ **The collapse of Northern Rock:** The bailout of the UK bank by the government following the failure to foresee the severity of the world economic crisis has many causes. One of these was the common belief of the people involved that a policy based on economics was the only way (encouraged by the UK Treasury), so they ignored any other risks (such as sociological risks) to the banking system.

So why do groups and teams make such terrible decisions every so often?

One of the most common ways that team decision-making can go wrong is *groupthink*. Psychologist Irving Janis first proposed the idea when he was trying to understand why a team reaches an excellent decision one time and a disastrous one the next. He found that in highly cohesive teams, where members have similar backgrounds and values, they're so concerned with agreeing with each other that they fail to evaluate alternative ideas and opinions.

Spotting groupthink

Understanding how groupthink happens, and what you can do to overcome it, is crucial for effective decision-making in teams and consequently vital for profitable businesses. To spot groupthink, managers need to watch out for the five main signs:

- **The team chooses the first-agreed option.** Members go with the first solution they all agree with, rather than the best, and don't consider the potential risks.

- **One person dominates the team.** All it takes is one strong individual to manipulate the outcome.

- **The team is highly cohesive.** The members seem more concerned about agreeing with each other than making the right decision because they want to stay in the team.

- **The team is insulated from other opinions.** Members won't listen to people outside the team or to any contradictory opinions. Consequently, they fail to consider alternative options or listen to outsider's objections.

- **The team is under pressure to reach a decision.** Members rush into a decision due to outside pressures and fail to work out contingency plans.

Combating groupthink

What can you do if you spot the signs of groupthink? Or what can you do to stop groupthink happening in the first place? Some measures you, as a manager or team leader, can take to prevent or reduce groupthink are to

- Appoint an independent leader who encourages participation.

- Assign a devil's advocate role to someone in the team to challenge ideas.

- Discuss plans with impartial outsiders to obtain reactions.

- Encourage each team member to express any doubts and objections.

- Invite experts to join the meetings to raise doubts.

- Plan second-chance meetings for members to express doubts before decisions are implemented.

You may have spotted that most of the ideas to fight against groupthink focus on encouraging critical thinking and dissent, which isn't easy, because most organisations prefer to appoint 'yes' people and team players instead of those who are always squabbling.

So how do you, as a team member, become an effective dissenter?

- Avoid making your attacks personal.

- Present alternative viewpoints in a calm and neutral way.

- Practice disagreeing within a secure group of friends . . . but be careful to let them know what you're doing!

Communication among aircrew

It can be difficult to grasp the importance of how you communicate within teams. A number of psychological studies have looked into reasons for air crashes and found communication and the *cockpit authority gradient* (respect for the captain's experience and authority) to have a significant impact on the disastrous outcomes. For example, a Boeing 737 crashed in Washington, DC in 1982, after the captain ignored the unassertive co-pilot's concern about the performance of the aircraft during take-off. More worrisome, a UK study found that nearly 40 per cent of first officers surveyed stated that, on several occasions, they failed to communicate to the captain their legitimate doubts about the operation of the aircraft.

Why does this lack of assertion happen? Usually, it boils down to a desire to avoid conflict, regard for the captain's status, and personality characteristics, such as an arrogant captain (Chapter 3 looks at personality in more detail).

Apparently, if the captain uses achievement-oriented language, like 'try', 'effort', and 'goal', flight crews will perform better and make fewer errors. So, the next time you take a flight, if you get a chance, listen carefully to the way the flight crew talk to each other, and if they're arguing as well it may be a good sign!

Making risky decisions

If you put eight people together and ask them to design a car, what do you think the design would look like? Would it look like a Ford Fiesta or the flying car from the film *Chitty Chitty Bang Bang*? You're likely to expect the team design to be based on the average view, a sort of safe compromise car, and end up with something more like a Ford Fiesta. However, psychological research suggests that team discussions lean towards a *polarisation* of views – teams and groups often make more extreme decisions than would be suggested by the average of their original preferences. Not all group polarisation, though, is toward the riskier decisions. Cautious shifts do happen, but not as often.

Surprisingly enough, groups and teams often come up with more extreme decisions than individuals.

Shifting to the extreme (polarising groups)

Risky shift isn't really just about risk but part of a general phenomenon known as *group polarisation*, where a group or team discussion strengthens the average inclination of the members. Many worldwide studies have confirmed group polarisation. For example, jury members who initially feel that the defendant is innocent or guilty will be even more certain of these beliefs after any discussion; after a team discussion, people who already support capital punishment will become even more supportive; and a team with a slight preference for one job candidate become even more certain of their choice.

These shifts toward the extreme have all sorts of implications for government, business, and justice systems. For example, psychologists Main and Walker looked at the decisions made by US Federal District Court judges. Judges who sat alone took an extreme course of action only on 30 per cent of occasions, whereas those who sat in teams of three made extreme decisions in more than twice as many cases.

Why does group polarisation occur? Psychologists have identified two possible explanations:

- ✔ **Social comparison:** You're likely to conform to socially desirable norms. In other words, you want to be the same as other people, only more so.

- ✔ **Persuasive argumentation:** You've a tendency to develop stronger views when you hear rational (and correct) arguments, particularly if these are the majority view.

Although group polarisation isn't inherently a good or bad thing, it seems logical that a team benefits from discussing all relevant ideas and arguments and not just going along with the first preferred option. You also need to avoid conformity, which you see in the nearby sidebar 'Conforming and obeying'.

Polarisation is more likely to happen when you're in a newly formed team with a new task. But you can prevent it from happening by

- ✔ Including individuals who are likely to represent different viewpoints because they're less likely to polarise

- ✔ Nurturing dissent by encouraging team members to discuss alternative viewpoints

If you've read the earlier section 'Thinking as a group', you may notice that a common theme runs through our advice. Remember, a good team member needs to disagree! So the tips we provide in the section on groupthink can also help reduce group polarisation.

Influencing as a minority

So, what do you do if you're in the minority in a team or group decision-making situation? You struggle to persuade the rest of the members that you're right and they're wrong, but how do you increase your chances?

Here are a few pointers:

- ✔ **Be consistent and confident.** Behave in an independent way.

- ✔ **Be prepared to disagree.** Don't be too unreasonable or inflexible, but state your case and back it up with evidence.

- ✔ **Identify common ground.** Find something that you all agree with, however small, and build on it.

✔ **Get appointed as the team leader.** You have more influence.

✔ **Have principles, rather than you own interests, at heart.** If your views are in keeping with social trends, such as liberalisation and tolerance (popular in Western cultures today), you have more success.

✔ **Make sacrifices.** Give in a bit to the majority while maintaining your position.

✔ **Stimulate discussion.** Conversation opens up opportunities to consider alternative ideas.

TECHNICAL STUFF

Conforming and obeying

Conformity (also known as *majority influence*) has a very powerful influence in society, and psychological experiments show that people even refuse to accept the evidence of their own eyes in order to conform to the majority. Two classic experiments, carried out by psychologists Solomon Asch and Muzafer Sherif, demonstrate the power of conformity in groups. Sherif used the auto kinetic effect, where participants sit in a dark room and stare at a small dot of light projected onto a screen. The dot appears to move, although this movement is just a visual illusion. When individual participants were asked to judge how far the dot moved, their estimations varied widely (20 to 80 centimetres or 7.9 to 31.5 inches). Sherif then put the participants in groups of three, with two people with similar estimations, and one with very different estimations. Over a number of trials, the group's estimate converged to a common view, with the person with the different estimate conforming to the majority view.

Asch gathered groups of eight people together, with all but one acting as his co-conspirators. They were shown a series of pictures of vertical lines and were asked to decide which of three lines was the same length as the standard line. When the accomplices (who had been instructed to choose the wrong line a number of times) chose the wrong line, the lone participants also chose the wrong line on up to 75 per cent

of occasions (an average conformity of 33 per cent of trials), even though later they admitted they knew it was wrong. They did it because they didn't want to be different from the majority, especially if the majority were unanimous. By the way, it was an easy task, and when people were tested individually, very few errors were made.

Conformity can lead to obedience when faced with an authority figure. Studies of obedience by social psychologist Stanley Milgram show that people will administer electric shocks to complete strangers when asked to by an authority figure in a white coat in a laboratory setting. This prospect is quite scary as participants administered 'shocks' (not real shocks, but the participants didn't know this) on an average of 62 per cent of occasions, and on 100 per cent of occasions when they couldn't see or hear the 'victim'! When groups were asked to give shocks, the behaviour of others was influential depending on whether they were in favour of, or opposed to, giving shocks.

If you check out the Internet, you can find many video examples of these famous, but controversial, experiments. Do keep in mind that although psychological research seems to indicate that conformity is a bad thing, think about how society (or the armed forces for example) would function without it.

If you're in the minority, you may be annoying, but by speaking up, you ensure that the team functions better, even if you're wrong. If you think about real life, society needs to have people with different points of view, or it wouldn't change. What rights would women have without the suffrage movement?

Developing Teams That Perform Well

Managers tend to believe that all they need to do is split their employees into teams and the organisation becomes more productive and effective. If only it were that simple! Teams are not always the right answer, especially where decisions need to be made quickly. Consideration also needs to be made about the team members – their cultural backgrounds and the roles they prefer to play within a team, for example.

In this section, we explain how to develop a high-performing team.

Choosing a team over individuals

In the earlier section 'Troubling Teams: When Things Go Wrong', we explain that lots of problems can occur in teams and groups. Yet many organisations continue to leave important (and minor) decisions up to teams of people rather than individuals (although in Chapter 8, you see that domineering managers still run many businesses). The million dollar question is why?

One reason is that, if you're in a team that makes a decision to reduce the number of coffee breaks to help your company during the recession, you'll be more committed to the idea than if your boss just told you not to have as many cups of tea.

On the other hand, making all decisions by committee takes time and money. We have no definitive answer to whether teams are better than individuals because it depends on the circumstances, mainly on the tasks undertaken.

Psychologists have debated hotly the comparative benefits of teams versus individuals in problem-solving situations. Overall, the general consensus is that teams win in a number of ways because they

- ✔ **Find things out faster:** They provide support for each other.
- ✔ **Make better decisions:** They can pool expertise and resources.
- ✔ **Make fewer errors:** They're more likely to spot errors because they've a greater mix of knowledge and experience.
- ✔ **Produce more:** And this production is often to a better quality.
- ✔ **Recall better:** They don't rely on one person's memory.

Teams are better than individuals due to *process gain* (as opposed to *process loss,* which we discuss in the earlier section "Troubling Teams: When Things Go Wrong"), which happens when team discussions inspire you to come up with new ideas. For example, if you need to decide the best way to solve a problem, a team is more likely to recognise and reject wrong solutions.

You also have the motivation aspect of team work. When you're working in a team and other team members support and encourage you to do well that also contributes to process gain. But when you work by yourself and feel apprehensive about whether you're doing something right or are afraid of being judged a failure, this fear can mess up your performance.

Although teams are likely to be more productive than individuals, remember that plenty of evidence suggests that they're not as good as they could be, due to process loss and diminished creativity. (See the nearby sidebar "How groups can kill creativity.") But overall a team is probably going to perform better than one individual.

Working with diverse teams

As the trend toward increased workforce diversity grows it becomes all the more important for organisations to understand the influence of diversity on the day-to-day interactions of work teams and groups. You're likely to work alongside many people who are different from you in terms of gender, age, race, ethnicity, sexuality, national origin, and other characteristics.

If you consider broad cultural differences, for example, you can break societies down into two kinds:

- ✓ **Individualistic:** Western societies tend to be in this category, where independence and self-sufficiency are seen as the ideal characteristics, and the focus is on "I."

- ✓ **Collectivistic:** Asian, Latin American, and African (to some extent) countries prioritise the importance of the family and larger social group, with the focus on "we."

How teams can kill creativity

Despite teams being generally better than individuals at problem-solving, psychologists tend toward the view that teams rarely come up with great ideas because people in them are shaped by *group or team norms* (unwritten rules that guide how people ought to behave in a group or team – see Chapter 4 for more detail). Creativity is about being different from other people and doing things in a different way, which is at odds with following group or team norms.

You can see from these descriptions (which we discuss more in Chapter 15) that a manager is likely to find it difficult to bridge the gap between the different team members. Asian employees place importance on saving face, keeping friendships, avoiding conflict, and taking time to make decisions. Western employees, conversely, are more likely to express conflicting ideas and tend to focus more on individual goals than group or team goals.

So, what can a manager do to overcome potential difficulties in diverse teams? Psychologists Johnson and Johnson suggest

- **Adaptation:** Encourage team members to accept the cultural differences and work to their strengths. You can initiate cross-cultural training to improve communication and understanding of the cultures.

- **Structural intervention:** Reduce the source of the problems. For example, employees from collectivist cultures work better within smaller teams because they feel more comfortable about expressing their opinions.

- **Managerial interventions:** Agree ground rules at the beginning and be prepared to make the final decision when a team can't agree.

- **Exit:** Remove a team member when they can't adapt to the challenge, and all else fails.

Diversity is hard to manage well because individuals have different values and beliefs about how to behave. And although diverse teams have the potential to perform well, due to the mix of viewpoints, it doesn't always happen. But diversity in teams is a good thing because it can help reduce the risk of group-think. (See "Thinking as a group," earlier in this chapter.)

Teambuilding

When you think of teambuilding, certain pictures spring to mind. A few weeks ago, the author Lynn saw a group of people walking in a line, one behind the other, with all but one of them with buckets over their heads (not a normal sight in a European city!). They had their hands on each other's shoulders and were shuffling along, following directions shouted by the bucketless person at the back of the line. A teambuilding exercise, Lynn thought to herself and took no more notice. But teambuilding doesn't have to be as extreme as this example. Every team is unique, and you must find your own way of working together productively. No single right way to work as a team exists.

Building a high-performance team

A number of psychologists and management specialists have spent many years looking for the holy grail of high-performing, or dream, teams – in other words, how to get teams performing to the best of their abilities. Management consultants Katzenbach and Smith propose a number of essential steps for you to follow as a manager or team leader:

✔ Communicate clear high performance standards.

✔ Create a sense of importance about meetings.

✔ Investigate individual skills (see the next section "Creating a balanced team").

✔ Set clear agendas.

✔ Set ground rules about behaviour in the first meeting.

In addition, we recommend that you lead by example:

✔ Admit to your own mistakes.

✔ Allocate tasks and set clear, agreed-upon deadlines (read more about goal setting in Chapter 9).

✔ Don't dominate, but listen and contribute.

✔ Give positive feedback and encourage others.

✔ Review the team process and reflect on what works and what doesn't; make changes where needed.

✔ Share your knowledge and continue to introduce new information.

In summary, just telling people to cooperate and work well together won't create successful teamwork. You need to encourage them to develop the skills of high-performing team members.

Recognising a high-performance team when you see it

But what does a high-performing team look like? Psychologists Johnson and Johnson suggest that in a high-performing team, each member

✔ **Demonstrates good interpersonal and team skills, through feedback and building positive relationships:** This helps the team reach higher levels of achievement and productivity.

✔ **Encourages, supports, and cares about others.** You can do this by

- Challenging other people's decisions

- Giving constructive feedback to others

- Motivating others to try harder

- Providing others with efficient and effective help

- Swapping resources and information effectively

- Trusting others and act trustworthy

✔ **Takes personal responsibility and feels individually accountable for decisions and outcomes:** Members do their share of the work and help others.

> ✔ **Thinks in terms of 'we instead of me':** Members realise that they can't succeed by themselves because they need to work with the team to achieve the goal. Everyone sees their contribution as vital to the success.

Creating a balanced team

Considering the makeup of a team is important because not all teams work well together. Starting in the 1970s, Meredith Belbin, a management theorist, observed teams and started to develop a theory that suggests that nine (increased from the original 8) distinct team-role types exist. Psychologists use the *Belbin Team-Role Self-Perception* (BTRSP) today when selecting, counseling, and developing management teams. The idea is that excellent teams tend to have members who take on the following roles within their team:

✔ **Completer finisher:** Acts as quality control by checking for errors, especially toward the end of a task.

✔ **Co-ordinator:** Ensures that the team focuses on the objectives, delegates roles, and encourages all members to contribute.

✔ **Implementer:** Plans practical matters and routine jobs.

✔ **Monitor evaluator:** Evaluates ideas in a logical way.

✔ **Plant:** Is creative and comes up with imaginative new ideas.

✔ **Resource investigator:** Gathers information from outside the team.

✔ **Shaper:** Provides the drive to keep the team moving toward the task goals.

✔ **Specialist:** Provides specialist knowledge of a key area.

✔ **Team worker:** Maintains the team spirit.

You probably have a strong tendency toward one role, but you may take on different roles in different settings or take on several roles to compensate for the missing roles in a relatively small team. You can take on more than one role but have a natural team role that reflects your distinct preferences for behavioural characteristics and thinking style.

If a team misses a role or has too many of the same types, the team is less effective. For example, what would happen if a team has too many team workers or shapers? Too many team workers may ensure that the team has an enjoyable time, good communication, and little conflict, but few decisions get made. On the other hand, being overrun with shapers is exhausting because they constantly hassle the team to get things done and may get in a bad temper about it.

Chapter 6

Reducing Stress, and Improving Health and Wellbeing

*T*he 1970s heralded major industrial relations problems, with many confrontations between unions and management. Then came the enterprise culture of the 1980s with major industrial and organisational change. The 1990s and early 2000s saw the Americanisation of most of the UK and Europe, with major restructurings, such as mergers/acquisitions, downsizings, outsourcing of functions, and the undermining of the concept of jobs for life. These activities transformed the UK economy, but at substantial personal cost for many individual employees. You can encapsulate this cost in a single word: *stress*. The problem, of course, has become much worse with the recession and post-recession period, with major job and resource cuts in the public and private sector, and more outsourcing of activities and functions now endemic to most workplaces.

Stress, then, has found as firm a place in the modern life as iPads, tsunamis, and frequent flyer miles. Although a little stress can be positive and motivating, even increasing performance, when levels become too high, detrimental effects can result.

This chapter focuses on the negative outcomes of stress and explores the many causes of workplace stress. We explore the cost of stress to individuals and organisations, as well as how both individuals and organisations can manage and reduce stress.

Understanding the Causes of Stress

People use the word *stress* casually to describe a wide range of health outcomes resulting from the hectic pace of work and life. You've probably heard someone say, 'I feel really stressed' or explain away someone's irritating behaviour because 'he's under a lot of stress'. Indeed, people even use the word to award an odd sort of prestige to a job: 'It's a high-stress job.'

The word *stress* is now in common vocabulary because the ability of people to cope with day-to-day problems is gradually depleting, leading to a range of behaviours that lead to ill health. An enormous amount of research has explored the main sources of stress at work. In this section, we look at the key causes of stress at work, and how people can experience stress differently depending on their personality.

The word *stress* can relate to both causes ('she's under stress') and outcomes of pressure at work ('I feel stressed'). Those who study organisational behaviour call the causes of stress the *stressors* and the effects of stress the *strain*.

Factors intrinsic to the job

Every job is different, so you need to identify which factors intrinsic to that job are different from all others and how they affect the health and wellbeing of the occupants of that role. For example, being a neurosurgeon is very different from being a bomb disposal officer in Afghanistan, although you may describe both jobs as stressful!

Every job has unique factors that may be very stressful and don't translate to other jobs. For example, a neurosurgeon has the stress of the risk of making a mistake, which may cost the patient's life. A bomb disposal officer has the stress of risking her own life.

Understand the stresses that are intrinsic to a job when you hire employees. You want to ensure a person-job fit so that you can select the most resilient people to do what may be a very stressful job. (We discuss person-job fit in Chapter 13. You can find out more about recruiting the right people in Chapter 17.)

Examples of some intrinsic job characteristics that can increase stress are

- ✔ **Long hours:** Not having free time and working excessively long hours, particularly over long periods of time, can be incredibly stressful.
- ✔ **Poor working conditions:** Working in high or low temperatures or simply not having the right tools to do your job properly can cause stress.

- ✔ **Risk and danger:** A job that involves risk and danger – for example, you work with potentially aggressive or violent people – can raise your stress levels.

- ✔ **Shift work:** Much evidence shows that *shift work* (work activity outside standard daytime hours where an employee, or group, hands over a work task to others) can be stressful and have a detrimental effect on your health.

- ✔ **Work overload and underload:** Simply having too much, or not enough, work to do can cause stress. Have you ever been unable to complete a task because you simply had too much work to do? Remember how it made you feel?

Job role

The role you play in your organisation is vital for your health and wellbeing. If you've a well-defined role, without much built-in conflict, with clear-cut organisational boundaries and a great deal of autonomy and control, then the likelihood is that you don't suffer from much stress.

Research seems to suggest that the key issue is control. The more people feel valued and trusted by their bosses, and the more they can exercise autonomy over their job, the less likely they are to suffer ill health outcomes, and the more likely they are to be satisfied. (Chapter 12 gives you the low-down on effective job design.)

Three job role factors are major sources of stress. Think about how having control over your work can help in each of these areas:

- ✔ **Role ambiguity:** You've inadequate information about your work role. You aren't clear about the scope and responsibilities of your job. If you don't know what your objectives are, how can you achieve them?

- ✔ **Role conflict:** You're given conflicting job demands. For example. a customer service worker is told to keep all customers happy and also to spend only five minutes with each customer. The employee can't always do both, so a conflict emerges. Other role conflict demands include being asked to do tasks you dislike or that aren't within your job specification.

- ✔ **Role responsibility:** Generally, having more responsibility can lead to higher stress at work. Having responsibility for people can be more stressful than having responsibility for things.

Relationships at work

Probably the most important relationship you have at work in terms of your own wellbeing and stress is the relationship you have with your boss. The better this relationship, the more you get along with your boss, and the more beneficial to your job satisfaction and health. A poor relationship can cause ill health effects.

In his humorous book *Something Happened* (Vintage), Joseph Heller's opening page illustrates the significance of work relationships:

> *In the office in which I work there are five people of whom I am afraid. Each of these people is afraid of four people, for a total of twenty, and each of these twenty people is afraid of six people, making a total of one hundred people who are feared by at least one person. . . . In my department, there are six people who are afraid of me, and one small secretary who is afraid of all of us. I have one other person working for me who is not afraid of anyone, not even me, and I would fire him quickly, but I'm afraid of him.*

Bosses aren't the only relationship that can cause problems; colleagues, customers, and suppliers can as well. The primary relationship stressors are the ones in your own workplace, though, because you interact with these people a lot.

Poor relationships at work can make your job harder and less enjoyable. You may have a boss who expects you to work harder than you feel possible, or an unhelpful, unsupportive colleague. Studies of workplace stress have shown that

- Bad relationships make stress worse.
- Supportive relationships reduce pressure and levels of stress.

We talk about fairness at work in Chapter 11, so check it out for discussion of extreme relationship problems at work, such as discrimination and bullying, and consideration of the stress that can be caused if you're unfortunate enough to experience it. Also check out Chapter 8 for more on leadership and how to be a good boss.

Career development

Career-driven issues, such as being overpromoted or underpromoted or fearing job loss or early retirement, can be stressful. These career events are now more common because people are much more mobile between employers and sectors.

Some areas relating to career development that can affect stress levels are

- ✔ **Fear of redundancy:** Especially important post-recession, fearing you may lose your job can be highly stressful.

- ✔ **Performance appraisals:** Stress can increase if you feel that you're unfairly appraised. (Chapter 18 covers appraisals.)

- ✔ **Reaching a career ceiling:** Not progressing in your career can be frustrating.

- ✔ **Retirement:** Worrying about retirement can cause stress. (See Chapter 11 for more on retirement.)

Job security

As we are entering an era of leaner organisations, intrinsic job insecurity and a culture of longer working hours, adverse stress effects on employee attitudes and behaviour are emerging. In 2001, the Chartered Management Institute's Quality of Working Life survey of 5,000 managers found that downsizing, outsourcing, and delayering in the workplace led to substantially increased levels of job insecurity, decreased morale, and eroded motivation and loyalty.

In addition, substantial research shows that job insecurity leads to ill health. Between 1985 and 2000, job security among British workers dropped from 70 per cent feeling secure to only 45 per cent feeling secure. In 2007, 66 per cent of 10,000 managers reported that as a result of all the structural changes in their organisation, they now felt significantly less secure. This trend of intrinsic job insecurity is of great concern for two reasons:

- ✔ A person's sense of job security is related to job satisfaction.

- ✔ A strong link exists between job dissatisfaction and mental and physical ill health.

We talk more about job satisfaction and dissatisfaction in Chapter 9.

Related to job security is the issue of short-term contracts. Many organisations are moving toward creating a short-term *contract culture* where people are hired in for the short term, or they outsource work to outside agencies or freelancers. This move has enhanced the stress levels of staff, as the permanence of their job is under threat. The insecurity of a short-term contract, as well as the more tenuous relationship an agency worker has with the organisation, is a real problem in these settings.

A survey in 2006 of a cohort of 10,000 UK managers compared the years 2000 with 2005 and discovered the following:

- ✔ The use of short-term contract staff rose from 41 per cent to 57 per cent.
- ✔ Cost-reduction programs went from 47 per cent to 63 per cent.
- ✔ Twenty-five per cent of managers reported that their organisations were engaged in major outsourcing.

And these figures were before the recession! Are we going to see greater use of contract staff and outsourcing post-recession as organisations seek to cut manpower and reduce costs?

Culture and climate

The organisation you work for has its own culture and climate, which can make work life pleasant or unpleasant and stressful. Some cultures are more bureaucratic or restrictive, but others may have effective consultations and be more engaging. A great deal of research has shown that work environments that create a culture of engagement produce greater productivity and health and therefore support a more trusting climate.

Check out Chapter 13 for more on organisational culture. There we discuss the importance of values and attitudes and explain how, if your values and attitudes clash with those of the organisation, you can find yourself not fitting into the organisation's culture. This conflict can cause you stress and lead to you performing less well and even leaving the organisation.

Work–life balance

As countries like the UK and the US create long-hours cultures, the stresses and strains between work and home life mount. Strong evidence reveals that working long hours not only damage your health and family life but also your productivity.

Since the early 1990s, the annual working hours across the globe have declined – by as much as 11 per cent for Japan, and 6 per cent for the UK, although only 2 per cent for the US. This decline is in part because more females are working, and as they often work part-time the average number of hours worked reduces. However, this trend is beginning to reverse with employees now reporting working longer hours than before the recession. According to a 2011 survey, 30 per cent of UK employees are working longer hours, with 42 per cent of this group working three hours extra per day and 26 per cent working more than three hours extra per day. And a survey of 300 organisations in the US and Canada reports that two-thirds of employees are working longer hours than three years ago.

Smoking breaks

Some employees appear to work fewer hours than others. According to a UK survey, smokers take about four 15-minute breaks a day to get their nicotine fix. This means that smokers work on average 240 hours per year less than non-smokers. The Chartered Institute for Personnel Development suggests that one way to overcome resentment between those who do and those who don't smoke is to restrict smoking to statutory breaks. A healthier option, though, is for employers to provide support to encourage employees to live a healthier lifestyle.

A survey in 2007 found that 56 per cent of managers reported that long hours damaged their health; 54 per cent said that these hours adversely affected their relationship with their children; 59 per cent said that it damaged their relationship with their partner/spouse; and 64 per cent said that it had an adverse affect on their social life.

The UK umbrella group Working Families did a study of 625 working people and found that nearly 40 per cent of those consistently working over 45 hours a week spent less than an hour a night with their children. In addition, a major discrepancy existed between their contracted hours and their actual hours. For women, 15 per cent were contracted to work over 40 hours, while only 44 per cent actually did. For men, 27 per cent were contracted to work over 40 hours, while 67 per cent actually did.

Work–life balance is now a major issue in most employee surveys carried out in both the public and private sector as a result of these long hours, and more employees are calling for more flexible working arrangements to deal with them.

In addition to long hours, another reason why work–life balance is seen as increasingly relevant to workplace stress is because of the increasing number of dual-career households, which makes balancing home and work life more difficult, especially if you've child or elder care responsibilities.

Work–life balance conflict can be in both directions:

- ✔ The demands of work can create problems at home.
- ✔ The demands at home can create problems at work.

Personality

People are different and react to stressors in different ways. The sources of stress influence the individual, and people's personalities influence what the likely effect of the stressors will be. (You can find out more about personality and individual differences in Chapter 3.)

Personality can affect stress in three main ways. It can have a

✔ **Direct effect:** If you're an anxious person, you're generally more likely to experience stress.

✔ **Moderating effect:** Some personality characteristics can lead to you being more likely to experience stress in a particular job. For example, if you're an outgoing extroverted person, you may find a job where you work on your own a lot more stressful than an introverted person would. On the other hand, your personality may cushion the affect. For example, being extroverted is linked to positive wellbeing, so a more extrovert employee may find a stressful job situation less stressful.

✔ **Direct perceptual effect:** Personality can affect your perceptions of your job. For example, if you've a high need for control, you'll be very conscious of being in a situation where you've low control and be more bothered by it than somebody else who has less need for control.

In Chapter 3, we introduce models of personality. Two are particularly relevant to discussions of stress:

✔ **Locus of control:** This trait affects the extent to which you think that you've control over your life. An internal locus of control is good because it can encourage you to do something about a stressful situation. However, if you can't change your situation, an internal locus of control can increase stress.

✔ **Type A behaviour:** If you're a high type A personality, you're probably very competitive, high achieving, and impatient. You're also at a higher risk of stress than Type B personalities, who tend to be more relaxed and less competitive.

Seeing How Stress Affects Employees and Employers

The financial costs of stress are high – and we mean really high. For example:

✔ The costs of ill-health in the working age population are estimated by us to cost the UK well over £100 billion a year.

✔ Mental ill health alone costs the UK around £28 billion.

✔ Stress was estimated to cost $3 billion in decreased productivity and $19 billion in lost employment annually in the United States.

✔ Effectively managing mental health at work in an organisation with 1000 employees can save as much as £250,000 per year.

✔ In 2009, workers in the UK took sick days at a cost of an estimated £3.7bn.

✔ Stress, depression, or anxiety is the largest cause of absence attributable to work-related illness in the UK and accounted for 13.8 million days lost in 2006–07.

You can look at the cost of stress from two angles:

✔ Individual costs, such as behaviour change and ill health

✔ Organisational costs, such as poorer performance and absenteeism

Impacting individuals

Table 6-1 outlines commonly reported feelings and behavioural symptoms of stress. If you've ever experienced stress at work, then you may recognise some of these symptoms!

Table 6-1	Common Signs of Stress
Feeling . . .	*Finding It Hard to . . .*
Like a bad person	Take an interest in others
Like a failure as a person, employee, or parent	Make decisions
Frightened of failure, illness, the future, or being alone	Concentrate
Neglected	Express true feelings, including anger
Like the target of other people's animosity	Have a sense of humour
A lack of confidence	Confide in others
Unable to cope	Be patient with people
Uninterested in life	Finish one task before rushing to another

The impact of stress at work on the health and wellbeing of individuals is huge. Stress follows a three-stage process:

✔ **Behaviour change:** Acting out can occur when you're near the dividing line between pressure, which is stimulating and motivating, and stress, which means that the pressure has exceeded your ability to cope. You may lose your sense of humour, have difficulty concentrating and become more socially withdrawn. Sometimes people can also become more aggressive when experiencing stress.

✔ **Physical symptoms of stress:** These symptoms can manifest themselves in a number of ways, such as feeling constantly tired, having frequent headaches and having difficulty sleeping at night. Stress-related behaviours, such as increases in smoking, alcohol consumption, and eating too much or too little, can worsen physical symptoms. Also, research indicates that musculoskeletal disorders have been found among call centre employees with high workloads, and premature births among women with low job satisfaction.

✔ **Serious illness:** If the sources of your stress are very deep-rooted and persistent, it can lead to a range of more serious illnesses, such as heart disease, gastrointestinal disorders, and migraines.

Obstructing the organisation: Absenteeism and presenteeism

Organisations experience a number of problems as a result of employees experiencing high levels of stress at work. Table 6-2 illustrates the problems stress causes and their cost for an organisation.

Table 6-2	How Stress Affects an Organisation
Result of Stress	*Cost to the Organisation*
Compensation claims by stressed individuals	Financial
High turnover of staff	Financial (cost of recruitment), disruption
Low morale	Performance problems and reduced commitment, so less effective and reliable employees who may work slower and produce work of lower quality
Sickness absence	Financial (loss of productivity, cost of sick pay, and replacement workers)

Of the problems described in Table 6-2, the two big factors that affect organisations are

✔ **Absenteeism:** According to estimates by the Chartered Institute of Personnel Development and the Confederation of British Industry, workplace stress is one of the biggest causes of absence in the UK workforce.

✔ **Presenteeism:** People are at work, but they aren't performing to the best of their ability or contributing to the bottom line.

Estimates of the costs of absenteeism and presenteeism range from £2 billion to over £20 billion per annum in the UK, depending on whether they're direct costs, such as sickness absence, and/or indirect costs, such as lack of added value to products or services and the costs to the NHS of treating people who have a stress-related illness precipitated by work.

Table 6-3 shows the estimated annual costs of poor mental health to UK employers. These figures are based on common mental health disorders, which include depression, anxiety, and stress (depression and anxiety can be outcomes of stress). Note that presenteeism costs the UK nearly twice what absenteeism costs.

Table 6-3	Estimated Annual Costs to UK Employers of Poor Mental Health		
	Cost Per Average Employee (£)	*Total Cost to UK Employers (£billion)*	*Per cent of Total*
Absenteeism	335	8.4	32.4
Presenteeism	605	15.1	58.4
Turnover	95	2.4	9.2
Total	1035	25.9	100

Source: Sainsbury Centre for Mental Health, 2007.

We can conceptualise presenteeism into a two-by-two matrix to get a picture of the extent of the problem. (See Table 6-4, which is based on a sample of 39,000 UK workers.) Table 6-4 shows that of these workers, 28 per cent of people turn up for work even if they're ill (sickness presenteeism). Thirteen per cent are healthy but not always present (job dissatisfied), whereas only 35 per cent of them are fully functioning.

Table 6-4	Presenteeism	
	Health Good	*Health Not Good*
No absences	Healthy and present – 35 per cent	Unhealthy and present sickness presentees – 28 per cent
Some absences	Healthy and not always present – 13 per cent	Unhealthy and not always present – 24 per cent

Source: Sainsbury Centre for Mental Health, 2007.

Rooting Out Stress in an Organisation

The Do-it-Yourself approach that we recommend organisations follow to identify and deal with stress at work isn't complicated. You follow four simple steps:

1. **Conduct a stress audit.**

2. **Identify stressed groups.**

3. **Involve affected groups in finding solutions to the stress problem.**

4. **Report on problems and recommended solutions.**

The following sections take you through each step in turn.

Conducting a stress audit

Before you start a stress audit, establish in the organisation a stress or wellbeing *working party*, comprised of management and representatives of workers/unions, to oversee the process and report back to senior management with the results and recommended actions.

To carry out a workplace stress audit, use an established stress psychometric. The most used stress psychometric is ASSET, an organisational stress-screening tool composed of a number of subscales. Each scale has several questions. The scales are aggregated up so that you receive a single score for each scale. Here are the three outcome measures:

- Job satisfaction
- Mental wellbeing
- Physical wellbeing

Seven scales represent workplace sources of stress:

- Control
- Job security
- Overload
- Pay and benefits
- Resources and communications
- Work relationships
- Work–life balance

These scales relate to the areas we detail in the 'Understanding the Causes of Stress' section, earlier in this chapter. For example, you may look at

✔ The extent to which employees are troubled by

- Their pay and benefits
- Their relationships at work (with their boss, colleagues, customers, clients, and so on)
- Aspects of their workload (whether overloaded or underloaded or unrealistic deadlines for the work)

✔ How much control or autonomy they have in their job

✔ How secure they feel in their organisation and job

✔ Whether they've adequate resources

✔ How effective the organisational communications are within the workplace

✔ Whether they're getting adequate work–life balance, including the hours they work and their feelings about the flexibility provided by the organisation

The final two ASSET scales look at the perceptions of employees in relation to

✔ How committed the organisation is to them

✔ How committed they are to the organisation

You can also download stress audit instruments developed by the Health and Safety Executive in the UK from www.hse.gov.uk and by the National Institute for Occupational Safety and Health from www.cdc.gov/NIOSH.

Identifying stressed groups

In order to identify which parts of the organisation, level, or group within the organisation has a stress-related outcome and what that problem is, you need to break down the audit data (see the previous section) by demographics.

Department 1 may have a problem of a long-hours culture that is causing stress. Department 2 may have a bullying boss, and Department 3 may have difficulties juggling work and outside life because employees have no flexible working arrangement options. Or perhaps no problem exists across departments, but a particular demographic within the organisation, such as older workers, experience more stress because they don't feel supported within the organisation. You can compare stress levels across numerous demographics, which can help you to identify any problem areas.

The stress psychometric ASSET (which we introduce in the previous section) has extensive norms from thousands of workers in a variety of sectors, so that each department or demographic can have their scores compared to the norms of the general working population or by the sector concerned (for example, IT, police, hospital, or finance sector). The norms help you diagnose accurately which part of the workplace has problems, as measured by poor mental or physical health, for example, and the source of that problem (for example, poor relationships, lack of control, or poor communications). Check out the ASSET publisher at www.robertsoncooper.com.

Finding solutions

After you know where the stress hot spots are and what they are, you can form focus groups of workers affected by the issue.

If the problem is a glass ceiling for women in Department 1, then form a representative group of women in that department. Ask them to consider how the organisation can deal with that issue to reduce the stress. If new staff have increased stress levels, then form a focus group of these staff and get them to come up with a solution to ease them into the organisation. This way, you've involved those individuals specifically adversely affected, and they've ownership in the solution.

Reporting and recommending

Get the working party on stress/wellbeing to put together a report on where the stress is, the sources of the problem, and their recommendations of how to solve the issue. This group can present their report and recommendations to senior executives, which hopefully includes the HR Director or some other senior role holder.

To ensure that the implementation has been successful, keep the working party on board as the recommendations are rolled out.

Intervening in Stress

So what can organisations do to manage the stress levels? Professor Cary Cooper and Professor Susan Cartwright, both leading work psychologists in the area of work stress, suggest a three-pronged strategy to deal with stress at work in their book *Managing Workplace Stress* (Sage Publications, Inc):

✔ **Changing the job (primary prevention),** such as carrying out stress or wellbeing audits and then intervening where a problem occurs.

✔ **Supporting the employee (secondary prevention),** such as stress management and resilience training.

✔ **Dealing with the fallout (tertiary prevention),** such as workplace counselling or employee assistance programs

A fully comprehensive strategy incorporates all three of these approaches.

Changing the job

Primary intervention strategies are often a means to change culture and are about taking action to alter or remove sources of stress inbuilt in the work environment, therefore reducing their negative impact on the individual. Possible strategies include

✔ Redesigning the working environment

✔ Setting up flexible working schedules

✔ Involving the employee in career development

✔ Improving managerial behaviour and competencies

✔ Providing social support

The critical focus of primary interventions is in adapting the range of factors, such as those we list here, in individual organisations that can help reduce stress. This type of approach is likely to need to be customised to a specific situation and as such should be guided by a prior diagnosis or stress audit (see the earlier section 'Rooting Out Stress in an Organisation') to find out what specific factors are responsible for employee stress.

Supporting the employee

Secondary prevention requires a quick response to find and manage the experienced stress. You can do so by making individuals more aware of the signs of stress and developing their skills to manage stress through training and educational activities.

Employees respond to exposure to workplace stress in different ways as individual factors can change how you perceive and respond to the working environment. And as everyone has their own personal stress threshold, which means some people suffer and others seem to flourish in the same environment, designing stress-awareness activities and skills training programs (for example, techniques to improve relations at work, and skills to change thought processes and modify work–life balance in order to improve an individual's physical and psychological resources) to improve how individuals cope is important.

Although the aim of secondary prevention is to help employees to adapt to their environment, this type of prevention is really a damage limitation exercise. In a number of instances the working environment is still stressful, so the individual has to develop their own strategies to resist the stress. This has been called a *band-aid* approach.

Dealing with the fallout

Tertiary prevention is all about getting individuals, who have suffered from, or are suffering from, serious ill health as a result of stress well again. This stage involves potential treatments that can assist the individual's recuperation and recovery.

Typical interventions include the provision of counselling services that help employees deal with work or personal problems. These services tend to be provided by in-house counsellors or outside agencies, and offer information, support, and counselling and/or referral to suitable treatment and support services. Research evidence indicates that counselling is an effective way to improve the psychological wellbeing of employees and has substantial cost benefits.

Taking Inspiration from Successful Stress Management Examples

Many organisations have carried out successful stress or wellbeing audits. The following sections give examples of different interventions in very different sectors, based on the work of Robertson Cooper Ltd, one of the leading providers of wellbeing solutions for organisations.

De-stressing the police

In 2007, a UK police force identified that numerous problems, such as relatively high sickness absence, reported work overload, and the like.

The police force decided to carry out a force-wide stress audit using ASSET online. (See the section 'Rooting Out Stress in an Organisation,' earlier in this chapter, for more on ASSET.) They discovered that they had high levels of overload, relatively poor physical and mental health (benchmarked against other police sector norms), worrying levels of bullying (which isn't uncommon in the police service), low levels of productivity, and a gap between commitment by the force to the officers versus their commitment to the force.

Following these results, the groups with the relevant problems designed interventions to tackle the stress problems identified. A range of interventions emerged from a bicycling to work and weight loss campaign to tackle the physical health issues, to controlling the work overload through 'switch off your mobile phone' scheme, to helping officers to prioritise their workloads. In addition, managers attended resilience training sessions to help them cope with many of the issues.

Two years after the interventions were implemented, a follow-up stress survey took place and found

- ✔ An 11.1 per cent decrease in reported work overload

- ✔ An 8.3 per cent improvement in physical and mental wellbeing

- ✔ A 6.9 per cent reduction in workplace bullying

- ✔ A 6 per cent increase in productivity

- ✔ A significant reduction in the commitment gap between the organisation and the individual

- ✔ A reduction in sickness absence figures from 6.3 per cent in 2003 to 3.0 per cent in 2010

Based on these numbers, this program was considered a success.

Improving absenteeism in a healthcare trust

Absenteeism from sickness, issues of engagement, and wellbeing in general tend to be high in the hospital and healthcare sector.

At one healthcare trust, a stress audit, using ASSET, identified hot spots sources of stress, with the goal of determining the nature, location, and severity and to develop follow-up activities for improvement. The stress audit discovered that 50 per cent of all staff reported having a major stressful event, with 66 per cent of these stressful events related to work. Employees had low levels of wellbeing scores and high levels of sickness absence in specific departments, which highlighted the need for targeted wellbeing initiatives.

After engaging their staff, the Trust developed action plans and implemented them, based on the ASSET stress-screening tool and focus-group discussions. A year later, staff turnover was reduced by 3.6 per cent, stress-related sickness absence was down by 7.0 per cent, and the reduction in sickness absence saved the Trust over £70,000 after only six months.

Looking to a stressful future

It is safe to say that we have, at the start of this millennium, all the ingredients of corporate stress:

✔ An ever-increasing workload

✔ A decreasing workforce

✔ A climate of rapid change

✔ Control over the means of production increasingly being exercised by bigger bureaucracies

✔ A downturn in the economy

✔ Emerging threats to stabilising and job security

The end result is that more people are working in job-insecure environments and fewer people are there to do the work.

And the pressures on everyone are likely to get worse. As we move away from our own internal markets and enter larger economic systems, individual organisations will have less control over business life. Rules and regulations are beginning to be imposed in terms of labour laws; health and safety at work; methods of production, distribution, and remuneration; and so on. These concerns are all laudable issues in their own right, but nevertheless, these workplace constraints will inhibit individual control and autonomy.

It appears, therefore, that stress is here to stay and can't be dismissed as simply a bygone remnant of the entrepreneurial 1980s and 1990s. The challenge for human resource management in the future is to understand a basic truth about human behaviour. Developing and maintaining a 'feel-good' factor at work and in our economy generally isn't just about bottom-line factors. This factor is, or should be, in a civilised society, about quality of life issues, such as hours of work, family time, manageable workloads, control over one's career, and some sense of job security.

As the social anthropologist Studs Terkel suggests in his book *Working* (published by The New Press), 'work is about a search for daily meaning as well as daily bread, for recognition as well as cash, for astonishment rather than torpor, in short, for a sort of life rather than a Monday through Friday sort of dying'.

Managing stress in the Council of Europe

The Council of Europe is an intergovernmental body based in Strasbourg, with 47 member countries throughout the whole of Europe. In December 2009, the Council commissioned an organisation-wide wellbeing audit. All employees throughout Europe, in 28 workplaces from Paris to Warsaw to Moscow, took the questionnaire. The Council's purpose was to assess their strengths and weaknesses in an effort to improve wellbeing among their employees.

The Council discovered lots of positives. It showed high engagement and commitment levels, a relatively physically healthy workforce, and relatively high productivity.

The Council identified two areas of concern:

- ✔ Employees were slightly troubled by their work relationships.
- ✔ Employees had high levels of presenteeism.

The Council then effectively and quickly communicated the results and got engagement from areas that needed improvement by localised action plans. The Council is still in the process of rolling out and implementing their action plans with the strong support of senior management and the employees themselves. Maud de Boer-Buquicchio, Deputy Secretary General of the Council of Europe, said of this exercise:

> *The work we have done with this study has enabled us to get to grips with the challenge of managing the wellbeing of a diverse workforce. Our organisation is complex and the work brings unique challenges, but we are now confident that the wellness of our people will contribute to, rather than hinder, its work.*

Chapter 7

Handling Emotionally Demanding Jobs

. . . .

In This Chapter
▶ Working with people and their emotions
▶ Getting all emotional with work
▶ Burning out and feeling down

. . . .

*H*ow many times do you reflect on a situation and think to yourself, 'I had to try not to cry,' 'I forced myself really hard not to laugh,' or 'I was determined not to show I felt hurt?' Often, controlling your emotions is part of behaving appropriately, such as feeling sad at funerals, happy at weddings, or not laughing during a serious work presentation. Or, you may want to keep your emotions in check because you don't want someone to know how you really feel. This control is all very well in your personal life, but think how you'd feel if your job depends on not showing how you really feel or having to fake your emotions.

In this chapter, we look at what an emotion actually is, what it entails within a work environment, and the types of work where you're more likely to use your emotions. We also explain the ins and outs of emotional labour; how and why, as an employee, it can be a problem; and how, as a manager, you can limit negative consequences.

Understanding Emotional Labour

Usually, you're careful about the emotions you show in social situations to protect other people's feelings or to avoid embarrassing yourself. However, you do have a choice to react how you want to, for example to show frustration to a friend who is making unrealistic demands on your time. Or, you can stay away from a relative who is distressed by a bereavement because it upsets you too much. However, in a work situation you may not be allowed to show your true feelings or to avoid emotional encounters. Your job description may require you to be polite and courteous to all customers at all times, or to act in a professional manner whatever is happening around you.

Jobs dealing with people can be stressful and emotionally demanding. For example, working in a caring profession as a nurse, or on the front-line in a service industry, can be difficult. Think about what it's like to tell a family that their mother is terminally ill, while maintaining a professional manner, or to put on a smile while dealing with an abusive and dissatisfied customer. Having to hide or fake emotions at work are what organisational behaviourists call *emotional labour* or *emotion work,* or the *have-a-nice-day syndrome.*

The reason organisational behaviourists and work psychologists are interested in emotional labour is because the requirement to display emotions at odds with your feelings is associated with high levels of stress, distress, turnover, and lower levels of job satisfaction, which, as we show you in Chapter 6, have enormous costs to the organisation and the individual.

Defining emotion

What's an *emotion*? Based on research by psychologists Bernstein and Nash, an emotion is something that

- ✔ **Is usually a temporary state:** In other words, an emotion has a clear beginning and end and lasts for a short time. Moods (and we all have them!) tend to last longer.

- ✔ **Is pleasant or unpleasant, positive or negative:** For example, feeling happy for most people is a pleasant experience, but feeling sad isn't an emotion you willingly choose. Happiness has a positive effect on your wellbeing, but being sad for a long time can lead to poor physical and psychological health.

- ✔ **Is triggered partly by weighing up a situation in relation to your goals:** The same event can create different emotions depending on how you interpret it. For example, an exam mark of 75 per cent may excite you if your previous marks were 50 per cent, but you may feel upset if your scores are usually more than 90 per cent.

- ✔ **Can alter thought processes:** The distress experienced by parents whose child is killed by a drunk driver, for example, may prompt them to alter their views on the importance of drink-driving laws.

- ✔ **Can motivate your behaviour:** Grieving parents' anger, for example, may motivate them to harm the driver who killed their child or fight for stronger penalties for drunk-driving.

- ✔ **Just happens to you:** Sometimes you just can't stop yourself feeling an emotion.

The author Lynn tends to react emotionally quickly, shaking her fist at bad drivers and feeling frustrated with poor service in restaurants. Her husband, on the other hand, always reacts calmly to every situation because he doesn't see any benefit in getting upset.

Despite Lynn's husband's ability to remain cool, even he can't decide not to experience emotions at all. How many people have the ability to resist falling in love or being overcome with grief?

However, some cultural differences exist in displaying emotions. For example, in Japan, importance is placed on not showing emotions. Nevertheless, when emotions are shown, they're the same across all cultures. The six main emotion categories are

- ✔ Happiness
- ✔ Disgust
- ✔ Surprise
- ✔ Sadness
- ✔ Anger
- ✔ Fear

Emotions determine your mood, which lasts longer than your initial emotional response. Moods influence your judgement and can affect the decisions you make.

Modifying feelings at work

When you carry out emotional labour, you're trying to manage or change an emotion or a feeling to be suitable for that particular situation. You base the suitability of the emotion on social guidelines, which are sort of basic rules you follow depending on your culture. For example, in the Western world, you're expected to feel happy at weddings and sad at funerals.

In the same way, work guidelines influence suitable emotions at work. As you'd expect, anything with the word *labour* involved means that you have to actively do something to your feelings. It takes an effort to produce a *suitable* emotion – for example, to hide your anger when someone is rude to you.

Technically, *emotion work* is the term psychologists use to describe the existing ability you have to control your own emotions, whereas *emotional labour* is used when management gets involved and makes demands on how you control your emotions to do your job. In reality, both terms do get used interchangeably, so in the interests of simplicity, we stick with one term, emotional labour, throughout the chapter.

Post-industrial societies, such as those in the West, are moving away from making things (manufacturing) to dealing with people (service work).

In doing so, more and more employees are constantly faced with emotionally charged encounters that need specific emotional reactions. Psychological research in America suggests that as many as a third of employees experience situations loaded with emotions, and research in the UK suggests that some workers spend around two-thirds of their workplace communications managing their emotions. All these jobs, whether you care for others or just serve members of the public, involve emotional labour, to some extent.

So what actually is emotional labour? Research by Dieter Zapf, a German psychologist, suggests the following characteristics:

- ✔ **Emotional labour is a significant part of jobs that require face-to-face or voice-to-voice interaction with clients or customers**. For example, a doctor with a patient or a call centre agent speaking on the phone with a customer both have jobs that require emotional labour.

- ✔ **Emotions in these jobs are displayed to influence other people's attitudes and behaviours**. In the doctor–patient example, the doctor may want to be empathetic and show sadness when explaining the negative results of a medical test. Or the call centre agent may express fear for the customer who isn't sufficiently insured, in order to sell more insurance.

- ✔ **The display of emotions has to follow certain rules**. For example, a medical code of conduct would not allow a doctor to laugh at a patient's predicament. Or the call centre organisation may instruct its agents to be polite and smile when speaking on the phone.

Looking at the characteristics of emotional labour, you can appreciate that it's an essential part of many jobs, but most prevalent in caring professions.

Seeing which jobs involve emotional labour

You probably have a typical view of the types of occupations that involve emotional labour – for example, healthcare, social workers, counsellors, police officers, and teachers. A police officer experiences strong emotions when faced with human sorrow in the form of violence, accidents, victims of crime, or death, as does a nurse when a young child is diagnosed with a terminal illness.

Often, the emotional challenges are what attract people to these types of careers. For example, in nursing, showing empathy and reassurance are key skills because nurses provide comfort to patients and offer reassurance to their relatives. The emotions involved with helping a patient can make the job worthwhile and give you a sense of accomplishment, which, as we explain in Chapter 9, can motivate you at work.

Dealing with people instead of things can result in unique stresses that many workplaces don't take seriously. Emotional labour can make you feel dissatisfied with your job. You may skip work, feel like leaving, or just be stressed out. In more extreme circumstances, you may become depressed, anxious, and burnt out. (See the later section 'Burning Out from Emotion Work.')

But jobs involving emotional labour aren't just restricted to caring professions. Most employees at some time experience a degree of emotional labour, especially, but not only, those in customer-facing, frontline roles. Psychological studies describe in depth the emotional experiences of flight attendants, debt collectors, hair stylists, and supermarket cashiers, but one of the highest levels of emotional labour (outside caring professions) is for those working in complaints or customer service departments.

Service employees are expected to be customer-friendly and to treat customers in a positive manner, even if customers are unfriendly or even rude or aggressive. If you visit a restaurant or retail outlet or contact a call centre, what makes you visit them or use them, again? It may be because the meal was wonderful, the jeans were a bargain, or your call was answered quickly. But, despite these positive outcomes, if the waiter was rude, the shop assistant scowled at you as you paid, or the call centre agent was offhand, would you still continue to use them? The chances are you won't (if you have a choice), and you'll tell all your friends about your bad experience. Organisations realise the commercial value in the impression their employees give, particularly in the emotions they show.

One of the main reasons organisations get involved with controlling employee emotions is the potential influence on their reputation. The emotion an employee shows directly influences the customer's impression of the service quality. For example, if you're a customer in a restaurant, you don't really care whether the chefs in the kitchen are pleasant or not, but if the waiters don't smile when they seat you and take your order, you may start to question the quality of the service.

Service work is growing rapidly and currently accounts for almost 70 per cent of jobs in advanced economies, so understanding emotional labour is increasingly important for organisations.

Recent research by organisational psychologists suggests that one of the most stressful parts of working in a call centre is being made to be cheerful to callers all the time (lack of control over how you do your work and constant monitoring of your output are also stressful for call centre workers – see Chapter 2). Because of the negative outcomes of emotional labour for the organisation and the employees (such as low job satisfaction, absenteeism, stress, and turnover), managers need to look at ways of reducing the impact of emotional labour and improving job satisfaction and employee wellbeing.

We give you some tips within this chapter for helping employees, but also check out Chapter 9 for more details on how to increase job satisfaction and Chapter 12 for information on designing jobs to have a positive impact on satisfaction and wellbeing.

Seeing Emotional Labour in Action

Emotional labour involves displaying emotions that your organisation wants you to, such as friendliness toward customers if you're a customer service worker. Emotional labour is a really important skill for the organisation because it affects the customer's view of the service quality.

In this section, we describe the way that organisations try to direct employee's emotions, the different ways employees perform emotional labour, and what happens when you've a conflict with your real emotions.

Displaying rules

If you interact with customers, your manager may expect you to behave toward them according to *display rules.* These rules may be as simple as instructions to smile or a specific greeting or farewell script to follow, or they may be more complex based on to how long you interact with the customer. You may not have even been told about the rules, but just picked up the expected behaviour from your colleagues. Generally, though, organisations are usually explicit about display rules, such as explaining to a new starter to smile at the customer. In other words, the friendly smile of a service worker becomes a job requirement!

Take a trip to Disney World for an example of more extreme explicit display rules. The new cast members are taught in classes, given handbooks, and reminded by strategically placed billboards exactly which positive and reputation-enhancing emotions they must show to guests at Disney World. The guidelines that must be adhered to for every guest is to 'make eye contact and smile' and 'greet and welcome each and every guest' are unlikely to appear genuine to every guest and can come across as fake.

How do you feel when you can sense that someone isn't genuine? Displaying fake or real emotions is the difference between using surface acting and deep acting, which we discuss in the section 'Handling conflicting emotions', later in the chapter.

On the other hand, some service organisations don't have explicit display rules and instead encourage employees to be themselves. This expectation is called *display autonomy.* Although these organisations don't enforce specific display rules, you can bet they still expect you to be courteous to customers or clients.

Hochschild's study of emotion at work

In her influential book *The Managed Heart* (University of California Press), American Sociologist Arlie Hochschild first coins the term *emotional labour* to describe emotion management for commercial reasons. She describes a study of female flight attendants who display emotions that are different from the emotions they're feeling. For example, the flight attendants have to put on a cheerful face and be nice to passengers regardless of whether they feel like smiling or how horrible the passengers are in return.

Hochschild's main contribution to the research on emotions at work is the importance she places on how managing your emotions can involve as much conscious effort and hard work as physical labour. Just think about the effort a flight attendant requires to speak calmly and smile while stopping herself from screaming at the obnoxious passenger – and not be able to leave the room to calm down! This study also shows that when pressures increase, due to quicker turnarounds for flights or low staffing levels, the flight attendants are even less able to cope with managing the emotional labour.

As a manager, think carefully about enforcing display rules. Instructing your employees to be enthusiastic and to hide frustrations is likely to result in more errors and exhausted employees.

Managing emotional labour

Emotional labour is important to organisations because

- ✔ Displaying emotions according to an organisation's display rules is directly related to a customer's view of the quality of service.

- ✔ Demands for emotional labour have a negative impact on your wellbeing at work and can make you feel emotionally exhausted, which is more likely to make you feel like leaving the organisation.

As a manager, you need to find ways to ensure that employees show acceptable emotions without ending up emotionally exhausted and stressed. The first step is to understand what can increase the level of emotional labour. Here are a number of causes of increased emotional labour:

- ✔ **Frequency of emotions:** Frequency of emotions means the number of times you have to smile at a customer.

- ✔ **Duration of emotions:** A flight attendant serving a drink needs to give only a brief smile, but a social worker visiting a child at risk of parental violence has to keep up a particular emotional appearance for longer.

✔ **Type of emotions:** Emotions can be positive, negative, or neutral. Positive emotions are most common, but a debt collector may have to appear stern to recover a debt, or a judge may need to appear neutral.

✔ **Control over emotions:** Some managers may enforce emotional display rules, whereas others may allow employees to tick off an abusive customer.

✔ **Conflict between emotions shown and felt:** For example, a receptionist is expected to smile even if she isn't in a happy mood. This display is called *emotional dissonance;* see the next section 'Handling conflicting emotions' for details.

If your employees often have no control over the emotions they show (and the emotions don't match how they feel) for long periods of time, the likelihood of their being negatively affected by emotional labour increases.

Handling conflicting emotions

Organisational psychologists tend to focus most on emotional dissonance as the main reason for the negative consequences of emotional labour. *Emotional dissonance* happens when your actual feeling is inconsistent with the feeling you show.

Emotional dissonance can happen for a number of reasons – for example when the organisation's rules expect you to

✔ **Suppress your true feelings.** Suppose that you had an argument with your partner in the morning before you left for work. You may be feeling down and find it difficult to hide how you feel.

✔ **Express neutral feelings.** A colleague, Rita, was on a train recently, and an elderly passenger had forgotten to bring his senior railcard (a discount card). As part of her job, the ticket collector had to ask the passenger to pay the additional fare. The passenger obviously had difficulty putting together the rest of the money. The ticket collector stood there expressionless. She couldn't let him get away without paying because the rest of the passengers were listening. Rita had no idea what the ticket collector really felt.

✔ **Show a negative feeling.** To do his job properly, a debt collector may have to show anger and hostility (if no money is paid) and appear heartless to people's personal hardships. Unless you're a nasty person and genuinely feel these emotions, you're likely to experience emotional dissonance.

✔ **Show a positive feeling instead of a negative feeling.** This situation is one of the most common experiences, particularly with difficult customers. If you've ever worked in a customer-facing role, the feeling you get when you stop yourself from showing your anger toward a customer and are pleasant to them instead is emotional dissonance.

So what do you do when you can't show your true feelings? Employees can control their own emotions and reduce any emotional conflict in two ways:

- **Surface acting:** Because you don't automatically feel the emotion you need to show, you fake it. For example, you smile although you don't feel happy inside. We cover surface acting in more detail in the next section.

- **Deep acting:** You change not only your physical expression, but also your inner feelings. See the later section 'Feeling on the inside'.

Surface acting focuses on outward behaviour and refers to actually acting out the emotions. Deep acting focuses on inner feelings and requires you to actually feel the emotion.

Research shows that although both surface and deep acting can have harmful effects on physical and psychological wellbeing, surface acting is particularly damaging.

Of course, you may also genuinely feel the emotions. A nurse may genuinely feel sympathy for a child with an injury, which means that she doesn't need to surface act or deep act to meet the organisations rules.

Smiling on the outside

Surface acting is about faking emotions you don't feel because you need to do so for your job. You need to put on an act to behave how your manager and customers expect you to. You may have to alter the tone of your voice, such as sounding sympathetic when you say, 'Oh, I'm so sorry.' Or you may need to change your facial expression, most often by giving a false smile. If you consider a doctor's role, he must spend a lot of time surface acting to hide negative emotions – for example, trying to appear optimistic when giving the patient abnormal test results.

You may think that faking emotions is easy to do, but if you do it frequently, it can get emotionally draining. In fact, research by organisational psychologists has consistently found that faking emotions can result in burnout, which is a type of chronic stress. (See the later section 'Burning Out from Emotion Work' for details.) As well as burnout, faking emotions can result in you

- Having low morale
- Feeling in a bad mood
- Leaving the organisation
- Providing poorer service quality
- Taking time off work
- Withdrawing from work

Check out Chapter 6 on stress, health, and wellbeing to see what these outcomes can really cost your organisation.

As a service employee, you're a lot less likely to get large tips and good customer ratings if you fake your emotions. If you try to feel the emotions that you need to show the customers, you'll be a lot more successful. (For tips, see the next section 'Feeling on the inside'.)

You will have times, though, when an employee may not put on the friendly face that, as a manager, you want them to. Psychologists call this *emotional deviance*. Emotional deviance may not be deliberate – the employee may not be experienced enough to control her emotions, or she may just be exhausted. On the other hand, an employee may work against the organisation. (For why, see the psychological contract in Chapter 10 and motivation in Chapter 9.)

Employees new to the job tend to show genuine feelings toward the customers and happily follow organisational rules. But, as time goes by, they show less of their true feelings and use more and more surface acting as self-protection.

Feeling on the inside

Deep acting involves trying to actually feel the emotions you need to show. You can deep act in a couple of different ways. For example, you can directly will the emotion by allowing yourself to genuinely feel the emotion. Or you can use your imagination and your own personal memories to produce the emotion. An example is thinking about a happy event, such as getting married or cuddling a child, to create a feeling of happiness.

The benefits to you of using deep-acting techniques, as opposed to surface acting, are

- An increase in job satisfaction
- A decrease in emotional exhaustion
- A decrease in stress levels
- More positive reactions from customers

As a manager, you may be thinking that deep acting is easy; just get your employees to discover deep-acting techniques, and all the problems are solved. And you're right up to a point!

Generally, any excessive or unreasonable demands for emotional labour can have a detrimental effect on your health, given that the demands are going to continue, but you can help your employees. We introduce techniques in the next section.

Burning Out from Emotion Work

Although job stress is a part of every worker's life, prolonged, chronic job stress can result in burnout, specifically in jobs that perform emotional labour. (Check out Chapter 6 for more details about stress.) *Burnout* is a state of emotional, physical, and mental exhaustion that results in you feeling emotionally drained, cynical toward work and customers, and like you can't do your job as well as you used to.

Managers in particular need to be aware of burnout as it can lead to an employee

- ✔ Becoming stressed
- ✔ Feeling demotivated
- ✔ Giving a poor level of service
- ✔ Taking sick days
- ✔ Leaving the organisation

In some service organisations, as many as one in five employees report symptoms of burnout.

Recognising burnout

Here are the three main elements of burnout:

- ✔ **Emotional exhaustion:** You feel physically and mentally drained. Everything just becomes too much of an effort, and you can't be bothered to try any more. You may get home from work and just collapse on the sofa and do nothing for the evening. Some symptoms you can recognise in yourself are
  - Feeling emotionally overloaded by other people
  - Feeling that customers need more of you than you can give
  - Not having positive feelings any more
- ✔ **Cynicism:** You begin to get bitter and develop an attitude toward work and customers, due to previous experiences. Symptoms you can recognise in yourself are
  - Having unsympathetic and negative thoughts toward customers
  - Being obnoxious or rude about customers – for example, making sarcastic and sneering comments to colleagues about customers
  - Behaving in a bad-mannered way toward customers

✔ **Feeling less effective at work:** Psychologists refer to this condition as *reduced personal accomplishment.* You become so totally dissatisfied with how you perform at work that you almost give up. Symptoms you may recognise are

- Feeling that you're a failure at work

- Experiencing a lack of control

- Being a lot less efficient

Although anyone can suffer from burnout, full-time workers are more likely to suffer from burnout than part-time workers, as they're more exposed to the emotional drain on them. And burnout tends to reduce with age, suggesting that life experience may be an important buffer against developing burnout.

Burnout isn't good for employees, managers, or organisations, but as a manager, you can take actions to reduce the likelihood of it happening. One of the best ways is to train your employees to better handle the demands of emotional labour.

Training emotions

When working in an organisation that needs a lot of emotional labour, training employees matters more than just relying on selecting the right people. However, recruiting people with a lot of emotional intelligence can help. (See later in this section and Chapter 3 for more details.)

Most organisations tend to focus employee training on how the customer feels, such as how to make them feel welcome in a hotel or calm in a hospital. But, also think about how your employees feel. Providing training programs to develop deep-acting skills to perform emotional labour can train your employees to give a more sincere impression to customers and create more job satisfaction. Perhaps, more importantly, training programs need to provide opportunities for your employees to talk about how they feel and to be open in discussions about the frustrations of the job. The benefits of doing open discussions are that

✔ Your employees realise that the organisation cares about their emotional roles.

✔ They provide an opportunity for your employees to talk about the real emotions they feel toward their jobs.

✔ The organisation examines ways of supporting employees who struggle with the expression of extreme emotions, by initiating non-tolerance of abusive behaviour, for example.

- ✔ Associated training can focus on developing the ability to keep anger inside and avoid frustration.

- ✔ You can use these opportunities for your employees (along with you as the manager) to exchange tips about the least offensive ways of showing negative emotions.

Tips for training

You can focus your training programs on developing and practicing deep-acting techniques in a number of ways:

- ✔ **Actively think about events to bring about the desired emotion.** For example, encouraging your employees to think about a funny film can make them feel more cheerful.

- ✔ **Go over unpleasant situations and reduce any emotional impact.** For example, in a study by psychologist Hochschild, flight attendants were taught to see difficult passengers as hungry children who need attention so that they don't feel as angry with them. (We give you the lowdown in the earlier sidebar 'Hochschild's study of emotion at work'.)

By practicing these techniques, your employees discover how to hide their feelings or create feelings whenever they need to.

Training managers in emotional intelligence

Front-line employees are not the only ones that perform emotional labour; as a manager, you do so as well. Dealing with employees, as well as being involved with customers, takes emotional labour, so managers can benefit from similar training.

A particularly good way to help managers is to train them in emotional intelligence. *Emotional intelligence* is about being aware of other people's emotions and responding to them appropriately, and understanding how your emotions impact on others and controlling them accordingly. Individuals with high emotional intelligence likely have a larger repertoire of emotional labour strategies at hand, so they can skilfully use the most suitable strategy for each situation. A trained manager can pass on these skills to their employees.

Having emotionally intelligent employees is an advantage for an organisation, especially when emotional labour is needed.

Being aware of the negative side

Training sessions should make your employees aware of the negative impact of surface acting on their general wellbeing. The negative effects of faking emotions are worse for women than men, and the positive effects of showing genuine emotions are greater for women. Women are more likely than men to work in caring professions and service industries, where more emotional labour is needed. This fact suggests that showing genuine emotions is even more important for women than for men.

So, as a manager, you need to

✔ Encourage employees to be as authentic as possible in the emotions they show through deep acting.

✔ Encourage female employees in particular to show authentic emotions and use deep acting.

Using other methods to improve emotional management

A training program by itself is going to have limited results. In addition, you should try to

✔ **Cultivate a supportive environment.** Encourage your employees to share their good and bad experiences with you and with coworkers. These discussions provide an opportunity to discover different approaches and give employees more confidence. Encourage older employees in particular to share their experiences with younger employees, as older employees are less likely to suffer from burnout. You can support this sharing by setting up mentoring schemes, which we discuss in Chapter 19.

✔ **Provide ways for employees to vent their anger and frustration.** You can encourage venting in a formal way. For example, a call centre we know actively encourages employees to take time out with a colleague after a difficult customer interaction. Informally, you can give employees extra time to let off steam.

✔ **Be aware of when an employee is having a bad day.** Encourage other team members to have a bit of banter between them to help them feel less frustrated.

✔ **Build trust between coworkers and managers in the workplace.** Trust is closely linked to your emotions because your emotions determine whether you trust someone. For example, if you feel that someone is telling the truth, you're more likely to trust them and others around them and feel positive emotions. As a manager, you can work toward developing a trusting environment by being consistent and honest in your behaviour and open about your concerns. Also, ensure that you've fair HR policies and practices. (You can read more about this topic in Chapters 10 and 11.)

- ✔ **Allow your employees to have more control over how they express their emotions.** We don't mean total freedom, but generally, individuals go along with how their colleagues behave. So, creating a culture that identifies what isn't acceptable behaviour should control any extreme actions. (Have a look at Chapters 4 and 13 for more information on attitude and culture.)

- ✔ **Create opportunities for your employees to have fun at work.** In other words, do things that put them in a good mood and trigger positive emotions. For example, providing cakes with candles to celebrate birthdays usually makes all but the most cynical smile and feel happy.

Part III
All About the Employer

"First of all, let me commend everyone on the teamwork displayed on this icebreaker. Secondly, let me apologize for some of the motivational language I used during this session..."

In this part . . .

Part III takes a look at organisational behaviour topics that relate primarily to employers. Leadership is a key topic when considering employers, and we explore different styles and think about how they can affect employees. We also look at motivating people at work, and the importance of the psychological contract that exists between employer and employee and the end result of breaking this contract. Finally, we consider the importance of fair treatment in the workplace.

Chapter 8

Leading the Way: Leadership in the Workplace

*W*hat's the point of leadership? Why can't you just get on with doing your job running the organisation, or your department, without any leadership nonsense? Well, the success of an organisation is all about attracting the most talented people to work in it and giving them all the help they need to meet the organisation's goals. Without effective leadership, there's no one to create the vision of what the future organisation will look like or to motivate and influence the employees to take it there. Therefore, the leadership skills of chief executives and their teams are extremely important to organisations.

You can find as many leadership styles as leaders. For example, think of the differences between Margaret Thatcher and Nelson Mandela. Margaret Thatcher was described as domineering and confident of her own opinion (at least by her enemies!) and expected her subordinates to follow instructions, whereas Nelson Mandela believed in consensus and used a general feeling against apartheid to empower and motivate the people of South Africa.

In this chapter, we look at the different styles of leadership and help you understand which styles are useful, and when to use them to be an effective leader. We explain what happens when you use a good leadership style badly so that you can avoid making those mistakes. And we take a look at how leadership is transforming with the times.

Leading or Managing?

Ten years ago, we'd have written this chapter all about management, and the best way to manage people, but now we focus on leadership instead. People often think that leadership and management are the same thing, but they're not. Table 8-1 lists the differences.

Table 8-1	Leadership versus Management
Leadership	*Management*
About behaviour	About processes
The *way* management methods and processes are used	The *type* of management methods and processes used
Sets a new direction and vision for others to follow	Controls or directs people/resources according to established principles/values
Relies on attitudinal qualities	Relies on management processes

In the words of Peter Drucker (a management guru): 'Management is doing things right; leadership is doing the right things.'

Leadership does involve many management skills, such as directing and instructing people and being decisive, but that's not all. Leadership also depends on less measurable things like personal character, attitude, trust, and inspiration. People follow good leaders because they trust and respect them, not just because they've good organisational skills.

Management is all about planning, organising, and controlling based on established principles. Leadership, on the other hand, is about setting a new direction, motivating, inspiring, and implementing change.

Take a moment and think about what happens if you've leadership without management and vice versa. Without management skills, a leader sets a new direction for others to follow but doesn't think about how to do it. The how-to part is left to other people to follow on behind and do all the work. Without leadership skills, a manager acts like a referee of a sports game – controlling resources and making sure that the rules and procedures are followed but not giving direction as to the best way forward.

Leadership skills are never a disadvantage to a manager; all managers should be leaders. However, not all leaders have the capability to be a manager.

Looking at Leadership Styles

A number of leadership types exist, and (conveniently!) they fit into four main categories:

- **Trait:** What type of person makes a good leader?
- **Behavioural:** What does a good leader do?
- **Contingency/situational:** How does the situation influence what a leader does?
- **Power and influence:** What is the source of the leader's power?

Table 8-2 shows the leadership types and how they're categorised and offers a general overview of why they're useful.

Table 8-2	Categories and Characteristics of Leadership	
Category	*Characteristics*	*Advantages*
Trait	Typical characteristics of effective leaders (for example, personality, ability, physiological, and so on)	Helps to identify the essential qualities in a good leader
Behavioural	Autocratic	Can offer control over routine and unskilled jobs
	Bureaucratic	Appropriate for safety-conscious jobs or dealing with money
	Democratic	Good in teamwork and when quality is more important than speed
	Laissez-faire	Useful if employees are experienced and motivated
Contingency/ situational	People-oriented	Encourages teamwork and creative collaboration
	Task-oriented	Helpful in early stages of planning, organising, and structuring
Power and influence	Transactional	Valuable on a daily basis to get things done
	Transformational	Highly effective for new initiatives
	Charismatic	Good for inspiring enthusiasm

The following sections look at the approaches in more detail so that you can make up your own mind about which style suits you or your organisation.

Investigating leadership traits

Trait theories dominated early thoughts about what makes a good leader. The idea is that good leaders share a number of personality characteristics and traits, so to find a good leader, you study them and make a list of what they're like. In Table 8-3, we compare a typical list from 1981 with a more recent list.

Table 8-3	Old and New Leadership Traits
Old	*New*
Tall	Integrity, maturity, energy
High socio-economic status	Business acumen
Good interpersonal skills	People acumen (for example, leading teams and coaching people; having empathy)
Decisive	Organisational acumen (such as building trust, sharing information, being decisive)
Intelligent	Curiosity, intellect, global mindset
Superior judgement	Superior judgement
High need for achievement (see Chapter 9)	Drive for results
Excellent verbal ability	Motivation to grow

You probably spotted the weakness in the old list! The suggestion is that unless you're tall or from a privileged background, you can't be a leader. The belief was 'You've either got it or you haven't' to be a leader. Luckily, (especially for short people!), we now know that you can do a lot to develop your own leadership qualities. However, even today, applicants for top jobs in organisations are likely to take a series of assessment tests for intelligence, judgement, verbal ability, and interpersonal skills. (Chapter 17 explains selection testing.)

Trait theories are about what people *are* and propose that leaders are born, not made.

Trait theory does help to spot certain qualities that are useful when leading others and suggests a generalised leadership style. But having a combination of these traits won't guarantee you success as a leader. They're not enough by themselves.

Behaving like a leader

The behavioural approach to leadership is about how leaders behave. For example, does the leader tell people what to do and just expect them to co-operate, or does she involve people in decision-making to gain support for the action? Table 8-2, earlier in this chapter, outlines the behavioural types of leaders, and here we look at them one by one.

REMEMBER

Behavioural theories are about what people *do,* and the idea is that these leadership traits can be taught.

TIP

How leaders behave impacts their effectiveness, and many of these leadership behaviours are appropriate at different times. So the best leaders are those who can use many different behavioural styles and use the right style for each situation.

Autocratic leadership

If you've an autocratic leadership style, you want absolute power over your team or employees. You make all the decisions, and no one else is allowed to contribute ideas, even when broader decision-making is in the organisation's best interest.

In some situations, though, the autocratic style is a useful approach. For example, some people choose to do routine and unskilled jobs because they don't want to be the person to make decisions or have any hassles at work – a number of times in our lives, we've just felt like stacking shelves in a super-market rather than be hassled and constantly making decisions at work!

The autocratic style is a rather outdated view of leadership, but the military and some industries such as large assembly-line factories often use it because it has some advantages:

- **Increased productivity:** While you're watching so closely, the team members are less likely to slack off.

- **Operational improvements:** Your being involved in all aspects of a project or task means that those you're leading deal with problems and meet deadlines.

- **Quicker decisions:** Fewer consultations over decisions mean that you can react faster, although this can backfire if the leader is overloaded and decisions can't be made because others aren't authorised to make them.

- **Reduction in stress:** If you're in control, then you know the task is going to get done.

Autocratic leadership isn't a style that's suitable for every occasion, but here are a few work situations where this approach is beneficial:

✔ A quick-changing business environment

✔ Low-skilled and monotonous tasks where employees aren't motivated to improve quality levels or work faster (although we advise you to read Chapter 9 on motivation!)

✔ Short-term projects with risky or complex aspects or tight deadlines

✔ When managing a large number of employees

How would you feel if you were managed by an autocratic manager? You're likely to object and not give your best, or even leave. As a manager, if you always use the autocratic style, you face a number of disadvantages:

✔ **Increased workload:** Controlling everything can result in high stress levels (see Chapter 6).

✔ **Poor perception of your leadership:** This style, which is favoured by ineffective managers, is disliked by employees.

✔ **Short-term approach:** Your employees aren't developing from making mistakes or gaining leadership skills, so you de-skill your workforce.

An autocratic style can be useful for demotivated employees, but often this leadership style is what demotivates them!

Bureaucratic leadership

If you're a bureaucratic leader, you like to work by the book. You make sure that your employees follow systems and procedures rigorously and provide detailed instructions. You gain authority through your position, as you ensure that you sign off on everything and reward only those employees who stick entirely to rules and procedures.

Using this style has a number of benefits:

✔ **Absolute control:** To be successful, employees have to follow rules, which makes keeping costs down and increasing productivity easier.

✔ **Increased health and safety:** Following rules and procedures is good in workplaces with serious safety risks, such as a nuclear power station.

✔ **High-quality results:** Drug trials, for example, have to follow exact procedures in order to ensure high-quality products.

A bureaucratic style is a useful style for potentially dangerous work or when you need to manage large sums of money.

If you've ever been blocked by an administrator telling you to 'go through the official procedure', you've hit one of the downsides of bureaucratic leadership. Here are some more disadvantages:

- ✔ **Inadequate communication:** If a customer service employee gets valuable feedback from a customer, the feedback is more likely to get stuck in the system than end up on the CEO's desk.

- ✔ **Lack of creativity:** Enforcing existing procedures means that employees have no incentive to try new ways of doing things.

- ✔ **Lack of job satisfaction:** Employees gain no personal satisfaction from deciding how to carry out a task and getting it right. (See Chapter 4 for more on job satisfaction.)

- ✔ **Waste of internal resources:** More employees are hired year to year but with no increase in efficiency.

If you work in a large organisation or a government body, you'll experience this leadership style. In many ways, this style can be to blame for the failure of some older organisations who were too slow to react to the fast pace of change in the 21st century.

Democratic leadership

A democratic leader asks the team what they think before making a decision. This approach is useful when you want other people to buy into a decision, but, of course, you can end up with a number of different points of view.

Here are a few tips on how to be an effective democratic leader:

- ✔ Credit individual employees for their ideas.

- ✔ Allow team members to set their own deadlines and work to their own pace.

- ✔ Ask all team members for their ideas and give feedback.

- ✔ Encourage creative thinking.

- ✔ Encourage team members to divide the work to suit their strengths.

- ✔ Give responsibility to all employees (even junior ones) and allow them to challenge themselves (see Chapter 12).

Being a democratic leader is a good approach when you have to work as a team and if quality is more important than productivity or speed. However, a good democratic leader is always prepared to make the final decision.

This style has a positive impact on your employees because it

- ✔ Decreases office friction and politics

- ✔ Develops skills and feelings of control

- ✔ Increases job satisfaction and motivation

- ✔ Reduces need for financial rewards

- ✔ Reduces the likelihood that employees leave

Democratic leadership can draw out processes, but the end result is often better. Using a consultation and feedback style with your employees can result in better decision-making and fewer disasters, and your employees will be motivated to work even when you're not there! (Chapter 12 discusses designing effective jobs, and Chapter 5 looks at teams.)

A team tend to tell a democratic leader when things are going wrong, whereas they often hide the fact from an autocratic leader.

It's not all roses being a democratic leader because every decision takes time and you may miss opportunities. But don't pretend to be democratic by asking employees for suggestions and then ignoring them – employees can see through that approach, and you lose their trust!

Democratic leadership works well in the following types of industries:

- ✔ **Creative:** This style encourages a free flow of ideas.

- ✔ **Manufacturing:** This style is appropriate when you need to involve employees in making processes leaner and more efficient.

- ✔ **Not-for-profit:** Democratic leadership encourages new fund-raising and cost-cutting ideas.

- ✔ **Professional:** This style works well when the emphasis is on training, professional, and leadership development.

Democratic leadership isn't effective in organisations where employees only have basic skills or have team members who tend to put things off.

If your instinctive leadership style is to be democratic, adopt some traits of autocratic or bureaucratic leaders and use them when you need to. Have a Plan B!

Hands-off approach

Laissez-faire is a French phrase meaning 'leave it be' and describes leaders who take a hands-off approach and leave their employees to get on with the job. The leader provides the tools and resources, but the employees make all their own decisions. This approach seems a bit a scary, but it can work in some circumstances, such as when

- ✔ The team is extremely capable and motivated.

- ✔ The team has highly experienced and hard workers.

- ✔ The leader is available for consultation and feedback.

However, in other circumstances, this style can be destructive. It can lead to a number of workplace stressors, such as conflicts between employees, uncertainty about the scope and amount of responsibility that comes with a role, and conflicting job demands (see Chapter 12). If the leader doesn't deal with these stressors, the hands-off approach can escalate into a bullying culture.

Generally, the laissez-faire style results in the lowest productivity among team members. And if a leader adopts this style because of laziness or because they're side tracked, it fails.

Leading to suit the situation

Saying that one leadership style helps teams and departments to work better than another is difficult. In the 1960s, Fred Fiedler (a business and management psychologist) suggested that the effectiveness of a leader depends on matching a leader's style to the situation (called *contingency theory*). Fred came to the conclusion that people tend toward two different styles of leadership:

- ✔ **People-oriented:** If you're a people-focused leader, you concentrate on organising, supporting, and developing your employees. This approach is where all the team joins in, and everyone collaborates; it encourages good teamwork.

- ✔ **Task-oriented:** This approach is the opposite of people-focused leadership. The task-oriented approach is all about getting the job done and is quite autocratic. (See the section 'Autocratic leadership,' earlier in the chapter.) This approach is all about defining the tasks, planning, organising, and supervising. Like the autocratic style, you're not that bothered about the well-being of your employees, which can cause difficulties with motivating and keeping staff.

The task-oriented approach to leadership presumes that an organisation should match a leader to the task and that a leader won't adapt or change style. It tries to explain why sometimes managers are promoted because they're doing well, but aren't suitable for the new situation. For example, a chief executive who's brilliant at turning around a failing company may be useless when everything is going smoothly.

Neither people- nor task-focused preferences are right or wrong because a good leader should use both styles of leadership depending on the situation. You may find it useful to think about recent situations and note whether you tend to show more concern for people or the task and try to adapt your style to stress both the people and tasks equally highly.

So how do you know which style is best for which situation? If you need to make a quick decision, what style do you use? If you need the support of the team, what approach is most effective?

Say that your new team member, Jim, has just finished the sales department's introductory training program. You ask Jim to contact key clients about a new product. Later that day, you discover that Jim hasn't contacted anyone. He was unsure about the new product details and didn't have the confidence to ask for more information. You're as much to blame as Jim because you didn't match your leadership style to Jim's maturity or the details of the task.

You can adapt your leadership style to a situation a number of ways. For example, organisational behaviourists Paul Hersey and Kevin Blanchard suggest that you adjust your leadership style depending on how confident and able employees are to carry out a task. Table 8-4 shows how to deal with a team member depending on her maturity level.

Table 8-4	Leadership Styles for Employee Maturity	
Leadership Style	*Maturity Level*	*Approach*
Telling	Employees lack the ability or experience to deal well with a task.	Say what is expected and give specific instructions on how to do it.
Selling/coaching	Employees are willing but lack certain skills to do it well.	Provide information and direction but sell the idea to them and allow some leeway to do it how they want to.
Participating/ supporting	Employees are willing and skilled but lack confidence.	Focus on working with them as a team, ask for their opinion, and share decision-making.
Delegating	Employees are confident and skilled and committed to the task.	Tell them what they need to achieve and let them get on with it, but keep an eye on their progress.

Not all teams, or team members, are the same, so to be an effective leader, base your style on the people you're leading. Ask yourself whether your employees have the skills and ability to do the task and are they confident and willing to do the work. Then use the most suitable leadership style.

Influencing and power

In the previous section, we describe a number of ways that you can get things done as a leader, but you can also use your power and influence. You can influence employees purely because of your position in the organisation – aren't you more likely to do what the chief executive of the organisation asks for than your team leader? Or you can use your personal power because of your personal appeal and charm or because you're an expert in the field.

Personal power works better than positional power to influence others, so building up your position as an expert makes sense.

Transactional and transformational

Leadership styles based on power and influence include transactional and transformational leadership. A *transactional* style is about assuming that employees work only to get rewards, whereas a *transformational* style is about communicating a vision, building trust, and leading by example. Table 8-5 describes the main differences between the two styles.

Table 8-5	Differences between Transactional and Transformational Leadership Styles
Transactional Leadership	**Transformational Leadership**
Leader is responsive but focuses on managing	Leader is proactive and enthusiastic
Leader ensures that routine work is done well	Leader looks to put in place new ideas that add value
Employees achieve organisational objectives through rewards or punishment	Employees are inspired by a shared vision for the future to achieve organisational objectives
Leader motivates employees by appealing to their own self-interest	Leader motivates employees by encouraging them to work for the good of the team

The transactional approach assumes that employees are motivated purely by simple rewards, whereas a transformational style assumes that employees are motivated to satisfy their higher ideals and moral values.

To understand the different styles, we describe the typical approaches. For example, a transactional leader has a preference for some (but not all) of these methods:

✔ Avoids taking responsibility and leaves the team to get on with it (like the *laissez-faire* approach; see the earlier section 'Hands-off approach')

✔ Leaves employees to it, but steps in when problems happen

✔ Sets SMART goals (see goal setting in Chapter 9) and provides rewards if employees perform well or try hard enough

✔ Watches employees closely in case they make mistakes

A transformational leader tends to use the following approach:

✔ Creates a clear and attainable vision to encourage employees to achieve higher things

✔ Encourages free-thinking and creativity

✔ Sets a good example, takes responsibility for actions, and shares any praise

✔ Treats each employee as an individual and develops them through mentoring, supporting, coaching, and delegating

If we ask you what type of leader you prefer (to be or to have), we're sure that the answer is transformational. A transactional style isn't bad, although this style is unlikely to develop any new leaders in the team and, if used exclusively, may create an environment based on politics, perks, and power. As with all leadership styles, which approach works best depends on the situation (see Table 8-6).

Table 8-6	What Situations Suit the Transactional and Transformational Styles
Transactional	**Transformational**
Leading efficiency drives: cost-cutting, productivity improvements	Creating a vision to transform the organisation (or part of it)
A stable environment	A radically changing environment
Routine work	New initiatives
Simple, or clearly defined, problems	Complex, uncertain, and ambiguous problems

Transformational leadership does have a down side. Passion and enthusiasm for an idea doesn't make the idea the right one, and employees and organisations can be led down the wrong path. These types of leaders can wear other people out with their energy, and eventually employees can give up. These leaders look at the big picture, but the devil is always in the details.

People with a transformational style are seen as true leaders, but in most organisations, both styles are needed. For example, routine, everyday objectives have to be met at the same time as value initiatives are moving the organisation forward.

A transactional style can be a useful, and effective, alternative option if you take care to

✔ Develop a clear and fair reward system – to prevent feelings of unfairness.

✔ Give rewards in a timely manner – if you wait weeks to distribute rewards, you destroy any trust.

✔ Provide regular, constructive feedback on employee's work – to monitor the quality of work and shape employee expectations.

✔ Understand what motivates each of your employees – so that you can reward them appropriately.

Look at Chapters 9 and 11 for more details on these behaviours.

No one right leadership style fits every situation. The best leaders switch between styles depending on what needs to be done and who's doing it. The key to success is to establish trust and to get the balance right between your team's needs and those of the organisation.

Charismatic leadership

A *charismatic* leadership style is similar to transformational leadership (see the previous section) because these leaders are charming, inspire enthusiasm, and are typically larger-than-life, superhero-type of characters. Their influence is based on their personal aura, and charismatic leaders play up this quality. Their team is likely to feel that the success of a project, or that of the whole organisation, is directly related to the charismatic leader's presence, which can be a disaster for the organisation if that leader leaves.

Charismatic leaders are persuasive speakers and have the skill to make everyone they meet feel special. It's an art that they can use for good (if the leader's heart is in the right place) or (if the leader is insincere and more interested in herself than others) can seriously damage an organisation. (See the section 'Avoiding the Dark Side of Leadership,' later in this chapter.) Martin Luther King was reputed to be charismatic, but on the other hand so was Adolf Hitler.

A charismatic leadership style works well on short projects (so if the leader leaves, her departure isn't too much of a problem), especially when energy and enthusiasm is important. Charisma is all about self-confidence and communication ability. You can develop charisma by building on these elements.

Avoiding the Dark Side of Leadership

The behaviour of leaders can cause problems, or even ruin organisations. For example, the collapse of Enron, one of the most disastrous business failures in recent years, can be put down to the leadership practices of its charismatic senior people.

Despite lots of investment in leadership training, many organisations feel that not enough effective leaders are available. Some suggestions estimate that between 50 to 75 per cent of leaders are failing to perform well, which explains why more leaders are being fired. Leaders tend to fail because of their personality (being aloof, arrogant, and perfectionists) and how they act (insensitive, selfish, and untrustworthy).

The problem with charismatic or transformational leaders (see the previous section 'Influencing and power') is that they can lose touch with reason. You can easily lose touch with reason when everyone thinks you're great and listens to your every word. These leaders can

✔ Hold back negative information so that people agree with them.

✔ Blame external forces when things go wrong.

✔ Exaggerate descriptions about themselves and claims about their vision.

✔ Pretend that they're the only one who can do the job in order to manipulate people.

And what do people do around them? They believe the leader and don't question them, so no one considers any other course of action.

To make sure that you don't fall into the same trap, encourage your employees to disagree and debate with you.

So what do you do with leaders who cross over to the dark side? Well, you can change dark side characteristics, but the process is difficult and involves intensive self-development. The leader needs to become more aware of the behaviour, and the best way is through feedback. Providing feedback is difficult because most leaders don't want to show weaknesses, and often employees are afraid to tell the truth. In Chapter 18, we write about the benefits of performance appraisals, which would be useful in these situations, but how many business leaders have performance appraisals?

Here are some organisational solutions:

✔ Put official feedback systems in place – this system can be something like a 360-degree feedback appraisal (see Chapter 18).

✔ Situate the leader's office next to other managers to reduce her sense of importance.

✔ Support employees and managers who are willing to give constructive criticism.

These steps work only if the leader is confident enough to accept criticism and isn't too arrogant.

If you're worried that you, as a leader, are leaning toward the dark side:

✔ Ask for feedback on what you can do better.

✔ Find someone you can use as a sounding board or get a coach.

✔ Talk with your management team about what sends you off the rails.

✔ Watch out for small failures, notice what you did wrong, and change.

Developing the Role of Leaders

In Chapters 2, 15, and 16, we discuss technological advances at work and the growing trend away from local traditional businesses, such as manufacturing and farming, toward a global service industry. Dramatic changes in industries impact the role and behaviour of leaders. In this section, we discuss the new challenges facing leaders, including leading a virtual team.

Coping with challenging times

The 21st century is raising a number of new challenges for leaders. For example:

✔ Increased competitive pressures

✔ More far-flung teams

✔ Move to a service economy

✔ Rapid change and new innovations

Challenging times bring changes to many organisations, and these challenges require higher quality, and different, leadership skills. An increasing emphasis on organisational performance results in a greater scrutiny of leaders' performance and, as a result, organisations often use personality measures to select potential leaders (see Chapter 17).

One of the most pressing issues for organisations today is the economic downturn. Leadership strategies exist, though, for getting organisations through it, as organisations have done when other such downturns have happened in the past:

✔ **Show energy and optimism**. Celebrate victories, however small, and inspire your employees. Don't appear down, or this will rub off on them, but be honest about the situation and explain your vision for the future of the organisation, and ask for ideas.

✔ **Be open to change**. Take the opportunity to move the organisation forward by improving processes and, as a result, productivity (see Chapter 12).

✔ **Communicate**. Keep employees up to date with what's happening in the organisation, and about future plans, to reassure them and avoid unnecessary stress caused by rumours (see Chapter 14 for more advice).

✔ **Empower employees**. Encourage employees to build relationships with customers and investors, and give them freedom (within boundaries) to negotiate new deals with customers.

✔ **Improve the organisation**. Look for ways to improve the organisation, however small. For example, introduce job sharing, flexitime or teleworking to reduce costs (see Chapter 16).

✔ **Develop talent**. Your best employees are the ones most likely to find new jobs in a poor economy, so reward this talent. Even if wages are frozen, find some way of giving token bonuses to employees you want to keep (see Chapter 9). Create a reputation for being a fair and honest organisation (see Chapter 11) so that when you hire again you attract the best talent.

Leading virtually

Organisations are constantly changing to meet new demands, and as a consequence, more and more activities are taking place across different geographic locations and even continents. In Chapter 16, we discuss the issues of selecting the right sort of people for virtual work and the more practical aspects of motivating the virtual team. In this section, we offer additional tips on leading virtual teams.

Leaders of virtual teams face a number of challenges to manage tasks across different time zones and physical boundaries. Based on studies of globally diverse teams, here are hints as to what you need to do to be a highly effective virtual team leader:

✔ Act in a mentoring role by guiding, encouraging, and challenging your team.

✔ Assert your authority without being bossy.

✔ Be adaptable.

✔ Be clear about roles and responsibilities among team members.

✔ Communicate regularly (and in detail) with your peers.

✔ Encourage team members to support each other.

✔ Show empathy to other team members.

You need to concentrate on being considerate to your virtual team members and ensure that they're satisfied with their job and that they know exactly what their responsibilities are.

Chapter 9

Motivating the Workforce

Motivation is a huge topic for organisational behaviourists because it explains a lot about why employees do what they do at work. Having motivated employees is important for the success of an organisation because unmotivated employees are unlikely to work as hard or be as productive as motivated employees. Motivating employees to focus their energy toward organisational goals is therefore a key task for a manager.

Motivating the workforce isn't straightforward because everyone is motivated by different things for different reasons. For example, you may be motivated to work hard by the promise of money, job security, responsibility to your coworkers, future career opportunities, a challenging job or something totally different. Motivation theories help a manager appreciate what makes an individual tick and as a result successfully manage and influence employee behaviour.

This chapter describes several theories of motivation and explains what causes you and your employees to behave in different ways. We discuss how you, as a manager, can understand the different influences on employee behaviour and, as a result, can motivate your employees.

Considering the Types of Motivation

No single definition of motivation exists, but the general agreement among organisational behaviourists is that *motivation* is a need, desire, or want that drives a person's behaviour and gives it a focus.

At work, motivation is all about encouraging employees to give their best performances. Everybody needs some motivation to work hard, or why would you bother? But you find individual differences in motivation due to factors such as personality (check out Chapter 3) and locus of control. People are motivated by different things and in different ways.

Think about people who are so motivated at work that they never stop, and those who look for any opportunity to do less. Why are some people more motivated than others, and what different types of motivation are there? Well, one distinction results from internal and external motivation.

Both internal and external motivation is important to ensuring that employees put their best into an organisation. The key is to understand the need of the employee and reward him appropriately.

Internal motivation

Intrinsic or *internal* motivation comes from inside you and is about feeling interested in, or getting pleasure from, doing a good job. If you're usually an intrinsically motivated employee, you may not be motivated to do a job you don't like even if you're offered more money.

Being intrinsically motivated doesn't mean that you want to work for nothing; it just means that material (extrinsic) rewards alone aren't always enough to provide sufficient motivation. And people's motivations can change depending on circumstances.

Where studies of motivation began . . .

Employers used to view their employees as just another component in the production of goods and services. No one thought that employees could be motivated to work harder to do their best in ways other than through increased pay. Then the Hawthorne studies, a research project conducted by psychologist Elton Mayo in the 1920s, changed the way that employers thought about their workforce.

The experiments in the Western Electric Company in Chicago measured the effects of changes in physical conditions, such as brightness of lights, on productivity levels. Mayo split a group of workers into a control group, where conditions remained the same, and a test group, where he manipulated conditions. Findings that productivity increased in both the test and the control group, regardless of the direction of change made to lighting levels, suggested that other factors were determining productivity. They concluded that employees worked harder when they were given attention and made to feel important – which happened because they were taking part in the study – so they were not totally motivated by money. The classic Hawthorne studies of motivation and performance demonstrate that employees' behaviour is linked to their attitudes toward work.

A good example of intrinsically motivated people is volunteer workers, who aren't being paid to work but are motivated by other types of rewards, such as feeling good about helping people.

As a manager, you can motivate intrinsically motivated employees by

- ✔ Making the job interesting
- ✔ Creating a challenging work environment
- ✔ Giving them responsibility for the task

When you provide this type of work environment and opportunities, an employee feels motivated to work hard because of intrinsic factors, such as personal recognition or opportunities for personal growth and advancement. You can read more about how you can design challenging, interesting, and responsible jobs in Chapter 12.

External motivation

Extrinsic or *external* motivation is motivation that comes from outside you and is about rewards that aren't part of the task itself, such as money, grades and promotion. If you're usually an extrinsically motivated employee, you work on a task you don't actually enjoy because you're satisfied by the idea of the expected reward. For example, you may not enjoy taking exams, but you do it for the end reward, such as a qualification.

As a manager, you can motivate extrinsically motivated employees by

- ✔ Providing monetary rewards
- ✔ Praising them for their efforts in front of other people
- ✔ Bribing or threatening them to do the job (although this kind of action can have other consequences, such as the employee leaving the organisation!)

Extrinsic motivation doesn't mean that an employee never gets pleasure out of finishing a task. Even if the task becomes boring, though, the extrinsically motivated employees are still motivated by looking forward to an external reward.

Have you ever persevered with a boring assignment and put the effort in to do well because you're motivated to get a good mark? Or worked in a job you don't enjoy in order to get enough money to go out with friends? If so, you're extrinsically motivated.

Introducing Theories of Motivation

Organisational behaviourists view motivation in two main ways:

- ✔ ***What* motivates your behaviour at work:** In other words, this view looks at what you need from your organisation in order to be motivated to work hard. For example, if an organisation provides a safe working environment or has a good reputation and you feel proud to work for it, it motivates you to perform to the best of your abilities. Theories that explain this approach are called *content theories of motivation* because the idea is that these motivators reveal the content of your mental makeup. These theories have been about for years.

    In the next section, 'All You Need Is . . . Content Theory,' we explain two of the most famous theories, Maslow's hierarchy of needs and Herzberg's two-factor theory. We also describe one of the more specific content theories to evolve from these two theories, McClelland's acquired-needs theory.

- ✔ ***How* motivation influences behaviour:** More recently, behaviourists have come up with a different approach to understanding motivation. These newer theories explain *how* you make the decisions you do in relation to your goals. In other words, you're a rational decision-maker and are involved in the actual process of motivation. These theories are called *process theories of motivation* and include expectancy, equity, and goal-setting theories.

    We look at process theories in the later section 'What's in It for Me? Process Theories.'

 Most leadership programs often cover content theories, such as Maslow's, so you need to be aware of them. But the newer process theories probably deserve more of your attention because they can be really useful in understanding employee behaviour and motivation.

All You Need Is . . . Content Theory

Content theories suggest that the way you behave at work depends on your urge to satisfy certain needs. When your needs aren't met, you experience a state of imbalance, which you try to put right.

The following sections explore two major theories – Maslow's hierarchy of needs theory and Herzberg's two-factor theory – that explain the importance of satisfying psychological needs in order for you to feel motivated to perform well at work. We also look at McClelland's acquired-needs theory.

Ascending the hierarchy of needs

Abraham Maslow, a professor of psychology at Brandeis University, Brooklyn and Colombia University, developed a hierarchical theory of motivation in 1943. Essentially, the hierarchy of needs model, shown in Figure 9-1, is as it sounds: a hierarchy. The premise is that initially you're motivated by basic, lower order needs that have evolved over tens of thousands of years (such as food and sleep). As these needs are satisfied, they no longer motivate you, and you move up the pyramid to the next stage, and so on until you reach the highest order need at the tip of the pyramid.

So how does the hierarchy of needs work? Well, when you've satisfied your basic physiological needs, you move up to the next level, and so on. Here's an outline of each level:

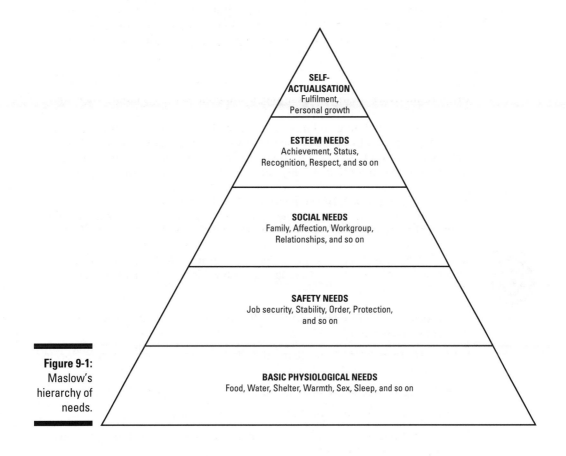

Figure 9-1:
Maslow's
hierarchy of
needs.

✔ **Physiological needs** are the absolute basics you need, such as food and shelter.

✔ **Safety needs** can include things like job security, a pension, and sick pay, or they can be associated with physical safety concerns, such as protective clothing.

✔ **Social needs** accept that most people want to belong to a group and can be met through offering opportunities such as teamwork or positive working relationships.

✔ **Esteem needs** reflect people's need for recognition that they're doing a good job. These needs can be met by gaining respect from others through a promotion, for example.

✔ **Self-actualisation** is about how you think about yourself in terms of success or your personal satisfaction with your achievements at work. These needs are about realising your potential. For example, you may have a strong desire to be the managing director of your organisation, or you may use work to fund your desire to win a gold medal at the Olympics.

As a manager, knowing where individuals are in the hierarchy is important in order to motivate them. For example, if someone earns minimum wage and is struggling to exist daily (at levels 1 and 2), he's unlikely to be motivated by the potential of winning an Employee of the Month certificate (level 4). On the other hand, an increase in the employee's hourly rate may be a strong motivator (although it may only be temporary; read more about money as a motivator in the section 'Money can't buy me . . .' later in the chapter).

When employees reach the self-actualisation level, this need continues to operate as a motivator. In fact, the more they experience this level, the more they want to experience fulfilment and personal growth.

Managers can use Maslow's principles to motivate employees, no matter which level they're currently at. Here are a few ideas to motivate employees at different levels:

✔ **Physiological needs:** Provide sufficient lunch and rest breaks; pay a basic living salary.

✔ **Safety needs:** Create permanent and secure jobs; provide a safe working environment.

✔ **Belonging needs:** Arrange social events; encourage teamwork.

✔ **Esteem needs:** Recognise achievements publicly.

✔ **Self-actualisation:** Create opportunities for career development; provide a challenging environment.

A problem with this theory is that individuals aren't always predictable. Employees may be driven by what they feel strongly about instead of what they need. For example, if employees feel that management are treating members in their work group unfairly (level 3), they may go on strike, despite knowing that this may mean that they can't pay their mortgage and their house may be repossessed (level 2), and they may fall out with their boss (level 2).

One organisation we know paid only minimum wage, but the work environment (assembling mobile phones) was clean and safe. A meat-processing plant opened next door, offering a higher wage, and tempted a number of employees to leave. A few months later, the ex-employees came knocking at the door wanting their jobs back. Despite the higher pay, the cold, unpleasant, and potentially more dangerous environment changed the priority of employees' needs. In this example, it seems the move from level 1 to 2 isn't straightforward.

The hierarchy of needs is one of the most famous motivation theories, and as it features in most management training courses; managers use it fairly extensively in workplaces. But because not everyone follows the exact steps that Maslow suggested, don't apply the model too rigidly.

Exploring satisfaction: Two-factor theory

What satisfies people at work? This question may not be interest you, but it fascinated the psychologist Frederick Herzberg in the 1950s and 1960s as he explored the effect of attitude on motivation. Herzberg went around asking people to describe times when they felt really good, and really bad, about their jobs. He found that people who felt good about their jobs gave different responses to people who felt bad about them. The main conclusion he drew was that satisfaction and dissatisfaction are caused by different factors at work – and aren't just opposite reactions. In other words, if you're not satisfied, it doesn't mean you're dissatisfied, strange as it seems!

The opposite of satisfaction is *no satisfaction,* not dissatisfaction. The opposite of dissatisfaction is *no dissatisfaction,* not satisfaction.

Job satisfaction involves two factors (hence the theory name), or needs:

> ✔ **Hygiene factors** relate to your need to avoid unpleasantness at work. These factors are the *dissatisfiers* and tend to relate more to working conditions or supervisory practices (rather like Maslow's lower order needs described in the previous section). Hygiene factors can make you feel dissatisfied when they aren't good enough, but don't make you feel satisfied with the job when they're okay. For example, you may feel

that you're paid a fair wage for your job, but that doesn't mean you're necessarily satisfied – most people would like more! It means you're *not dissatisfied* with your level of pay.

✔ **Motivator factors** are based on your need for personal growth. These factors are the *satisfiers* and relate to the nature and consequences of the work itself (like Maslow's higher levels; see the previous section). For example, if you feel pleased with the work you've done on an interesting task, you may feel satisfied with your job, but even without this sense of achievement, you may not feel dissatisfied.

An easy way to think about the two-factor theory is to consider high and low conditions, as shown in Table 9-1.

Table 9-1	Conditions of Hygiene and Motivator Factors	
	High Hygiene Factors: Not Dissatisfied	**Low Hygiene Factors: Dissatisfied**
High Motivator: Satisfied	Motivated employee + no complaints about the organisation = ideal situation for motivation	Challenging job + poor working /financial conditions = not ideal, may lead to demotivation
Low Motivator: Not Satisfied	Boring job + good money = not ideal, may lead to demotivation	Boring job + poor working/financial conditions = worst scenario for motivation

Look at Table 9-1 and consider what's important to you and what situation would satisfy you. For example, if you were on a year out from education or work and took a typical volunteer role, you may experience a high motivator + low hygiene situation and be working in a challenging job but in poor conditions or for low pay. You may be able to put up with this situation during temporary employment because your expectations of the job are influenced by its short-term nature and the experiences you hope to gain from it. How would you feel if the conditions were typical of your permanent job, though?

Managers should look within their organisations to identify potential satisfiers and dissatisfiers. A good place to start is to look at the types of factors in Table 9-2.

Table 9-2	Hygiene and Motivator Factors
Hygiene Factors: Causes of Dissatisfaction	*Motivator Factors: Causes of Satisfaction*
Company policy and administration	Sense of achievement
Supervision	Recognition
Interpersonal relationships	Responsibility
Working conditions	Opportunity for advancement
Salary and financial remuneration	The work itself
Feelings of job security	Status

You can see that when working conditions and salary, for example, deteriorate, it can lead to job dissatisfaction. In contrast, if the job itself allows you to grow and satisfies your personal needs, such as being recognised for your efforts, you can experience job satisfaction.

As a manager you need to be aware of potential dissatisfiers and ensure that they're fair in order to reduce any chances of employee dissatisfaction. (We talk more about fairness in Chapter 11.) But to motivate your employees, you need to focus on the satisfiers and change factors intrinsic to the job itself. Making a job more intrinsically satisfying is where the principles of job design come into play. (You can read about job design in Chapter 12.)

Reaching for success: McClelland's acquired-needs theory

One of the most influential need-based theories focuses on needs for achievement, power, and affiliation. Psychologist David McClelland suggests that you acquire these needs over time, based on your life experiences. He also asserts that these needs influence your motivation and effectiveness at work. The three needs are

✔ **Need for achievement:** If you've a need for achievement, you tend to

- Look for tasks that are reasonably difficult

- Prefer to work by yourself

- Need consistent feedback from your manager about how well you're doing

Most successful businesspeople and entrepreneurs have a high need for achievement.

✔ **Need for power:** If you've a need for *personal* power, you tend to take over situations and throw orders around. On the other hand, if you need *institutional* power, you guide the people working for you toward organisational goals. Most people don't like it when someone acts superior just because of his position, which means that managers with a high need for institutional power tend to be more effective.

✔ **Need for affiliation:** If you've a need for friendly relationships, you prefer to work where you can meet people. You want to be accepted by others and get along with them. People with a high need for affiliation work well in customer service situations, such as a sales role.

Understanding your needs is important so that your job is a good fit. For example, if you've a high need for affiliation, you won't be happy working alone.

As a manager, what motivates *you* can influence your employees. (Read more on leadership in Chapter 8.) For example, if you've a high need for achievement, you're likely to want to take the praise for any success, so you're reluctant to delegate. Also, you expect everyone to be as driven as you are and ignore the fact that other people may have a life outside work. But if you've a high need for affiliation, you've a totally different approach. You want to get along well with your team and believe that only you can bring out the best in them. As a result, you're unlikely to get good business results because you're more concerned about being liked.

A stereotypical leader is one with a high need for institutional power – a born leader. If this need is typical of you, you use your status to encourage employees to work toward the organisation's goals.

To be the most effective leader, you need to have a combination of all the needs – a high need for achievement, a need to influence others, and a small need for affiliation – to make up for the pressure you put on other people.

What's In It for Me? Process Theories

You can see a different take on motivation with process theories, or as we call them, *what do I get out of this?* theories. Generally, *process theories* focus on how people think and behave to get what they want. These theories can help managers to understand, anticipate, and motivate employees by increasing job satisfaction.

Expecting returns: Expectancy theory

Victor Vroom, a Canadian psychologist, based his expectancy theory on the principle that people want to believe that they'll be rewarded for the efforts they put in at work. He suggests that how hard you perform at work depends on the following questions you ask yourself:

- ✔ **If I try, can I do it?** This question is about your belief in your own capabilities. (Vroom calls this belief *expectancy*.) For example, you may wonder, 'If I work harder than everyone else in the factory, will I produce more?' But if you're operating faulty equipment, you're unlikely to perform well whatever your effort, so you won't bother trying too hard.

- ✔ **If I do it, will I get the reward?** This question is about whether you believe that your effort actually results in the reward you want (Vroom calls this belief *instrumentality*.)

We have a friend, John, who worked an average of 60 hours a week to bring in new business for his organisation. He was motivated by the knowledge that he would be rewarded by a percentage of his profits as an annual bonus payment. At the end of the year, he was told that overall the organisation had not performed well, so no one would receive an annual bonus payment, despite how well they had performed individually. John is no longer motivated to work as hard and is planning to leave the organisation.

- ✔ **Do I value the outcome?** This question is about how much you believe that you'll like the rewards. (Vroom calls this belief *valence*.) For example, if you've a young family, you may value time off and may not be motivated to work late nights on a task for more money. Or if you don't feel that you've support from colleagues and managers to perform a task, you won't be motivated, even when you're offered extra money. (For more on rewards, see the earlier section 'External motivation'.)

Employees think about what they have to do to be rewarded, whether they can do it, and how much the reward means to them, before they work hard.

Everyone is different, so an employee's motivation to perform is influenced by factors such as personality, self-esteem, previous experiences, skills, knowledge, and abilities. (See Chapter 3 for more details on individual differences.) So, when deciding what to do, employees choose the option that motivates them the most.

Just having one of the three beliefs (expectancy, instrumentality, and valence), though, isn't enough, because the amount of motivation depends on the three beliefs combined together. If any of these three beliefs are missing, your overall motivation is low. For example, if you think that you'll do a good job and trust the organisation to deliver on a reward, you may feel reasonably motivated. But if the reward is your photo on the Employee of the Month board when you'd rather get a bonus payment, you may not be as motivated to go the extra mile.

As a manager, you need to ensure that the message you and the organisation are sending encourages your employees to make the right decision – to work hard for the benefit of the organisation. Here are a few tips:

✓ **For expectancy:** Find out whether your employees need any training, resources, and information to do their tasks well. Providing this support ensures that any effort your employees put in shows in their performance.

✓ **For instrumentality:** Ensure that your employees can trust you and know that you do deliver promised rewards. Having formal written policies linking rewards to performance helps.

✓ **For valence:** Find out what type of rewards motivate individual employees. For a start, you can understand whether they're motivated intrinsically or extrinsically. (See the section 'Considering the Types of Motivation' at the beginning of the chapter.)

As well as these approaches, you need to make sure that the organisation's reward system is fair (see Chapter 11 for more detail) and that the jobs are interesting and challenging when possible (see Chapter 12).

Balancing up with equity theory

When you look at how employees are motivated, you can consider the idea that employees expect a fair balance between what they put into work *(inputs)* and what they take out *(outcomes)*. John Adams, a work and behavioural psychologist, proposed this equity theory of motivation. Adams explains that as an employee, you tend to be demotivated about your job and your employer if you feel that your inputs (ability, education, effort, commitment, tolerance, and so on) are greater than your outcomes (pay, benefits, rewards, recognition, responsibility, and so on) when compared to others around you.

At work, you're likely to compare your efforts and rewards with the efforts that other people in a similar situation are putting into their work and the types of rewards they get. Imagine that a colleague gets a 20 per cent pay raise and you get only 10 per cent, and you feel you've both worked as hard. Do you both remain as motivated, or does your colleague end up more motivated than you? Are you demotivated? How do you feel? Do you continue to work as hard? You can probably correctly guess the answers to these questions! (You can also read more about possible reactions to unequal treatment in Chapter 11.) But, conversely, if everyone gets a 10 per cent pay raise, you're likely to feel happy, even if you feel that you worked harder than everyone else.

Based on the principles of equity theory, as a manager you need to ensure that your employees receive

✓ A fair and reasonable return for carrying out their job

✓ Fair and reasonable benefits in relation to others

A key difference exists between equity theory and expectancy theory (see the previous section). Take this scenario: an employee feels that he isn't being paid enough. Expectancy theory suggests that the employee may still work as hard, if he really wants the outcome. Equity theory suggests that the employee may rebalance the unfairness by not working as hard. No theory has the one best explanation for employee behaviour, which makes things difficult for managers as every employee is different. (See Chapter 11 for more information on fairness at work.)

Being aware of employee perceptions

As a manager, you need to be aware that your employees may compare themselves to others inside or outside your organisation. They make the comparisons in the form of a ratio – what they put in and get out compared to what others put in and get out. But often these ratios are based on employee *perceptions*. The result is one of three situations:

- ✔ **Overpayment:** Your employee's outcome-to-input ratio is greater than the other person's. In other words, they don't feel that they deserve what they get in relation to other people. This perception leads to feelings of guilt.

- ✔ **Underpayment:** Your employee's outcome-to-input ratio is less than the other person's. They feel that they deserve more in comparison to others. This perception results in anger.

- ✔ **Equitable payment:** Your employee's outcome-to-input ratio is equal to the other person's. They feel what they get is on par with others. This perception results in feeling satisfied.

An interesting angle to equity theory is that it explains employee behaviour better when people receive less, rather than more, than their fair share. Basically, people are more likely to react to being under-rewarded than over-rewarded – wouldn't you? Organisational behaviourists have expanded these ideas into theories about fairness at work, and you can read more in Chapter 11.

Dealing with employee comparisons

What can you do as a manager when you know that employees are comparing their situations to others'? Keep these tips in mind:

- ✔ **Don't feel like you have to treat all employees the same.** Although an employee makes comparisons with other employees to see whether he's been treated fairly, it doesn't mean that he wants the same as the other person. For example, a father with young children may appreciate flexible working hours instead of higher pay; whereas someone wanting to buy their first house may prefer an increase in pay.

- ✔ **Look at an employee's contributions:** These contributions can be as diverse as effort, loyalty, hard work, commitment, flexibility, skill, ability, coworker support, and acceptance of change. Be willing to recognise the value of any of these employee contributions.

✔ **Consider what motivates each employee.** A good manager understands that people have different needs and motivators. For example, are employees intrinsically or externally motivated? (See the earlier section 'Considering the Types of Motivation.')

✔ **Reward your employees equal to their contributions and remember what motivates them.** For example, for some employees, extrinsic rewards, such as a pay increase, flexible working hours, or perks like discounts on health club membership, are suitable. Other employees may be motivated with intrinsic rewards, such as job security, extra responsibility, or a sense of achievement.

One way to understand what motivates your employees and to appreciate their contributions is to hold regular meetings to discuss personal development and goal setting. Appraisals can be a good opportunity to discuss these issues. (See Chapter 18 for more on performance reviews.) We discuss goal setting in the next section, and you can read more about equity and fairness in Chapter 11.

Striving for the goal

Goal setting is an approach to motivation that is so well established that practical management systems, such as *management by objectives,* are based on it (see the sidebar 'Seeing why goal setting works so well'). Goal setting is an effective way of motivating employees (and yourself) and is one of the most useful motivation theories in organisational behaviour.

The idea of goal setting is based on psychologist Edwin Locke's original research in the 1960s. Locke suggests that employees are motivated by having specific goals and being given appropriate feedback. Working toward a goal creates a motivation to achieve the goal, which as a result improves performance within the limitations of your ability.

Studies in organisations show that performance improvements related to goal setting can be between 10 per cent to 25 per cent.

Getting SMART with goals

The process of goal setting involves telling your employees what they need to achieve and where to focus their efforts. How often have you set yourself a goal – maybe a New Year's resolution – and failed to keep it? Every January 1, the author Lynn vows to get fit, but never does. Her resolution doesn't work because her goal doesn't follow the SMART rules for goal setting.

To make the most of goal setting, follow these *SMART rules:*

✔ **Specific:** Goals need to be specific to ensure that employees know exactly what to do. Suggesting that your employees 'increase sales by 10 per cent' is more specific than saying 'sell as much as you can.'

✔ **Measurable:** Goals need to be measurable, or how would you know when you've got there or done it? You can measure goals by looking at cost, quality, or quantity, for example. Providing feedback on progress is important to keep your employees motivated.

✔ **Agreed upon:** Agree upon goals with your employees or, better still, get your employees to choose their goals. This way, your employees have a vested interest in the success.

✔ **Realistic:** Goals should be difficult, but feasible to achieve. The employee should be able to achieve a goal in the time allowed and with the resources available. Employees given difficult goals outperform those with easier goals. But setting impossible goals demotivates your employees.

✔ **Time-bound:** Goals should include a time limit, or your employees may never get around to the task.

Although it seems a simple concept, many goals set in organisations are often not SMART. For example, an audit of goal-setting and performance reviews conducted by Microsoft discovered that only about 40 per cent of its goals were specific and measurable.

Seeing why goal setting works so well

Goal setting is one of the most useful tools a manager can use to motivate employees (and themselves) to work towards organisational goals. In fact, goal setting is so useful that some complete management systems, such as Management by Objectives (MBO), have been built around the principles. MBO is about all employees being clear about what they're doing and how it benefits the overall organisation.

Goal setting works because

✔ **Goals give direction.** For example, by setting a goal – for example, 'reducing the number of defective widgets by 5 per cent by the end of February' – gives your employees a focus for their energy and meets organisational needs.

✔ **Goals provide a challenge.** Reaching a goal provides a sense of achievement for your employees. Remember the motivators under the need theories, such as the highest level of Maslow's pyramid. (For more on these theories, see the section 'Ascending the hierarchy of needs', earlier in this chapter.)

✔ **Goals energise people.** How many times have you said to yourself something like 'I'll check Facebook when I've finished reading the chapter'? Setting goals encourages you to keep reading until the end of the chapter so that you can then do something you like. This response should be the same for your employees.

✔ **SMART goals encourage creativity.** Challenging goals require your employees to rethink different ways of doing things.

An example of a goal that ticks all the boxes may be 'Between this January and the end of March, aim to increase sales of blue cars by 10 per cent more than last quarter' – as long the goal is realistic (given market conditions and the supply of blue cars, for example) and your employee agrees that the target is fair.

Goal setting is essential for your employees to be successful. Using clear, challenging, but achievable, agreed-on goals and providing appropriate feedback results in improved performance.

Supporting employees to achieve goals

Setting SMART goals and just leaving your employees to get on with tasks isn't always enough because not all SMART goals are effective by themselves.

To motivate your employees even more effectively, follow these goal-setting tips:

- **Give feedback.** Tell your employees regularly how they're performing toward their goals. Don't wait until the deadline to tell them they've failed. Feedback not only provides information on how well they're doing, but it also provides ongoing motivation. Following are some tips for giving effective feedback:

  - Be specific about the focus of the feedback and use 'I,' as in 'I've noticed . . .'.

  - Focus on behaviour that your employee can control.

  - Deliver your message in a sensitive and straightforward way.

  - Be direct and give criticism in a helpful way.

  - Give feedback as soon as possible after the performance incident happens.

  - Give feedback frequently.

- **Ensure that employees have knowledge, skills, and abilities.** If your employees don't have the abilities to achieve their goal, they feel helpless and perform poorly. In these situations, set goals linked to learning activities. For example, in a sales situation, instead of a goal asking for a 10 per cent increase in sales, the goal can be to identify four ways to network with customers.

- **Think about goals based on *quality*, not *quantity*.** Managers find it a lot easier to set goals based on quantity than quality of work. For example, in call centres, measuring the number of calls answered instead of the number of satisfied customers focuses more on quantity. But the quality of the work task is often more important to the organisation, as disgruntled customers are bad for business.

- **Avoid conflicting goals.** In some jobs, achieving one goal may mean neglecting another. Call centres often have goals to restrict the length of a call as well as goals to satisfy the customer. Does the employee continue to sort out the customer's problem if the call lasts longer than the time limit?

✔ **Be careful when the task is new.** In situations where the task is new, give employees time out to think about their performance before agreeing on specific goals. In new situations, a 'do your best' goal can sometimes be more effective than providing more specific, detailed goals.

Give performance feedback through constructive feedback. Positive feedback is about giving an employee information about an effort well done. Negative feedback is about giving an employee information about an effort that needs improvement.

Motivating Employees: What Works?

We introduce a number of motivational theories in the previous sections of this chapter, and you may be wondering why so many different ideas exist and how you can use them. Well, in their work, organisational behaviourists tend to combine many of the theories because no one theory by itself is wholly successful.

Before we discuss whether motivation through money works, we look at how you as a manager can influence employee motivation. One reason that motivational approaches are unsuccessful is when your influence as a manager is ignored.

Understanding your influence

As a manager, you need to think about how the way you behave also motivates (or doesn't) your employees. Psychologist Douglas McGregor suggests two models of human nature that shape how managers behave toward their employees. He argues that managers hold one of two fundamental theories (X or Y) about the personality of their employees, as shown in Table 9-3.

Table 9-3	**Theory X and Theory Y of Human Nature**
Theory X Assumes That the Average Employee	**Theory Y Assumes That the Average Employee**
Can't be trusted	Wants to learn
Is inherently lazy and unreliable	Seeks self-development
Has no ambition	Seeks responsibility
Wants to avoid any responsibility or work	Wants the freedom to do challenging work by themselves

So, a manager who believes in Theory X wants to control employees and motivate them with rewards, punishments, and intimidation. Otherwise employees pursue their own goals, working against the organisation. This attitude is often called the *carrot and stick* approach to management and motivation.

A manager who believes in Theory Y presumes that employees take pride in their work and are generally self-motivated, so motivates them by using a more participative style, such as involving them in organisational decisions.

In your opinion, which of these approaches is appropriate to get the best out of your employees? Based on the motivation theories described throughout this chapter, your instinct may be to say Theory Y. But the answer is that neither one by itself is totally successful because they both have some use. (Check out styles of leadership in Chapter 8.) As organisational behaviourists, we've visited factories where employees working on low-skilled production lines are managed effectively with a carrot and stick approach. In these organisations, the employees are motivated to work hard because otherwise they lose their job.

Theory Y style of management tends to be adopted by organisations that value and encourage participation – usually knowledge work and professional services. Even highly structured industries like call centres can benefit from Theory Y principles to encourage continuous improvement and sharing of knowledge.

You can't use either approach, though, alone to successfully motivate employees all the time. Some employees thrive on a Theory Y management approach; others thrive on a Theory X approach.

You need think about what motivates your employees, take account of the specific situation, and consider the needs of your employees at that moment in time. Ask yourself whether your employees work better when you take control (use a Type X approach) or when you offer guidance and encourage them to do their best (use a Type Y approach).

Money can't buy me . . .

Many organisations focus on motivating their employees through pay. In particular, many organisations use *performance-related pay*, where pay is linked to actual performance. As an interesting point, studies tend to find that performance-related pay schemes based on group incentive schemes are more successful at improving performance than those based on individual schemes.

To what extent should you use money to motivate your employees? If you think about the motivation theories we outline in the earlier sections 'All You Need Is . . . Content Theory' and 'What's In It for Me? Process Theories', you can reach some conclusions:

- Maslow's **hierarchy of needs** suggests that pay is a motivator only for your employees functioning at the lowest level of the hierarchy of needs – for example, those struggling to get by on a day-to-day basis or want to be able to afford to buy a house.

- Herzberg's **two-factor theory** acknowledges that money isn't a motivator in the same way that motivators (satisfiers) such as achievement and recognition are. Money, in the way it's linked to your employee's achievements in the job, is a satisfier because money is a form of recognition and confirms progress in the job. But more often than not, money is a cause of dissatisfaction associated with unfair pay systems or lack of salary increase in line with promotion.

- McClelland's **acquired-needs theory** suggests that material status rewards, such as an expensive company car and a high salary, meet your employee's need for achievement because they demonstrate obvious success.

- Vroom's **expectancy theory** suggests that pay as a motivator works if your employees know what they're required to do to get higher pay and believe that their performance will result in more money. They also need to have confidence in their ability to perform the task.

- Adams's **equity theory** suggests that your employees are concerned with whether their pay is fair in relation to rewards given to others. In the earlier section 'Balancing up with equity theory,' we mention that employees who feel they're overpaid perform better than those paid fairly, but those who are underpaid perform worse than those who are paid fairly.

The sidebar 'Money: The greatest motivator' outlines research that shows money is a motivation at work, but not the greatest motivation. Money can improve performance, especially when money is felt to be fair, and money is a motivator if you lack a reasonable level of existence, or you're saving for a house or a holiday. But, for the majority of employees, money isn't a long-term motivator in itself.

Money: The greatest motivator?

Surveys and research studies repeatedly show that money isn't the prime motivator for employees. Many studies in the 1970s and 1980s identify job security as the most important motivator, followed by career advancement, type of work and being proud to work for an organisation.

A more recent study found that private sector employees place the highest value on good wages, whereas public sector employees value interesting work the most. Age also plays a part – as employees get older, interesting work becomes more of a motivator.

Chapter 10

The Unwritten Agreement: Psychological Contract

. . . .

In This Chapter

▶ Describing the psychological contract

▶ Knowing what happens when someone violates the contract

▶ Keeping a psychological contract in place

. . . .

*W*hen you start a new job, you get a contract of employment. This contract gives you lots of specific information about the deal between you and your employer. For example, you work 40 hours per week, your employer gives you £20,000 ($31,000), you get 20 days vacation a year, and so on. You know exactly where you stand.

But is this contract enough? Just think about certain behaviours and attitudes you may expect from your employer that aren't spelled out, such as opportunity for promotion or equal pay. Likewise, your employer may also expect certain behaviours from you, such as not spending all your working time updating your Facebook page.

Work psychologists call these unsaid or *implicit* contractual expectations between you and your employer the *psychological contract*. This contract is important because it can affect your impression of your employer and, as a result, your behaviour at work, which in turn affects your employer. In this chapter, we explain what a psychological contract is, why such a contract is important, and what can happen if you or your employer breaks it. We also look at the content of a contract, reasons behind the differing perceptions of it, and the changing nature of the contract over time.

Understanding the Psychological Contract

The psychological contract was first mentioned in the 1960s in the context of employment, careers, and early HR management. However, it wasn't until Denise Rousseau, a professor of organisational behaviour at Carnegie Mellon University in Pittsburgh, wrote her famous article in 1989 that the psychological contract became a subject of considerable and continuing academic research.

Definitions of the psychological contract vary, and the differences between versions are often subtle (and the subject of much debate in the bar at psychological conferences!). Rousseau defines the psychological contract as 'individual beliefs, shaped by the organisation, regarding terms of an exchange agreement between the individual and their organisation'. Or, put another way, the contract is between an employee and an employer and covers those things that neither says she'll do, but the other person assumes that she will. The psychological contract is a set of implicit and subtle expectations about work that employee and employer have about each other.

The key point in the definition is *implicit* – the psychological contract isn't written down or discussed explicitly! And because the contract hasn't been formalised and is based on assumption, employees and employers occasionally can have different opinions about 'what the deal is'. Here are examples of assumptions that employees may make:

> If I work hard, I'll eventually get promoted.

> If I'm loyal and work overtime when asked, I won't be laid off.

The concept is important for managers to understand because research suggests that taking time taken to shape and maintain the psychological contract leads to employees being motivated and satisfied and improves their commitment to the organisation, which means that they're less likely to leave.

Making and breaking promises

So what is the content of the psychological contract at work? Denise Rousseau defines it as being 'what employees expect to give and contribute and what they expect to receive in return'. And as with everything to do with the psychological contract, you need to consider the matter from two perspectives – the employee's and the employer's. Typical expectations from the employee are to have

- ✔ A safe and decent environment to work

- ✔ Equal opportunities and a secure job

- ✔ Opportunity for promotion after a suitable amount of time

- ✔ The going rate of pay for the job

- ✔ Training and development opportunities to improve personal skills

And the employer expects an employee to (at least):

- ✔ Be flexible

- ✔ Do extra tasks when needed without formal rewards

- ✔ Show loyalty to the organisation

- ✔ Work hard and be conscientious

Note than none of these points include hours and place of work, rates of pay, holidays, and other entitlements. These topics are all matters for an explicit employment contract.

The psychological contract beyond the workplace

The psychological contract doesn't just exist between employees and employers in a work context. Every time you enter into a relationship with another person, you subconsciously form a psychological contract. If you think about a relationship you've had with a partner, you can probably think of some agreements or contracts between you. Some of these contracts are explicit (formal), and some are implicit (assumed). The following table shows some examples.

Explicit (Discussed and Agreed)	Implicit (Assumed)
We 'share the household bills equally.	I'll buy flowers for the house for the weekend.
We'll visit each other's parents regularly.	I'll be polite, even though I don't like your parents.
We'll share household chores.	I'll do the outside chores; you keep the house clean.
We're going on a big holiday abroad next year.	I'll cut back on my spending.

Making every agreement explicit may lead to unnecessary conflict – you may find it better to go with the flow, both at work and in life!

If you're employed, think about the content of your psychological contract with your employer. What do you think the implied deal is? What do you think you owe your employer, and what do they owe you in return?

For example, Eric is a qualified mechanical engineer who worked for one of the big airlines. His work was exciting and challenging, and for more than 15 years he was happy working long hours and travelling around the world. However, one year the airline did poorly and chose to lay off some people, including one of Eric's closest colleagues. Eric's job was fine, but he felt so badly about how the process was handled that he applied for a job with one of the airline's competitors and left soon afterward. Eric was unhappy about the way the organisation handled the layoffs, in particular:

✔ Announcements of upcoming layoffs were made by email.

✔ Interviews with employees were done by HR, not line managers.

✔ The company made little recognition of previous efforts and experience.

✔ No time was given to colleagues to say goodbye to friends before they left.

The firm had worked within the law. But Eric felt let down. His psychological contract with the firm had been broken (*breached,* in psychological terminology; see the later section 'Breaking the contract: How and why?'). And instead of speaking to his boss about how he felt, he simply decided to leave and take his 15 years of experience to another company. The firm didn't want Eric to go, but he felt so strongly about the lack of respect shown to employees that he couldn't be persuaded to stay.

Seeing how the changing nature of work affects the contract

In the old days (or at least before 1970!), people used to live and work close to where they were born, in a job or with an organisation that was often found for them by parents, close family, or friends. As long as you turned up when expected and worked relatively hard, you could expect to remain employed for a long time, often for life. Firms were stable, often bureaucratic organisations, with well-defined management structures and corporate behaviours. Change, when it occurred, was slow and limited in scope, and loyalty between employees and employer was perceived to be a joint commitment. This old style of psychological contract was based on the assumption of permanent employment and a long-term career within the same organisation.

However, remarkable improvements in information technology and telecommunications, the relative reduction in the costs of travel and transportation, and the increasing globalisation of commerce have all affected the type of work done and the attitudes of employees toward employers (and vice versa). Competition has increased considerably, and many firms have reduced the number of workers employed in order to survive. Decades of continuous improvement initiatives have led to flatter managerial structures with fewer opportunities for promotion to positions traditionally linked to length of service. And legislation to address inequalities of opportunity at work has led to a welcome rebalancing of the workforce, with many more women now employed.

All these changes have changed the nature of work. The chance to be able to remain in a similar job with a single organisation for life is now relatively small. And discussions about an appropriate work–life balance, multiple careers, and part-time working are becoming more familiar. As a result, employees are no longer loyal to one organisation and need to look out for themselves. This all means that the new style psychological contract is no longer as clear cut and is more likely to change without warning as organisations respond to shifting economic pressures and employees have different career priorities.

Delving Deeper into the Contract

The psychological contract isn't the same for everyone in all organisations and is made up of differing amounts of two types of contract, which overlap and complement each other. Each contract has a *transactional* part that covers more specific details of the compensation package, and a *relational* part that is non-specific and includes expectations about interpersonal relationships. To confuse matters, who the contract is specifically between isn't always clear.

Understanding the types of psychological contract

Two different types of psychological contract exist:

- ✓ **Transactional:** If I give you things, you 'give me things. A *transactional* psychological contract has the following characteristics:

    - **Economic and explicit:** If I do this for you, you'll pay me.

    - **Enforceable:** Because you know what the agreement is, you can enforce it more easily.

    - **Fixed term:** You know how long the agreement is.

    - **Public:** All parties know what the agreement is.

    - **Static/fixed:** The agreement isn't likely to change.

✔ **Relational:** If I am good to you, you 'be good to me. A relational psychological contract has the following characteristics:

- **Difficult to enforce:** Because the terms of the agreement aren't generally known, and they're not based on a simple exchange, they're harder to enforce.

- **Dynamic:** The agreement may change over time.

- **Non-economic and implicit:** The agreement isn't based on a simple exchange, so it can be more difficult to understand.

- **Open-ended:** The agreement has no fixed term.

- **Subjective:** People may have different ideas of what the agreement is because the agreement is not publically known.

You can have either type of contract with an employer and also movement between these types of contracts. For example, if an organisation merges with another, contracts can become less relational, and employees can see their contracts as more transactional in nature. Or an individual on a temporary contract may start with a transactional view, which may change into a relational contract when she becomes a permanent employee after a probationary period.

Relational and transactional contracts aren't exclusive, so it's not always the case that you have one or the other. Sometimes, both types of contract are in place at the same time. For example, an organisation can provide pay for performance as well as career development and job security.

Knowing who's contracting with whom

Almost all the research examining the psychological contract is from the perspective of the employee. This one-sided perspective is probably because it can be easier to tell who the employee is and much more difficult to find someone who's qualified to speak consistently and accurately on behalf of the employer. However, a contract implies an agreed exchange between two parties, and so someone must be able to express opinions on behalf of employers, for no other reason than to shape your expectations. This person may be a line manager or, more likely, the firm's HR department and associated HR policies and procedures.

Individuals have psychological contracts rather than organisations. So as an employee, your psychological contract is (usually) with your line manager rather than the whole organisation.

The importance of good HR practices

David Guest, a Professor of Organisational Psychology at King's College London, demonstrated a significant link between the psychological contract and employee–manager relations. Working with Neil Conway from Birbeck College, he studied more than 600 people in different organisations in the UK and measured the extent that the organisations had kept their promises. They found that organisations with progressive human resource practices (such as an appraisal process – see Chapter 18) had employees who had a more positive psychological contract and therefore more commitment to the organisation.

Undermining the Contract

The most important practical implication for managers is the effect on a working relationship when parts of the psychological contract are broken. Think about how you feel when you make an agreement with someone that the person then goes back on. Not a good feeling, is it? When the contract breaks down in the workplace, it can create big problems for the employment relationship, so much so that an employee may withdraw goodwill, be less productive or even leave the organisation completely.

Exploring contract change

Many things can trigger a change in the psychological contract. Table 10-1 shows some different reasons for change from both organisations and individuals.

Table 10-1	Things That Can Lead to Psychological Contract Change	
Organisational Changes	*Individual Changes*
Changes in policies and procedures	Birth of children
Change of management	Change in career goals
Downsizing and restructuring	Demands from other areas, such as family
Mergers and acquisitions	Job change
New performance targets and measures	Midlife crisis
Relocation	Skill change

You can describe contract change in three ways:

- **Contract drift:** A gradual change in beliefs about what is expected from each party
- **Accommodation:** Small, limited changes
- **Transformation:** Radical change

Contract drift

With *contract drift,* changes aren't usually explicit and can be one-sided where one party isn't even aware of the change. An example of contract drift may be moving from working late occasionally to help your company finish an important task to working late nearly every day. You may be willing to work late occasionally but become resentful if you think that the extra work is being expected of you all the time.

Contract drift is one of the most dangerous types of psychological contract change, and it can be difficult to define and correct.

So how can you manage contract drift? Here are a few tips for managers:

- If you notice contract drift, talk about it so that people are aware of what's happening.
- Talk with your employees so that the situation is clear to everyone and you've the opportunity to explain why any changes have happened.
- Hold regular meetings with your employees to provide opportunities to discuss potential contract drift – for example, through job appraisals.
- Provide updates on what your organisation is doing that may affect employees – for example, through updating and sharing policies and business plans.

Accommodation

Psychological contract *accommodation* is where small and limited changes are made. Change is often seen as unavoidable, which may mean less resentment because people can often appreciate the need for the change.

Examples of psychological contract accommodation include small changes to pay and benefits or working hours. Voluntary layoffs can also be seen as an accommodation change because employees have control over whether they engage with the change or not.

The employee decides whether a change is small or not and whether she is happy to accommodate it. Say, for example, that an employer changes working hours, so people start and finish work half an hour earlier. Not a big change, right? However, if that earlier half an hour in the morning means that you can't take your kids to school, then this change may be huge to you, so you won't see it as small and easy to accommodate!

Psychological contract accommodation is the least threatening type of psychological contract change.

Here are a few tips for managing accommodation change:

- Make sure that people know that the organisation has a necessary reason for the change.
- Try not to change basic values and so maintain the aspects important to an existing agreement.
- Consult with employees throughout the change process and encourage participation wherever possible.
- If the change is short-lived (for example, employees need to work long hours to reach a target), make sure that people know when the change is going to end.

Transformation

Transformational psychological contract change means that major changes are taking place, so much so that sometimes you can't just change the old contract and so you must introduce a new contract altogether. This type of major change can often lead to employees feeling that their contract has been breached and violated. (See the next section 'Breaking the contract: How and why?'.)

Examples of contract transformation include major changes to pay and benefits, downsizing, restructuring or mergers, changes in promotion requirements, and major changes to organisational culture (for example, following a merger or acquisition).

Here are tips for managing transformational contract change:

- Clearly explain the reasons why changes are being made.
- Recognise the old contract and acknowledge that it's ending and things are changing.
- Be fair in the way you introduce changes.
- Give people the opportunity to tell you what they think about the changes.
- Show concern for people negatively affected by the changes.
- Where needed, provide training to people to help them meet the requirements of a new contract.
- Reward news skills and behaviours to reinforce the terms of the new contract.
- Monitor the change so that you know what's happening and what people think about it.

Breaking the contract: How and why?

Here are two terms associated with psychological contract breaking:

- ✔ **Breach:** One party to the agreement believes that the other has failed to live up to their side of the deal.

- ✔ **Violation:** Feeling that your psychological contract has been violated is an emotional reaction to breach and can involve feelings of anger and betrayal.

Breach and violation can occur in relation to a vast range of different issues at work. How much you react to a breach depends on how important that aspect of your work is to you. If something changes that you don't really care about, you probably won't react negatively. However, if something you value is changed, you may well experience feelings of violation.

Here are some examples of different types of breach and violation:

- ✔ **Compensation:** A difference exists between the pay you were promised and the pay you received. Similarly, differences in expected and received benefits and bonuses can result in breach.

- ✔ **Feedback:** You were promised feedback on your work to help you develop your skills, but you never receive it.

- ✔ **Job security:** You were told that you could expect job security with your organisation, but now you hear talk about layoffs.

- ✔ **Nature of job:** When you were hired, you believe that your employer misrepresented the organisation or job so that you're not doing what you thought you would be.

- ✔ **Promotion:** You were promised a promotion that hasn't happened, and you're starting to think that it never will.

- ✔ **Responsibility:** You were hired to manage a new store, but it hasn't happened, and you're stuck in a deputy manager role.

- ✔ **Training:** Promised training doesn't happen or it isn't what you were promised.

Reacting to broken contracts

So how do people react to the breaking of a psychological contract? Table 10-2 shows what you may think and do if you experience psychological contract breach and violation.

Table 10-2	Things You May Think and Do Following Psychological Contract Breach	
Think	**Do**
I can't trust this organisation any more.	Don't work as hard.
My job is at risk.	Don't work outside your specific responsibilities.
They promised me a promotion, and now they've promoted someone else.	Get your own back – turn up late, leave early, take days off, or email friends instead of working.

According to studies, breaking the psychological contract can result in

✔ A desire for revenge or retribution

✔ Higher stress levels

✔ Increased absenteeism and turnover

✔ Lower employee commitment, motivation, and job satisfaction

✔ Reduced organisational citizenship behaviour – a reluctance to do things beyond what you have to just to help out

✔ Reduced performance

After promises are broken, mending a relationship can be hard, especially if you feel violated and are angry and mistrustful of your employer. However, just as you may forgive a friend who upset you, you may be prepared to forgive an employer who treated you badly. A lot depends on how the breach occurred – for example, was it a wilful decision of your employer, or did she have no choice about the breach that occurred? And is the employer making any effort to address the problem and build bridges of her own?

Strong relationships and frequent interactions can create resistance to feelings of violation following psychological contract breach. Violation is most likely to occur when a history of conflict and low trust exists in the workplace and where one of the partners in the relationship places little value on it.

As a manager, treating employees fairly after the breach occurs is perhaps the most important strategy for making amends. See Chapter 11 for more about treating people fairly at work.

If you're a manager, avoid making empty promises. A broken promise can lead to psychological contract breach and doesn't go down well with your employees. If you know that you're promising something that won't happen, then you're just storing up problems for the future when employees realise that they've been misled.

Managing the Psychological Contract

If you've read the previous sections in this chapter, we hope that you're convinced that the psychological contract between an employee and an employer is important. But how can you effectively manage this contract? And what should you do if the contract has been been broken? Well, it depends from whose perspective you look.

Strategies for managing the psychological contract need to consider the *content* and *causes and countermeasures* for breach. Content is fairly straightforward – if content is important, talk about it, act like you mean it, and maintain your behaviours to reinforce what you say. Managing breach – whether accidental (through misunderstandings), deliberate (often when an organisation is failing or realises that it has overpromised), or due to factors beyond the organisation's control – is trickier.

Here are some things for employees to consider in the context of managing the psychological contract:

- ✔ Talk openly to your boss about your expectations and ambitions, hopes and fears, goals and ambitions, and your opinions on those policies and plans that affect you.

- ✔ When something happens that you don't like or that doesn't seem fair, discuss the issue quickly with your boss to understand the reasons why.

- ✔ Don't assume that the company is out to get you – at least not initially!

- ✔ Cut your boss and the organisation some slack – they can't get everything right all the time.

And if you're an employer, keep in mind the following:

- ✔ Be clear about the behaviours you expect from your people.

- ✔ Communicate often, especially when situations change.

- ✔ Check understanding regularly so that misunderstandings don't occur.

- ✔ Be consistent with your requirements.

- ✔ Trust what you're told and assume the best of people (until proven otherwise!).

- ✔ When someone does something that annoys and surprises you, think about why they've done it – from their perspective.

- ✔ Realise that not everyone shares your commitment to work, and that little things may be hugely important.

If you're an employer and you believe that the psychological contract *needs* to change, here are four stages to successfully transform the contract:

1. **Question the old contract.**

   In doing so, you justify the change.

2. **Plan for change.**

   Describe what's going to happen and how and make up for possible loss.

3. **Create a new contract.**

   Involve employees in the design of the new role and discuss what the organisation needs.

4. **Deliver the new contract.**

   Keep promises, behave consistently, and communicate.

Chapter 11

Ensuring Fairness at Work

*O*rganisational behaviour and work psychology have contributed enormously to the understanding of how important it is to people that they believe they're being treated fairly at work. Why is fairness so important? Well, if you've ever been badly treated at work, remember how that made you feel and how you wanted to react. Perhaps you wanted to get even with your boss after he was rude to you, or you've even left a job because you weren't treated well.

In this chapter, we talk about some of the likely responses people have to unfair treatment in the workplace and the impact that these responses have on organisations.

Unfairness can be born of discrimination, and discrimination can lead to bullying – two subjects we explore in detail in this chapter. We also cover the importance of fairness in selection, the benefits of building a diverse organisation, and how organisations can deal fairly with the issue of retirement.

Being fair in the workplace isn't a choice but a legal obligation. A key message in this chapter is that legislation covers many fairness issues, and as a result, employers can't afford to ignore them.

Looking at the Consequences of Unfairness at Work

Research into fair treatment at work has provided explanations and examples of what can happen when people feel unfairly treated. For example, if you compare yourself to your colleagues at work and decide that you're not being treated equally, you become dissatisfied. Organisations suffer directly as a result of dissatisfied employees, be it through less productive workers or claims in the courts. The following sections explore the negative impact that unfairness at work has on both individuals and the organisation they work for.

For the employee

Employees expect to be treated fairly at work. They compare themselves to people in similar job roles (either at their own workplace or similar workplaces) to see whether they're receiving the same treatment as other people. They don't necessarily want to be treated the same as others, but they do expect to be treated fairly in comparison to others.

Pay is an important part of feeling equally treated, but other things are also seen as important. For example:

- ✔ Being treated with respect
- ✔ Not being bullied (see the later section 'Tackling Bullying at Work')
- ✔ Receiving the same opportunities as fellow workers (see the discussion of reduced training opportunities for older workers in the later 'Avoiding age discrimination' section)

Imagine that your boss always asks you to deal with the most difficult customers and generally do the hardest tasks at work. Now imagine that your boss gives your colleague, Sally, simple tasks and even allows her to choose what tasks she wants to take on. You'd probably decide that you were being treated unfairly and would wonder why your boss chooses to treat you and Sally differently. This unfairness probably makes you angry, and you may want to redress the balance in some way to make things more equal.

Equity theory research (see Chapter 9) has shown that people make changes at work to make their situation 'fairer' in their eyes. These changes can be simple, such as putting less effort into work, or may involve finding a new job where the boss treats them better.

One general reaction to unfairness is the development of negative attitudes toward work. (Take a look at Chapter 4 to see how negative attitudes can affect your experience of work and your work behaviour.) Negative attitudes can result in

- ✔ Decreased morale, motivation, and commitment
- ✔ Lower job satisfaction
- ✔ Poorer performance
- ✔ Withdrawal of *organisational citizenship behaviours* – that is being less helpful at work

Work becomes less fun and something employees *have* to do rather than something they *want* to do. And employees may experience higher levels of workplace stress (see Chapter 6).

For the organisation

If your organisation treats employees unfairly, you can expect

- ✔ **Dissatisfied employees:** They're harder to manage, more likely to under-perform, and more likely to leave their jobs, leaving you to foot the bill for recruiting and training new employees, and with a knowledge gap to plug.

- ✔ **Bad press:** Organisations that treat employees badly run the risk of receiving bad press as a result. Think about extreme examples, such as child labour in sweatshops.

    Bad press can also exist on a smaller scale. Think about the places where your friends and family work. If they tell you tales of unfairness where they work, you've a more negative opinion of that workplace and the organisation's products and services.

- ✔ **Legal challenges:** Employees can take an organisation to court for unfair treatment. In the UK, the amount paid out for discrimination claims almost doubled from £4 million to almost £8 million between 2007 and 2009, with average awards of just under £21,000. In 2009, in the United States, it was reported that awards were also high, with the Federal Court having median bench trial awards of around $71,000, and median jury verdict awards of $150,000.

If a business focuses only on making money, unhappy employees, high staff turnover, reputational damage, and legal wrangles can all add up. Organisations need to take fair treatment of employees seriously.

Managers take note: Fairness at work isn't about being soft with workers; it's about managing your workforce to get the best possible results. Treating people badly is bad for business.

Hiring Fairly

Much of the unfair treatment in the workplace we discuss in this chapter, such as the bullying and discrimination issues, occurs when you're actually working in the job. But one area of fair treatment occurs prior to the start of employment: the *selection process*, when you're advertising job vacancies and hiring new employees.

In this section, we detail why paying attention to fairness during the selection process is important. (For more on hiring, see Chapter 17 where we discuss the different types of selection methods that organisations commonly use.)

Avoiding discrimination when hiring people is a legal requirement. People can pursue a claim against you if they believe they were not offered a job as a result of unlawful discrimination. These claims can damage your organisation's reputation and lead to compensation payouts.

Watching for selection bias

Attribution bias means that you incorrectly interpret people's behaviour, and it can affect the way in which you expect people to behave. Attribution bias can affect the selection process. (See Chapter 18 for more details on attribution bias.)

The best way to illustrate attribution bias is with an example. Imagine that you're a boss hiring to replace your project manager. Years ago, you held this post yourself, so you've a good idea of the skills the candidate needs to do the job. The bias comes in if you mistakenly think that only a certain type of person has those skills – for example, that only a person over the age of 40 can be a manager because you yourself weren't promoted to management until you reached that age. You may believe that you weren't ready for that level of responsibility when you were younger, so a candidate under the age of 40 wouldn't be able to perform well in the job. You assume that other people think and behave the same as you do. But if, when you're assessing candidate applications, you decide to discount applications from people under the age of 40, you'd be conducting an unfair selection process because you've no grounds for your age rule other than your own incorrect assumptions.

Selection interviews in particular are vulnerable to attribution bias. In fact, psychologists know that the majority of managers make a decision about whether to hire somebody in the first few minutes of an interview. This finding suggests that the interview is used not as a way to accurately assess candidate's skills but to justify the manager's snap decision. Chapter 17 discusses how structuring the selection interview can make it a fairer and more successful selection method.

Investigating unfair selection and adverse impact

To prevent unfair selection, you need to use a method that avoids both direct and indirect discrimination:

✔ **Direct discrimination:** An applicant is treated unfavourably because they're a member of a particular group, gender, or ethnicity. (For more on this topic, see the later section 'Avoiding Discrimination at Work'.)

✔ **Indirect discrimination:** One group of applicants have more difficulty complying with a selection requirement. For example, if you ask everyone applying for a job to take a written English test, it may adversely affect candidates whose first language isn't English, resulting in less job offers to non-English speaking candidates. Indirect discrimination is often unintended.

Indirect discrimination has an *adverse impact*, which means that a selection procedure results in a difference in employment rates for members of certain groups. Adverse impact is usually determined using the *four fifths rule,* which means that if you select a group at less than four fifths the rate of the highest selected group, they're adversely affected by the selection process.

You can justify adverse impact against a particular group if you've a job-related reason for the selection process you're using. For example, if the job is to help people complete paperwork and forms in English, then your selection method of a written English test is justified, even though non-English speakers are adversely impacted and less likely to be offered a job.

Think of it this way: a test or selection method isn't unfair because different groups receive different scores. After all, men and women have different mean heights, but this difference doesn't mean that a tape measure is an unfair measurement tool! The fairness of a measurement tool relates to whether or not you use it appropriately. So, if a job requires people to be of a certain height (for example, a racing car driver who can't be over 6 feet because he won't fit in the racing car), then a tape measure is a fair measurement tool for you to use. If, however, height is unimportant to the job (as with most jobs), a tape measure is an unfair tool for you to use.

Steering clear of unfairness in the selection process

Unfairness in the selection process is a problem for your organisation because it can:

✔ Prevent good candidates being selected, causing you to miss out on the best people to do the job.

✔ Lead to complaints and legal action against you.

Here are a few suggestions for how you can reduce or eliminate unfairness in the selection process:

- **Ask relevant questions in the interview.** When interviewing people, ask only relevant questions. For example, don't ask whether the candidate is married or plans to have children in the future. Similarly, ask only health or disability questions that are relevant to the job – for example, if a disability prevents somebody from doing the job.

- **Invest in training.** Train managers in good selection techniques to reduce the risk of discrimination.

- **Keep good records.** Keep good records of the selection process. Make sure that you include your justification for hiring a particular person. You can use the records to defend yourself if a rejected candidate later accuses you of unfair treatment.

- **List essential and desirable requirements.** Listing how each candidate matches the '*essential requirements*' and '*desirable requirements*' of a job vacancy can help you to map a candidate's skills and compare him on that basis, thus reducing bias.

- **Make reasonable adjustments.** If an applicant informs you that he is disabled, you should make reasonable adjustments to the selection process to ensure that he's able to attend and participate.

- **Request minimal personal details.** Ask only for the minimum of personal details on an application form to reduce the risk of bias when applicants are being compared. Remember that you're interested in the candidate's skills, not his personal life.

- **Set appropriate tests.** Make sure that any tests you use in selection are appropriate to the job.

- **Write accurate, fair job listings.** When advertising a job vacancy:

  - Be clear about the tasks you require people to do and the skills they need.

  - Don't include any applicant requirements that aren't related to the tasks they undertake in the job.

  - Don't include discriminatory requirements, such as gender (unless gender is a requirement of the post). Don't include phrases such as 'young and enthusiastic' or 'must have at least ten years' experience' because they can be discriminatory on the grounds of age. (See the later section 'Avoiding Discrimination at Work'.)

Tackling Bullying at Work

Bullying at work is an extreme example of unfair treatment. Defining *bullying* isn't simple because the term covers an array of different actions and behaviours that range from verbal abuse to ignoring people. But you can look out for three aspects of behaviour that indicate a person is bullying:

✔ Abusing or misusing power

✔ Being offensive, intimidating, malicious, or insulting

✔ Intending to undermine, humiliate, denigrate, or injure the recipient

Because bullying involves a misuse of power, those who bully are often in positions of authority over people. You most often see bosses and supervisors accused of bullying behaviour; indeed, about three quarters of reported incidents are linked to managers and supervisors.

How your boss/supervisor treats you and how you treat other people determines whether or not bullying is an issue in your workplace.

Looking at types of bullying behaviour

If you've been unfortunate to work with a bullying boss or colleague recall how his behaviour made you feel. If you've been lucky enough not to experience this scenario, just imagine what it would feel like to be picked on at work through no fault of your own. For example, you're not working badly, but the boss doesn't like you and is determined to make sure that you know it. He may shout at you, prevent you from receiving rewards or bonuses that you deserve, and even stop you from progressing in your career.

Here are some of the common complaints of bullying behaviour:

✔ **Spreading gossip:** A colleague has started to spread rumours about you having an affair with a senior colleague at work. This colleague has a history of spreading rumours about people in the organisation. You think that this pattern of behaviour is an attempt to discredit you so that he has a better chance of receiving a promotion over you.

✔ **Humiliating or ridiculing you:** Your boss regularly singles you out for criticism at work. Last week, he talked about a piece of your work in a team meeting, highlighting in detail all your errors to your colleagues. What makes this situation worse is that he doesn't seem to treat other people this way. You wonder why he always picks on you.

✔ **Ignoring opinions:** Your supervisor listens to some members of the team, but when you make suggestions, he doesn't listen to you. He makes you feel as if your opinion is worthless.

✔ **Creating impossible deadlines:** Your boss regularly sets impossible targets for you to meet. You feel it makes you look like an underperformer, especially because your team members are given easier targets to reach.

✔ **Being assigned inappropriate tasks:** You've worked in your current job for ten years and are highly experienced. Despite your background, your new boss keeps giving you the junior tasks. You feel that your experience isn't valued and worry about progressing in the future if you don't get more challenging work.

✔ **Reassigning responsibility:** You haven't made any mistakes, but your boss has announced that he's removing you from your role of team leader. He hasn't given you a reason, but you believe that this action is simply because he doesn't like you.

✔ **Withholding information:** A work colleague deliberately fails to inform you of a change in work rules. As a result, when the boss checks your work, he believes that you've made mistakes.

Knowing who gets bullied

Unfortunately, bullying at work isn't the unusual occurrence it should be, and fairly high numbers of people report that they've been mistreated at work. In 2000, a UK research survey into workplace bullying asked whether people had experienced persistent and long-term exposure to negative behaviour at work. The results showed that

✔ Eleven per cent of people believed that they had been bullied in the previous six months.

✔ Twenty-five per cent of people believed that they had been bullied in the last five years.

✔ Forty-seven per cent of people reported witnessing bullying in the last five years.

Some groups of workers are more at risk of bullying than others, often because they're a minority group in the workplace and others may see them as different or an easy target. Although not an exclusive list, these groups are examples of why you may be a target of bullying at work:

✔ **Age:** You're a younger worker and one of your colleagues is always making you do jobs that you haven't been trained to do and then laughs at you when you make mistakes.

✔ **Disability:** You're being overlooked for promotion. Because you've all the skills you need to do the job, you believe the lack of promotion is because of your disability.

✔ **Ethnicity:** You're isolated at work because you're from a different ethnic group than the majority of the workforce. You're never asked to attend team events or nights out.

✔ **Gender:** You've a male boss who's sexist and rude toward female employees (or vice versa).

✔ **Sexual orientation:** You got on really well with your supervisor until you told him you were gay. Now he's ignoring you and you're certain that he's spreading rumours about you at work.

Some groups are at higher risk of bullying than others, which is why laws are in place to try to prevent it. So although it's not a crime to be mean to people as long as you treat everybody in the same manner, it is against the law to be horrible to particular groups of people purely because they belong to that group. (We also discuss minorities in the later section 'Avoiding Discrimination at Work'.)

Counting the cost of bullying

A friend of ours (we'll call him Daniel) recently experienced bullying behaviour at work – he was humiliated and ridiculed by his boss in a team meeting. The day before the meeting, Daniel had a one-on-one meeting with his boss, and none of these issues were raised. Daniel felt that his boss had deliberately targeted him in front of his colleagues with the sole goal of showing Daniel and his colleagues that he was calling the shots at work. Daniel was shocked and upset by the behaviour of his boss and left the job because he wouldn't accept such treatment. Luckily, Daniel found another job within a week. The loser in this situation is the organisation, which now has to replace Daniel and also deal with the remaining workers' lower morale and distrust of the boss. This situation doesn't make for a happy and productive workplace.

Losing good employees is only one consequence of bulling. Table 11-1 outlines some of the consequences of bullying at work.

Table 11-1	Individual and Organisational Consequences of Workplace Bullying
Individual Consequences	*Organisational Consequences*
Anger	Absenteeism
Job departure	Financial costs
Isolation at work	Litigation
Inability to concentrate	Need to investigate complaints
Irritation	Reduced productivity (from both the bullied employee and potentially observers of the bullying)
Poor health and time off for sickness	Reputation of organisation negatively impacted
Mood swings	Turnover and need to replace staff

Many organisations now have *anti-bullying policies* that detail examples of bullying behaviour and explicitly state that such behaviours aren't acceptable. These policies outline procedures for reporting bullying and assure complainants of bullying that they won't face recriminations. Such policies can help to raise awareness of bullying at work and demonstrate to employees that they don't have to accept this kind of treatment. Having an anti-bullying policy in your organisation can help prevent bullying at work because it demonstrates that your organisation takes a serious view of such behaviour. Having, and adhering to, anti-bullying procedures can also reduce the risk of your organisation facing legal action as a result of bullying behaviour.

The value of an anti-bullying policy lies in whether or not the policy is adhered to. If your organisation has a policy but doesn't act on it, then the policy itself is worthless.

Avoiding Discrimination at Work

Discrimination means that you treat somebody differently purely because of who they are. Lots of different types of discrimination can exist at work, and both the US and the UK have laws to prevent workplace discrimination. These laws cover discrimination resulting from

- Age
- Disability
- Gender
- Marriage/civil partnership
- Pregnancy
- Race
- Religion/belief
- Sexual orientation

The US also protects against discrimination due to colour, creed, and national origin. The UK doesn't specifically mention these words in its discrimination laws; instead they're included under 'race'. Basically pretty much the same discrimination protection exists in the UK and US but the laws and the terms used differ a bit.

The law protects these groups against discrimination. If you treat somebody differently because you think that they belong to one of these groups, then you're being discriminatory. (You may have even crossed the line to bullying, which we discuss in the earlier section 'Tackling Bullying at Work.')

Paying the price for discrimination

The average claim for compensation resulting from discrimination at work is in the tens of thousands. Some claims, however, are much, much higher. Here are some examples of race discrimination claims:

✔ In 2005, a consultant employed by the National Health Service in the UK was awarded £1 million ($1.5 million) compensation following her unfair dismissal and discrimination on the grounds of race.

✔ A record payout of £2.8 million ($4.3 million) was awarded to a former UK bank trader in 2009 who claimed that he was made redundant on the grounds of race.

✔ Famously, in the US in 2000, Coca-Cola paid out a record $192.5 million (£123.5 million) in a class action suit brought by African-American employees who successfully claimed that they had been systematically held back from pay raises and promotion on the grounds of race.

Discrimination, then, is not only unfair but can be costly to your organisation!

Treating both genders the same

It is unfair (and unlawful) for you to discriminate against somebody on the grounds of their gender unless gender is a requirement of the job. For example, you can't refuse a woman a job as a bus driver because you think that all bus drivers should be male. You can, however, refuse to hire a woman for a job as a male model because male models need to be, well, male. Another acceptable reason for discriminating on the grounds of gender is on privacy and decency grounds, such as when a care assistant who helps to dress his client needs to be the same gender as the client.

You generally shouldn't consider gender during the selection process, or when you agree to terms of employment, such as pay or holiday entitlement. Given that both the UK and US have laws to prevent gender discrimination, everyone should be being treated the same in today's workplace. Unfortunately, although things are better in terms of equal treatment, claims of sex discrimination still go through the courts, and plenty of evidence suggests that women still aren't receiving the equal treatment they're entitled to. (See the sidebar 'Gender equality facts and figures'.)

Although more women are in employment, many struggle to progress past a certain point – the *glass ceiling* – and into managerial positions. Often, the higher up an organisation's hierarchy you look, the fewer women you see, as some of the statistics in the sidebar 'Gender equality facts and figures' clearly demonstrate.

Some explanations that work psychologists propose for this glass ceiling effect despite the existence of gender discrimination laws include:

- ✔ **Lack of role models:** With a shortage of women in top positions, it can be hard for women to find good role models or mentors.

- ✔ **Leadership stereotypes:** People attribute the stereotypical qualities of a leader as tough and direct to men more than women. We discuss leadership qualities more in Chapter 8.

- ✔ **Societal expectations:** Women are traditionally expected to manage a home in addition to their job. This viewpoint can lead to the belief that women are more unreliable and less committed to their job than male counterparts. This expectation of lower commitment from women can lead to organisations being less willing to invest long term in women's careers.

- ✔ **The old boy's club:** Some people argue that women are excluded from existing networks dominated by male members. (Think about business decisions being made on the golf course or in a bar.)

Gender equality facts and figures

The following facts and figures give you a picture of the continuing gender gap at work:

- ✔ In 2007, a study by the Equal Opportunities Commission in the UK reported that full-time female employees earn on average 83 per cent of average hourly earnings of male full-time employees.

- ✔ In 2008, the Equality and Human Rights Commission in the UK reported that at the current rate of progress, it will take another 27 years for women to reach equality in civil service top management.

- ✔ Despite a rapid increase of women in paid employment in both the UK and US over recent decades, care responsibilities can lead women to accepting poorly paid part-time jobs that they can fit around their family responsibilities.

- ✔ Global statistics reported in 2004 showed that women were under-represented in managerial positions, although some countries (in North America, South America, and Eastern Europe) have more women in management positions than other countries (East Asia, South Asia, and the Middle East).

- ✔ In 2009, a study reported in the *Harvard Business Review* found that

  - Only 29 (1.5 per cent) of CEOs in 2,000 of the world's top performing companies were women.

  - In the US, despite women comprising 57 per cent of all college students, only 26 per cent were full professors and 14 per cent university presidents.

  - Despite women comprising 50 per cent of law graduates in the US, only 18 per cent were law partners and 25 per cent judges.

These points show how easy it can be to discriminate on the grounds of gender. Being aware of gender discrimination and knowing what can cause it is a good first step in reducing the risk of you being discriminatory, though.

Maintaining equality for minority employees

Many of the laws in place to protect employees from discrimination are designed to prevent minority groups from experiencing unfair treatment at work. Minority employees include those who are

- Disabled
- Lesbian, gay, or bisexual
- Members of an ethnic group
- Religious

Research shows that some groups are more likely to experience discrimination than others. For example, studies in the UK have shown that employees with a disability, members of ethnic minorities, and gay, lesbian, or bisexual employees are more likely to experience unfair treatment at work.

Organisations should be aware of the risk of discrimination and ensure that they've good rules and procedures in place that can protect them from claims of discrimination.

Of course, in an ideal world, you wouldn't need laws to protect people at work. The way you're treated at work should be dictated by your behaviour and performance at work and not whether you're different in some way to others, especially when it has no impact on your work. Unfortunately, though, such discrimination does happen, as demonstrated by the cases brought to court under discrimination laws. So all organisations must take minority discrimination seriously.

Avoiding age discrimination

Discriminating against people because of their age is against the law. In the US, a law protecting workers over the age of 40 against discrimination has been on the books for many years. And the UK recently introduced a law that prevents any person being discriminated against because of their age.

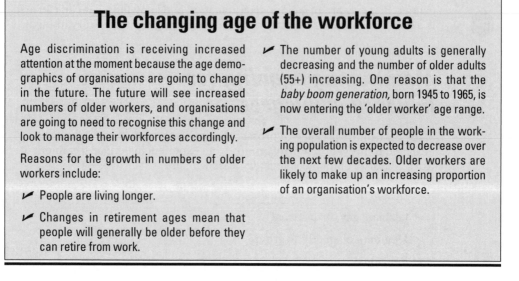

The changing age of the workforce

Age discrimination is receiving increased attention at the moment because the age demographics of organisations are going to change in the future. The future will see increased numbers of older workers, and organisations are going to need to recognise this change and look to manage their workforces accordingly.

Reasons for the growth in numbers of older workers include:

✔ People are living longer.

✔ Changes in retirement ages mean that people will generally be older before they can retire from work.

✔ The number of young adults is generally decreasing and the number of older adults (55+) increasing. One reason is that the *baby boom generation,* born 1945 to 1965, is now entering the 'older worker' age range.

✔ The overall number of people in the working population is expected to decrease over the next few decades. Older workers are likely to make up an increasing proportion of an organisation's workforce.

Some examples of age discrimination are

✔ Advertising a job that specifies you're looking for a 'young' person. This descriptor is clearly discriminatory to older candidates who probably won't apply for the job.

✔ Not offering training to older employees because you believe they'll be leaving the organisation sooner than younger employees and therefore you don't see their training as a good investment.

✔ Overlooking people for promotion purely because you believe that they're either too young or too old. You must base promotion decisions on ability and not age.

Stereotypes against all age groups exist (think about attitudes toward teenagers, for example), but older workers seem to bear the brunt of negative stereotyping at work. These stereotypes imply that older people

✔ Are less able, and less willing, to pick up new skills and technologies

✔ Are more likely to leave an organisation

✔ Are not interested in training opportunities

✔ Have poorer cognitive functioning (for example, the ability to solve problems)

✔ Resist change

These are stereotypes, not facts. Indeed, evidence supports the unfairness of these stereotypes:

- ✔ Little evidence exists to support a decline on performance with age, and some research shows that performance improves with age.

- ✔ General ability to do a job and resistance to change are much more likely to be linked to individual differences (see Chapter 3) than age.

- ✔ Older workers are actually less likely to quit.

Stereotyping can lead to unfair treatment at work. To abide by age discrimination laws and to get the best performance out of your employees, raise awareness of these stereotypes in your organisation and show that they're unfounded. Lots of organisations now do this by offering employees *diversity training,* where stereotypes can be explained, explored, and reduced.

Managing Diversity

A *diverse workforce* is likely to be one that employs men and women, people of different ages, and people with a variety of ethnic and racial backgrounds. In addition to abiding by laws and preventing discrimination, some organisations see increasing the diversity of their workforce as making good business sense. The business case for increasing diversity in your workplace proposes that a diverse workforce is better able to understand the marketplace and therefore is better able to perform in that marketplace.

Imagine an organisation that employs mainly middle-aged men. What insight are they likely to have into the requirements of their female customers or their young customers? Having a diverse workforce of both genders and a variety of ages should help the organisation understand its customers better.

So what can you do to try to ensure equality and better manage diversity at work? Well, no quick-fix solution exists, but you may consider the following:

- ✔ **Assessing diversity:** Formally assessing the diversity situation in your organisation may help you determine where you may need to take steps to improve diversity.

- ✔ **Developing mentoring schemes:** Use mentorship as a way of helping people progress in an organisation. Mentors can be especially useful in introducing mentees to useful networks that they may not be privy to.

- ✔ **Ensuring promotion procedures are transparent:** Have a clear promotion planning process so that promotion is decided on clear terms, which leaves less room for discrimination to creep in.

- ✔ **Giving the message from the top:** The importance of equality and appreciating diversity at work should be a message that comes from the management of your organisation.

✓ **Making diversity a goal:** Diversity must be a business target and not just something your organisation 'should' or 'has' to do.

✓ **Providing training on diversity issues:** Make people aware of their own potential biases.

Dealing with Retirement

In the UK, changing retirement ages and age discrimination laws mean that retirement is no longer a simple matter of leaving work when you reach the age of retirement (traditionally 65 years for men and 60 years for women). The UK is now in line with the US, which doesn't have a compulsory retirement age. The absence of a specific retirement age means that organisations don't know exactly when to expect people to retire from work.

The earlier section 'Avoiding age discrimination' explains the importance of treating older workers fairly – and that includes handling their retirement. In the following sections, we detail two important issues in relation to retirement: early retirement schemes and how retirement can affect individuals and organisations.

Handling early retirement

Although we explain in the earlier 'Avoiding age discrimination' section that the workforce is getting older and that in the future people will retire later in life, the current economic uncertainty means that early retirement schemes are prevalent. (Of course, it may also have the knock-on effect of more older workers looking for jobs in the future.)

Organisations use early retirement schemes as a way of reducing salary costs without having to resort to redundancies. This approach can make economic sense, but it can also mean that good workers leave your organisation. Early retirement schemes can have a negative impact on the people left behind in three main ways:

✓ **Fairness perceptions:** Employees consider how fairly you've managed the retirement process, which influences their attitude toward the organisation. Some employees may have *survivor syndrome* – a negative reaction following a spate of early retirements (or redundancies).

✓ **Increased workload:** The workload of your remaining employees is likely to increase because the organisation has fewer employees.

✓ **Loss of knowledge:** Employees leaving can result in the loss of knowledge important to your business. (We talk about this issue in the following section.)

Organisations offering an early retirement scheme should take care to manage the process fairly and make decisions based on a clear and defendable basis.

One thing that can cause major unrest within an organisation is if people apply for early retirement and are turned down, and then the organisation goes on to make compulsory redundancies to people who don't want to leave. From an employee perspective, this decision can be seen as particularly unfair. If you need to make this sort of decision, then provide an explanation to reduce any negative impact.

Managing the impact on individuals and organisations

Retirement is an important decision in people's lives, and planning to retire can cause anxiety and uncertainty. An employee who's thinking about retirement probably has questions about

- ✔ **Money:** Will I be able to manage financially after I retire?
- ✔ **Timing:** When is the right time for me to retire, and how will I know?
- ✔ **Health:** How can I maintain my wellbeing both during and after retirement?
- ✔ **Support available:** Where can I go to get help and advice?

By supporting employees as they retire, organisations demonstrate to the people leaving and the employees who are still working there that it cares about its employees, appreciates the work they've done, and wants to support and help them in the retirement process. The more organisations do to help employees, the more loyal, committed, satisfied, productive, and motivated employees will be. (Chapter 4 discusses employee attitudes in more detail.)

Organisations can provide assistance to people who are nearing retirement in various ways:

- ✔ **Offering pre-retirement courses:** These classes provide information and advice on retirement issues (both financial and emotional).
- ✔ **Putting positive policies in place:** Offer HR policies that cover retirement and retirement planning.
- ✔ **Valuing knowledge:** A problem with people retiring, from an organisational point of view, is the loss of valuable expertise and knowledge. One way to minimise the loss of key knowledge from your organisation when people retire is to put in place mentoring programs where your experienced workers can pass on their knowledge and skills to others. Not only do you retain important knowledge in an organisation, but you also recognise the retiree's contribution to the organisation.

Part IV
All About the Organisation

The 5th Wave   By Rich Tennant

"Apparently, no one told you about the dress code here, Mr. Dunn, but we don't wear ties."

In this part . . .

*I*n Part IV, we discuss the organisation as a whole and cover general organisational behaviour topics that we don't address in the individual and employer parts. We talk about how best to design jobs and the importance of establishing an organisational culture. We also take a detailed look at change in organisations and consider the best ways in which to manage change. Finally, we look at the impact of increasingly global workplaces and the technology changes that are transforming the way in which organisations work.

Chapter 12

Designing Jobs

• •

In This Chapter

▶ Increasing motivation and performance

▶ Detailing approaches to job design

▶ Fostering empowerment

• •

*M*ost people want jobs that are interesting and varied and that make a real difference. But why are so many jobs boring and monotonous? Does it matter to employees and organisations if jobs are designed to be challenging? And what can work psychologists do to improve things?

The principle of job redesign has been around as long as work itself. A typical approach is to look at a job and see how you can simplify the processes to make better-quality products, quicker and cheaper. However, organisations also look at job design for another reason – jobs that people find satisfying motivate them to work harder and better. Many employers now realise that the design of a job can have a considerable influence on employee behaviour and how they perform. Jobs that offer variety and responsibility and provide an interesting challenge tend to be more satisfying and motivating for most people.

As work psychologists, we look at how a job is designed and focus on how a redesign may improve the quality of people's lives. Employers, however, are unlikely to accept our suggestions unless the changes also improve productivity and the bottom line!

In this chapter, we discuss the benefits of job redesign to the employee and organisation. We describe the different features of job design and the basic principles you can follow to improve employee satisfaction and motivation and, as a result, performance.

Understanding the Need for Job Redesign

Job design is always a work in progress, and you need to make adjustments as conditions and tasks change. The main purpose for doing so is simply to get employees to work harder and better – but we suggest doing it in a nice way. Instead of threatening employees to make more widgets or else, a better way of increasing productivity is to create jobs that people are happy to do. Unhappy workers can become stressed, take time off work (through stress-related illness or just skiving off to avoid work), leave, become destructive, or just work less hard – all at a cost to organisations. To get the best out of people, you need to look at the relationship between employees and the nature and content of the job they do. You need to create jobs that employees find satisfying and are therefore motivated to work to the best of their abilities.

Don't confuse *job design* with *workplace design*. Job design is about administrative changes to improve working conditions, whereas workplace design is about sorting out the workstation, tools, and body position that affects how a person does her work.

Motivating through job design

In Chapter 9, we explain motivation and how to motivate employees, with the focus on the individual. For example, people have different needs, and therefore motivators, at different times in their life. The promise of a promotion and more pay may motivate you to work harder, but perhaps all you need right now is to be congratulated for a detailed report that you've just submitted. This chapter considers motivation (or the lack of it) as being down to the nature of the job itself. So in this chapter, we look at the job itself rather than the employee.

How well you perform your job can boil down to something as basic as how the job is designed. Some people are satisfied by doing the same thing at work every day; they want to follow instructions and not make decisions. But to motivate many other people requires a lot more effort from the employer. Many employees want a varied job that offers a challenge, gives responsibility, and allows them to do the job the best way they can.

The sorts of problems a job redesign can address include

- Feeling isolated
- Having too much or too little work to do
- Lack of control over work
- Uninteresting and repetitive work

Job redesign practices are also useful for more practical issues, such as planning shift work and covering for delays in filling vacant jobs.

Motivation won't happen magically when you redesign a job. In Chapter 9, you can read about how to motivate employees in much more depth. But basically, the idea of job redesign is that someone who's involved in their job views the role as important and is highly affected by their task experiences and therefore more likely to feel satisfied. A satisfied person is more likely to put in effort to work toward the organisation's goals, be more positive, and feel more confident.

Impacting on the organisation

Many jobs are designed based on common sense from an organisation's point of view – to spend as little money as possible in order to make as much money as possible. But focusing on the economic benefits can cost organisations a lot more in the long run, and not just in money, but also in a personal cost to employee health. (Check out Chapters 6 and 9.) Managers often look to design jobs to be simple by

- ✔ Minimising the number of skills needed
- ✔ Minimising the time it takes to perform a task
- ✔ Maximising the amount of control by managers

This approach benefits organisations because it reduces the skill and training needed and decreases the cost of staffing.

Taylorism

The traditional approach to job design is called *scientific management* or *Taylorism*. One of the earliest attempts at job design was based on ideas from Frederick Taylor in 1911, in his book *Principles of Scientific Management* (published now by Forgotten Books). This book played a major part in how work was organised for many years. After watching employees work inefficiently (for example, labourers who used their own shovels rather than a standard design), Taylor suggested that managers should follow more scientific methods to increase productivity. By providing training and specific instructions, Taylor showed a dramatic reduction in the number of labourers needed to do each job.

This approach progressed to the use of *time and motion studies,* where each job was broken down into minute activities to work out the most efficient method. Employees were paid to do the jobs using these exact methods, and often different employees were each given a simple part of the job to do (called *job specialisation*). Many organisations still follow these principles today – just think about McDonalds, and the 19 carefully worked out steps it takes employees to prepare and bag your French fries!

The problem with designing jobs along these principles is that it can backfire on the employer. Rather than increasing productivity, the employees become demotivated and dissatisfied, making them feel stressed (we cover stress in Chapter 6) and therefore less productive.

For example, we recently walked around a meat-processing factory that practiced job specialisation. (See the sidebar 'Taylorism' for details.) In the packing area, ten people worked on each conveyor belt. Each person did one small task. For example, some employees straightened the beef burgers as they landed on the line, others stacked them into piles of two, others put them into individual containers, others straightened the containers as they went through the vacuum wrapping machine, and others packed them into pallets. The process was efficient and quick, but not satisfying. Not surprisingly, the organisation had a high turnover of employees in this department. (Have a look at the later section 'Looking at Different types of job design' to see what action you can take if you face a similar challenge.)

Creating jobs that can motivate employees is important for an organisation because it can

- Improve performance
- Increase commitment to the organisation
- Increase job satisfaction
- Reduce absenteeism and turnover

Affecting employees

An employer may presume that an employee is motivated only by pay, and how they do their job doesn't matter (within reason!). But for many employees, the design of their job matters as much as getting paid. If you think about a job on the conveyer belt of the meat-processing factory (see the previous section), these types of jobs are boring and repetitive and can make you feel dissatisfied and demotivated. As a consequence, the job can have a negative effect on your physical and psychological health and lead to absenteeism or even employee turnover.

See Chapter 9 and Herzberg's two-factor theory of hygiene factors and motivators to appreciate what can lead to satisfaction and dissatisfaction at work.

Although you can become skilled and capable of doing a repetitive job, the lack of variety can also drive you up the wall. You feel bored and totally removed from the overall goals of the business. You're not really bothered about how your job contributes to any organisational success. As long as you do your job passably, nothing else about the business matters to you.

A potential solution to this problem is to provide employees with more variety in their work, and we look at ways to do provide this variety in the next section.

Successful job design is about creating jobs that are more intrinsically satisfying and motivating.

Looking at Different Types of Job Design

To design jobs well, you need to consider the following:

- ✔ What does the employee actually do?
- ✔ How long does the employee do the job?
- ✔ When and where do they do the job?

Job design doesn't have to focus on a single job; it's mainly used on groups of jobs. When we go into organisations, we often use employee attitude surveys (see Chapter 4) to assess job satisfaction among groups of employees and use these findings to inform job design ideas.

Job design can take a variety of forms:

- ✔ **Rotation:** Varying the tasks
- ✔ **Enlargement:** Providing more and varied tasks
- ✔ **Enrichment:** Giving some responsibility

Creating variety

Job rotation is one of the most basic forms of job design used to increase variety. It involves moving employees around different jobs at regular intervals. Job rotation can reduce the monotony of work and create a team with a wider range of skills.

Even with job rotation, if all the tasks involved are rather similar and tedious, when the novelty wears off, the work may end up boring again.

Supermarkets use this technique to move employees from checkout duties to stacking shelves. As well as reducing aches and pains from continually swiping products at a till, job rotation allows management to adjust checkout levels to meet customer demand. For example, in a laundry facility, employees can rotate between sorting the washing, operating the washer or dryer, and ironing. Table 12-1 outlines the benefits for the employee and organisation.

Table 12-1	Benefits of Job Rotation
Organisational Benefits	*Employee Benefits*
Increase overall skill levels	Acquire new skills
Increase flexibility of employees to meet demands	Reduce boredom
Transfer knowledge between departments	Increase identity with finished product/service

You may be thinking that job rotation is a good idea for supermarkets and manufacturing, but how is it relevant to higher levels in an organisation? Well, international organisations such as Nokia often rotate senior level managers around their different sites. Nokia feels that these managers bring new perspectives to old problems. Organisations also rotate future company leaders through different jobs.

Increasing the scope of the job

Job enlargement is all about giving employees more and/or different tasks of a similar level to do. The idea is that giving employees several different tasks to do, rather than limiting activities to a small number of tasks, reduces boredom and makes the most of human resources.

Job enlargement involves adding tasks that are simple and similar to the tasks an employee carries out. These additional tasks may add interest but may not give people more responsibility (having more responsibility is called *job enrichment* and you can read more about it in the later section 'Making work more challenging'). Job enlargement really means giving more of the same.

If your manager gives you extra tasks, you may take it one of two ways. You may be pleased that you get to carry out a broader range of skills and feel a sense of achievement. Or you may be irritated by just having even more boring and monotonous tasks to do. You may just prefer to do the same simple task because you've got it down to a fine art and don't need to think about it, so you can get on with chatting with colleagues or day-dreaming.

Managers should avoid adding tasks that are simple because it won't increase job satisfaction. However, giving employees tasks that increase their knowledge in different areas *will* increase satisfaction.

As a manager, don't assume that everyone wants to take on more work – so unless you've no other option, ask first!

If you enlarge an employee's role, you need to be careful about creating the following:

- ✓ **Role ambiguity:** When employees have inadequate information about their role. Employees aren't sure about the scope and responsibilities of their jobs because the job guidelines are unclear. For example, if an employee in a department store is told to work on the kitchenware counter, but a customer asks her about wine glasses in a different part of the store, she may be unsure whether she can help the customer or not. Role ambiguity often happens because the manager fails to tell the employee exactly what her role is.

- ✓ **Role conflict:** When employees are given conflicting job demands. For example, in a sales role, an employee may be encouraged to sell as many special products as possible, but he knows a product is the wrong one for his major client. He finds it impossible to do what's right for both manager and client. Or an employee may experience role conflict because she just doesn't want to do part of the job.

In Chapter 6, we give more examples of conflict and ambiguity and explain how they can be major sources of stress at work. To avoid conflict and ambiguity, managers must clarify with the employee the following:

- ✓ What is the task?
- ✓ What are they responsible for?
- ✓ How much authority do they have?
- ✓ How will their performance be evaluated?

Managers should encourage their employees to ask for more information when they're given unfamiliar tasks or are unsure about new roles.

The level of uncertainty in tasks, expectations, and roles is directly related to employee stress.

Making work more challenging

Building on the ideas of job rotation and enlargement (see the previous sections) is a method called *job enrichment* (also called *vertical job enlargement*). Job enrichment gives employees more control and authority over how they go about doing their work. This approach allows employees to take on more responsibility and gives the employee a more meaningful and challenging job. It's like *empowerment,* which we discuss in more detail in the section 'Empowering Employees', later in the chapter.

Job enrichment has a number of benefits for organisations:

- ✔ Increased productivity
- ✔ Reduced sickness absence
- ✔ Reduced turnover

Just think, if you were given more authority and responsibility for your job, would you change things for the better, or would you just carry on doing as you were previously told? We bet you'd soon be more efficient and stop doing unnecessary tasks, such as attending meetings that have nothing to do with your tasks.

As a manager, you can enrich jobs by allowing your employees to have responsibility for some of the following:

- ✔ Checking their own work
- ✔ Deciding how to go about doing their work
- ✔ Developing new skills
- ✔ Planning their own work schedules

Job enrichment features motivating factors, such as an increase in responsibility and involvement, and offers opportunities for advancement and a sense of achievement.

Job enrichment isn't suitable for everyone or for every type of job. Not everyone will thank you for enriching their job. It depends on what motivates an employee. If an employee isn't solely motivated by a sense of achievement, he may expect more pay or other sorts of compensation for taking on the extra responsibility and control and be frustrated to not receive anything.

Job enrichment may also be risky for an organisation because although motivation increases, productivity can go down. When people are new to a task, you may need to deal with issues of training, efficiency, and performance. You have to decide whether the benefits are worth it.

Designing for High Performance

A good job design helps both the employee's physical and mental characteristics, but we'll leave the physical characteristics to the psychologists who are experts in human factors (often called *ergonomics*) and instead focus on mental characteristics.

Good job design provides employees with some enjoyment and encourages them to care about what they do. One of the most famous ways to design motivational jobs was proposed by organisational psychologists Richard

Hackman and Greg Oldham who devised the *job characteristics model*. This model suggests that the following five main characteristics of good job design influence how an employee feels in relation to her experiences at work:

- **Skill variety:** The job offers a variety of tasks and a chance to use different skills.
- **Task identity:** The job is complete in itself.
- **Task significance:** The job has a purpose in the organisation.
- **Autonomy:** The employee has control over how the job is done.
- **Feedback:** The job needs to provide performance feedback.

For example, the employee may ask herself a number of questions:

- Does my job have a purpose?
- Am I responsible for what happens as a result of my job and how things turn out?
- Do I know whether I performed the task well?

The answers to these questions determine how motivated and satisfied you are with your work, how well you perform, and whether you're likely to stay with the organisation. However, asking yourself these questions is only worthwhile if you're interested in improving yourself (called *high-growth need*).

The following sections look at each element of the job characteristics model in turn.

Don't just follow these ideas as a whole package because they won't work in every situation. Think about the practicalities of your workplace and your organisation's objectives. If you're a manager, it's your responsibility to work out which combination of job design features increases productivity and performance. But keep in mind that different employees working in the same job have different feelings about how much variety the job offers. So, however you redesign a job, you won't please everyone!

Varying skills

Skill variety means designing the job to include a number of high-level skills. Skill variety is somewhat different from job rotation and job enlargement. (See the earlier section 'Looking at Different Types of Job Design'.) Those approaches can mean just giving an employee an extra number of low-level tasks. For example, at a car wash, an employee who directs drivers to the automated car wash doesn't need a high level of skill, but if the same employee also takes the money, maintains the car wash equipment, and orders the replacement chemicals, then her job has a higher level of skill variety.

Identifying tasks

Increasing task identity is where an employee follows a job from start to finish. This approach allows the employee to use a variety of skills and makes the job feel more meaningful and important. For example, if an employee on an assembly line usually does one task, you can change the process so that each employee assembles a whole unit. Likewise, if a website designer is responsible for parts of websites, the work blends in with all the other designers, and they can't take responsibility for the final product. Instead, if a website designer designs the whole site, she has high task identity.

You can use these techniques wherever you have people or groups who perform a small part of an overall process. You don't have to give them responsibility for the entire process – just a bigger part.

Making tasks meaningful

Task significance is the amount of impact an employee's job has on other people. If you work in medical research looking for a cure for cancer, you know how important your work is to the world. On the other hand, if you're a cleaner in an office block, you may think that your job isn't important. However, if you're an office worker in that office block, you certainly appreciate that your bins are emptied every night and the crumbs you spilt are cleaned up. If the cleaner knows how important his work is to your working environment, she will have a better opinion of herself.

A simple way to improve task significance is to get the person performing the service to meet the recipient. If the cleaner meets with the office workers, she gets feedback about her work and the job becomes more meaningful to her.

Giving control

Autonomy is about the extent an employee has freedom to decide how to do her job. For example, if a teacher is given a list of specific classroom activities and told which textbook to use, she has low autonomy. On the other hand, if a teacher has freedom to choose the textbook and can decide how to teach the subject, she has high autonomy. Autonomy has loads of benefits:

- Allows employees to be more creative
- Improves productivity – if employees have more control, they can work out how to do the job more effectively

✔ Increases motivation (see Chapter 9), resulting in more proactive employees who are less likely to have the 'it's not my job' attitude (see Chapter 4 on attitudes)

✔ Reduces stress (see Chapter 6)

Autonomy is one of the main qualities of empowerment, which we describe in later section 'Empowering Employees.'

Providing feedback

Feedback lets employees know how effective they are at work and as such improves their effectiveness. Feedback doesn't have to come from a manager; colleagues, subordinates, and customers can also provide feedback.

An example of low feedback is if you're a salesperson and you give a presentation to a client, but you never hear what her decision is. If you're told that your organisation made a sale due to your effort, however, then feedback is high. (Take a look at Chapter 9 to find out how to give effective feedback.)

Feedback doesn't improve performance if given in a critical and unhelpful way, or the employee isn't ready to receive feedback.

Autonomy (see the previous section) and feedback are the most important elements to provide motivation. If these qualities are completely missing, regardless of levels of variety, significance, and identity, employees won't be as motivated.

Implementing a Job Design Program

When we're invited into an organisation to evaluate how jobs are designed, we usually work our way through the following steps:

1. **Find out why people are dissatisfied with their job.**

   Surveys are particularly useful for this step (see Chapter 4).

2. **Think about the job design features you can provide.**

   You don't have to make drastic changes, but you need to strike a balance between increasing motivation and operational needs. If you do need major changes, think about using a team of employees and give them responsibility for deciding on the best options.

3. **When you've designed your program, communicate.**

   Tell employees the purpose of the job redesign, and what you're doing and why. They may be worried that jobs may be lost or skill sets reduced.

4. **Regularly monitor and evaluate how well the job design is working.**

   Carry out surveys annually (or ask individual employees) to make sure that the job design maintains or increases employee satisfaction, and make any necessary adjustments.

Make sure that you've a fair work environment as a basis before you enrich jobs in your workplace. First, fix any problems with pay, working conditions, how employees are supervised, and expectations placed on them. (Chapter 11 helps here.)

Empowering Employees

Empowerment is a contemporary approach to motivating job design. It's about extending the idea of autonomy (see the earlier section 'Giving control') by giving employees more authority to make decisions in order to do their job more effectively. Organisations need to create an environment where employees thrive, feel motivated, and have the responsibility to make decisions about how they go about doing their job. To feel empowered, you have to feel

- ✔ **Competent:** You believe in your ability to do the job. For example, the organisation provides adequate training and support.
- ✔ **Impact:** You've a sense of accomplishment and feel that you're contributing to the organisation. For example, you can influence strategic, administrative, or operating outcomes.
- ✔ **Meaning:** You feel that you're doing something that's worth your time. For example, your job doesn't conflict with your values.
- ✔ **Self-determination:** You've the freedom to choose how to do your tasks. For example, you can decide the importance of each task and do them in that order.

These characteristics reflect personal experiences and beliefs about your role in the organisation that make you feel powerful. Employers can't make you feel this way, but they can create a work environment that enables you to feel empowered.

To feel empowered, employees must see themselves as having freedom and discretion; be personally connected to the organisation; confident about their abilities; and capable of having an impact on the organisational system.

Benefitting from empowerment

As a manager, you can't make employers feel empowered because empowerment is down to employee perception. Employees can choose whether to feel empowered, and not all want to be.

If organisations can't be sure that employees are going to feel empowered whatever they do, why do it? Empowerment is beneficial to organisations because it's related to positive outcomes on two different levels:

- ✔ **Employee-level:** Innovativeness, organisational commitment, job satisfaction, improved job performance, and reduced stress

- ✔ **Organisation-level:** Managerial effectiveness; competitive advantage; attraction of more competent and effective employees; lower sickness, absence, and turnover; and customer satisfaction

Empowerment isn't suitable for all employees. Employees with *low-growth need* (little interest in improving themselves) or *low achievement needs* (check out Chapter 9) may not benefit as much. Some employees may not be ready for increased responsibility, such as when they first join the organisation or department. So, selecting the right employee (see Chapter 17) and providing training (look at Chapter 19) are important.

Tapping into empowerment

Some organisations support high levels of empowerment where employees decide what to do and how, basically managing themselves. For example, at Toyota, any employee can stop the assembly line if she spots a blemish on a car. However, organisations can go too far. For example, one rumour is that a parcel delivery company 'empowered' its workforce to do anything it needed to satisfy its customers. One salesman took it literally and bought a jet plane to ensure that his customer's parcels arrived at their destination on time!

Don't just think that supporting high levels of empowerment means letting the employees run loose. Our own research suggests that too much empowerment can result in a highly stressed workforce.

Having the right approach to leadership is also important. Bossy, micro-managing, and controlling managers won't allow empowerment to happen. They'll be worried about letting go of their power and authority. In many cases, a manager's power is based on the information she has, and she's reluctant to give it up. Access to information, though, is key because empowered employees need information to make informed decisions.

Here are a number of tips for managers to empower employees:

- ✔ **Change the company structure.** Remove procedures where employees need to ask a manager for permission for every decision so that employees have more discretion within their jobs.

- ✔ **Ensure that employees can do their job.** Select the right people for each job (see Chapter 17 on recruitment) and provide continuous training and development.

- ✔ **Introduce a climate of empowerment.** Discourage managers from regularly stepping in and taking over decisions.

- ✔ **Provide information.** Employees need information about organisational goals and strategies to do their job well.

- ✔ **Support employee decisions.** Don't undermine employee decisions, unless it threatens the whole organisation or employees won't believe in the genuineness of the empowerment program.

The empowerment process starts with the organisation creating a structure and climate that can support empowered employees and, if consistent, eventually leads to employees feeling empowered.

Chapter 13

Fitting In: Organisational Culture

*I*n this chapter, we look at organisational culture. We explain why understanding culture helps you make sense of what's going on in an organisation and where an organisation is going in the future.

We also explore the amount of influence that culture has on an organisation's success or failure, especially during times of great change – for example, during mergers and acquisitions. Finally, we look at a specific example of culture – safety – and show the effect that transforming culture can have – in this case, decreasing the number of accidents and making work a safer place to be.

If you haven't read Chapter 4 where we explore attitudes, you may want to read it now. There we explain how attitudes at work shape the culture of an organisation. We also discuss changing attitudes and the things that can influence attitude change. This chapter looks at shared work attitudes in more detail, which form the basis of organisational culture.

Explaining Organisational Culture

Organisational culture (or *climate*) is one of those terms that you may find difficult to clearly define and yet you probably know what is meant by it. We're talking basically about the *feel* of an organisation. Think about the culture of a large profit-making company compared to a small family firm, for example. These two companies are likely to have different cultures because of their different values and the way that the workplaces are managed.

Culture as personality

One way for you to think about culture is to see it as the personality of an organisation. When you're at work, you're surrounded by the culture of the organisation. It affects your working life as it influences both the way in which things are done at work and your work relationships.

Of course you can't see culture, but you can see signs of it throughout an organisation:

✔ **Language used in an organisation:** For example, is it formal, or does the organisation have a 'jokey' atmosphere?

✔ **Decisions that are made in the organisation:** For example, what are the aims and priorities of the organisation?

✔ **Symbols of an organisation:** Consider symbols such as employee uniforms, mission statements, and other corporate images.

✔ **Stories that are told in the organisation:** For example, do you hear stories about past glories or times when things have gone badly wrong.

✔ **Daily work practices:** For example, are there group meetings, and do people participate?

The decision-makers in an organisation influence culture especially because they're the power to influence the culture of the organisation through the way they manage their employees and the direction they choose to take the organisation in.

For example, when people display positive work behaviours (such as meeting high sales targets), they usually receive rewards. Likewise, they receive punishment for negative behaviour, such as showing up late for work. Through this reward/punishment process, people discover the culture of an organisation. Managers can therefore affect the culture of their organisation via the way they treat employees and whether they reward the behaviours they want people to display and punish inappropriate behaviours.

Culture, then, influences the behaviour of people within an organisation: it affects their attitudes and behaviour at work. (We discuss attitude in Chapter 4.) The culture of an organisation informs people what behaviour is expected of them, or the *behavioural norms*. People tend to fit into these expected ways of behaviour (except when a *person-culture clash* occurs, which means that a person doesn't agree with behavioural norms). See the section 'Fitting in at work' for more information.

Before the 1980s, managers and organisational psychologists paid little attention to organisational culture. If improvements were felt to be needed in a workplace, the focus was usually on how to make the equipment or processes better and faster. Today, though, experts widely recognise that organisational culture has a huge impact on the performance and success of an organisation.

Considering types of culture

Many different types of culture exist:

- ✔ Customer-focused culture (emphasis is placed on customer satisfaction)
- ✔ Learning culture (emphasis is placed on training and retaining employees)
- ✔ Open or closed culture (for example, is everybody invited to meetings, or are meetings conducted behind closed doors so that employees don't know what's going on?)
- ✔ Safety culture (see the later section 'Ensuring Safety at Work')
- ✔ Sales culture (emphasis is on hitting sales targets)

In addition to an organisation's overall culture, *sub-cultures* – groups within an organisation that have different cultures – often exist. Organisational culture has been described as an umbrella under which multiple sub-cultures exist. Although you may have an overall opinion of a large company's culture, many different workplaces and working styles exist within that company (particularly if the company is based in different countries) that sub-cultures simply have to exist.

For example, imagine two work groups based in the same organisation. One has a domineering boss who's reluctant to give praise and rewards. The other group has an approachable boss who talks to his employees and always says thank you and good job when they perform well. Do you think that the culture of these two groups is going to be different?

Modelling culture

Psychologists have proposed numerous models to explain organisational culture, and we introduce three prominent ones here:

- ✔ Schein's three levels of culture
- ✔ Hofstede's four cultural layers
- ✔ Harrison's four culture types

You can use these models to understand what culture is and how you can describe organisations in terms of their culture.

Schein's three levels of culture

Edgar Schein, former Professor of Organizational Development at MIT Sloan School of Management, describes organisational culture as having three main levels:

- ✔ **Artefacts:** The external signs of an organisation's culture. Artefacts may be behaviour you see in a workplace or the procedures and rules that are stipulated at work. You can also see artefacts in policies such as dress codes and organisational ceremonies, such as formal meetings or informal group gatherings in the pub.

- ✔ **Espoused values:** Things that influence how people act at work and what behaviours are viewed by other people within the workplace as acceptable or unacceptable. Values are often driven by the leader of an organisation because he has the power to establish what values are important. *Espoused values* can become shared organisational values and over time can become shared basic assumptions. Examples of espoused values are acting professionally when representing your company or putting customer service above other tasks.

- ✔ **Basic assumptions:** This deepest level of culture (in Schein's eyes) consists of unconscious assumptions about what behaviour is appropriate at work. An example is the assumption that all people deserve to be treated with respect, which influences the way that people interact with each other at work. As well as being based on general human characteristics, basic assumptions can develop from organisational values. Basic assumptions can become so ingrained in the culture of an organisation that people are not consciously aware of them.

The first level (artefacts) is the most superficial and easiest to change in an organisation. The third level (basic assumptions) is the deepest and can be hard to change. Most research into culture, and culture change, focuses on the middle level (espoused values).

Hofstede's four cultural layers

Geert Hofstede, a psychologist and anthropologist, based his work on organisational culture on his research into national cultures (see Chapter 15). Hofstede described cultural layers in organisational culture:

- ✔ **Heroes:** People, often the founders, who are particularly important to the company. Think about people like Bill Gates and Richard Branson and how they're come to represent their companies.

- ✔ **Rituals:** Collective activities, such as group meetings or social events.

- ✔ **Symbols:** Dress codes, flags, and status symbols (for example, a company car).

- ✔ **Values:** What is seen as important in the workplace and what behaviour is acceptable. Hofstede saw values as important to organisational culture and believed that people within an organisation hold similar values.

According to Schein's model (see the previous section), heroes, rituals, and symbols are visible, so they're cultural artefacts. Values equate to Schein's middle level of espoused values.

Harrison's four culture types

Roger Harrison, an internationally recognised consultant in organisation development, used four types to describe organisational culture, which he viewed as existing on a continuum. Table 13-1 explains Harrison's four culture types.

Table 13-1	Harrison's Four Culture Types		
Power Culture	*Role Culture*	*Task Culture*	*Person/Support Culture*
Often a small family firm	Organisation viewed as a collection of roles to be filled rather than a group of individuals	Emphasis on the tasks that are to be completed	The emphasis on the individual employee
Decision-making is done from the top of the organisation	Jobs have clear role descriptions	Expert knowledge is valued	Value is placed on employee growth and development
Can adapt quickly to respond to market demands	Lots of formal procedures exist	Team cultures are common (because of team-based projects)	May be a non-profit-making organisation
Employees motivated by loyalty or fear	Employees see organisation as secure and predictable	Employees usually have flexibility in their roles	
Low morale common in employees	Employees can feel under-challenged	Employees have autonomy over their work	
Employees feel they're little control over their work		A lack of formal authority can cause problems	

A power culture is at one end of the continuum and person/support at the other. The power culture seems to have the highest constraints on employees, while the person/support culture (the least common of the four types) has the lowest constraints.

Sharing attitudes and beliefs

One person doesn't make the culture of an organisation, although the more powerful people in an organisation (such as the leaders and managers) tend to have more influence than others.

Culture is the shared attitudes and values of the people within an organisation. People who work together usually work

- In the same working conditions (that is, they usually work in the same place)
- Toward a common goal
- Under the same organisational rules and regulations
- With the same group of people

Not surprisingly, then, people have a *shared understanding* of the workplace and share some of the same attitudes toward work.

In addition to written rules and regulations in a workplace, people often have unspoken and unwritten rules for working together. These rules develop through, and influence, the culture of the organisation.

For example, imagine three colleagues, Jo, Flo, and Mo, who take turns making the tea and coffee for the morning break, with each contributing to a shared pot of money to buy what's needed. This informal agreement becomes part of their work culture. Now imagine a new person, Bill, starts to work for the organisation, and he upsets this routine by not contributing money and just helping himself to their drinks at break time. This behaviour clashes with the existing culture. The outcome may be that the existing group of workers feels like Bill really doesn't fit in.

Culture is acquired by people through interaction with others in the workplace. You pick up on the culture of an organisation by watching how other people behave at work. Bill may not have realised at first that there was an unspoken shared agreement over tea breaks. But when he does (and we hope that Jo, Flo, and Mo have the heart to tell him his mistake), he may join that group and so become more a part of the existing culture of the organisation.

Figuring Out Why Organisational Culture Matters

Organisational behaviourists and psychologists investigate organisational culture to gain insight into an organisation so they can understand what people think about the place they work and why they act in certain ways in their workplaces. Some research indicates that culture is linked to the performance and success of a company. Knowing how culture influences the success or failure of organisations can help an organisation make changes for the better.

If you want to understand what's going on in an organisation, what makes people tick at work, and how people are likely to behave (to help you manage employees or roll out changes, for example), you need to take the organisational culture into consideration. Understanding the job roles and job content isn't enough. You need to find out what people feel and think about their work.

In the following sections, we outline two key reasons that organisational culture matters:

✔ Culture impacts on employee behaviour, which has a ripple effect on organisational success.

✔ You need to project a positive impression of your organisation to the outside world.

Seeing the connection between employees and organisational success

Employees are integral to an organisation's success. How useful employees are to an organisation comes down to how well they fit in and how they behave.

Fitting in at work

An employee's relationship with the culture is highly important. The employee needs to fit in. The *person-culture fit* refers to whether the values and attitudes of an employee match the values and attitudes of the organisational culture. In the section 'Sharing attitudes and beliefs' we provide an example in which an employee, Bill, doesn't contribute to the tea fund. We may say that he had poor person-culture fit.

An employee may fulfil the *person–job fit* (meaning that he has the skills and abilities needed for the job), but clash with other workers and management. That clash causes the employee not to perform as well as he could. In fact, this cultural mismatch may even affect the performance of the existing work group. (This situation works the other way around, too, of course. A person may fit into the culture of an organisation perfectly, but if he lacks the skills for the job, he won't perform well.)

Person-culture fit has been linked to

- Job satisfaction
- Organisational commitment
- Staff turnover

All are important to the productivity and economic performance of organisations and also to the wellbeing of employees. For example, one outcome of having a poor person-culture fit is that an employee is more likely to leave the job. This departure can cause disruption in an organisation, negatively affecting the wellbeing of remaining employees, especially if their workloads become heavier as a result. Additionally, high turnover of staff can be expensive to an organisation because advertising and recruiting new people takes both time and money.

Considering person-culture fit carefully during the selection process can help to improve person-culture fit and should reduce turnover, which is good news for the organisation. We look at matching personality to the job in Chapter 3 and at recruitment more generally in Chapter 17.

Influencing behaviour

Throughout this chapter, we give examples of how culture affects behaviour. For example, you know that culture affects what behaviours are tolerated and those that are frowned upon at work. Our understanding of the impact of culture on behaviour comes from various studies conducted in organisations. Culture impacts attitudes and behaviour, affecting an employee's

- Ability and willingness to work in teams
- Decision to stay with or leave the organisation
- Decisions in general
- Feelings
- Morale
- Motivation
- Objectives and aims
- Reactions to change
- Safe working environment (see 'Ensuring Safety at Work')
- Satisfaction
- Stress level
- Work performance

In Chapters 8 and 9, we discuss how you, as a manager, can encourage or discourage certain behaviours, thereby influencing employees. For example, consider the impact on behaviour if a leader encourages or discourages the following scenarios:

- ✔ Teamwork or attainment of individual targets
- ✔ Reduced costs, resulting in poor service
- ✔ Keeping the customer happy at all costs
- ✔ The ability of employees to approach him with problems

Culture affects attitudes and behaviour, and behaviour and attitudes affect culture. The relationship works both ways. The culture of an organisation affects employee and organisational performance. A long-term study of 160 organisations revealed that culture is linked to the success or failure of an organisation. An organisation with a strong (positive) organisational culture is more likely to be successful. Don't forget, though, that culture can also be negative – for example, if workplace bullying is being tolerated (see Chapter 11 for more on bullying at work).

Knowing how outsiders view the organisation matters

In the previous sections, we explain how organisational culture affects those people working within the organisation. But what about the way the organisation is viewed by people outside the organisation? Customers, investors, and potential employees form an opinion of a company based partly on the organisational culture.

Outsiders can gauge the culture of an organisation based on external signs and the way in which the organisation and its employees behave.

Two key groups of people evaluate an organisation from the outside looking in: potential employees and customers/investors.

Volkswagen and a healthy culture

The German carmaker Volkswagen has recently announced that emails are no longer being sent to employees' smart phones when they're not working a shift. This action is in recognition of the negative impact dealing with work emails at home can have on your work–life balance (see Chapter 6 for more on why protecting work–life balance is a good idea). Moves such as this one can help to create a healthy working culture where employees feel that their organisation does actually care about their health and home-life.

Potential employees

Potential employees assess whether they can fit into an organisation when they apply for a job.

You want to hire someone who fits in with your organisation. Likewise, employees are looking for the best place to work, and culture is an important part of this search.

As a job seeker, when you assess whether you want a job, you're looking not just at the tasks you'll do and the pay you'll receive but also whether the values of the organisation match your own and whether working there is going to meet your expectations. For example, you're probably more impressed with a company that has a training culture and provide a development opportunities for you than one where training isn't typically offered, and your career development is a non-issue.

Customers and investors

Some companies make it a priority to hold a certain culture and promote their culture to the outside world. For example, an organisation may display a service, ethical, or trustworthy culture. As a result, people have certain expectations of an organisation because they view it in a particular way. For example, a company that promotes itself as having a strong service culture is expected to actually provide good customer service. As long as the behaviour of an organisation matches the external culture they portray, this behaviour is likely to have a positive impact on outsider perceptions of the company.

The risks of behaving contrary to the culture are high, especially if an organisation actively promotes itself through its cultural values. If you interact with an organisation that promotes a service culture and it treats you badly as a customer, it reflects badly on the organisation. You may think even less of the company _because_ it portrays an image of good service that it doesn't live up to. You may see this company as lying to you. Organisations should take care to live up to the cultural image they portray.

Investigating Organisational Culture Change

Change is an inevitable part of organisational life. Sometimes the culture of the organisation needs to change in order for the organisation to adapt. This section looks at organisational culture change in terms of why it happens, how you can manage it and what you can do to make the change more likely to succeed.

Knowing why you may need to change the culture

The culture of an organisation may need to change in order to

- ✔ **Become more competitive:** Changing becomes even more important when you're facing external threats from competitors.

- ✔ **Change employee behaviour:** This change is usually done with a view to improving performance.

- ✔ **Fall in line with changing goals and aims of the organisation:** For example, a small company may expand to become a national rather than local business.

- ✔ **Meet changes in technology:** These changes occur when you need to change the way jobs are done or retrain people so that they're new skills.

- ✔ **Provide better customer service:** For example, you may need to make a change if customer complaints are high.

- ✔ **Reduce employee turnover:** Cultural issues can often cause high turnover.

Understanding the hurdles to change

You can change the culture of an organisation, but the process is often difficult and time consuming. Culture change isn't something that you can do overnight. People need time to get used to changes that happen at work before they see the new way of working as the *norm*.

People are often resistant to change, particularly if the change contradicts existing attitudes and cultural values. Understanding why people resist culture change and the ways you can minimise this resistance is important. If you don't carefully manage change, your employees may not want to change and may refuse to accept changes. This lack of co-operation can cause conflict in the workplace and can result in people leaving the workplace altogether.

 Sometimes people change their behaviour temporarily, but if the change isn't reinforced, they revert back to old ways of working. For change to be successful, you must implement it consistently and pay attention to getting and keeping employee buy-in.

Planning for change

Understanding the existing culture of an organisation is an important first step to changing it. You can investigate organisational culture through

✔ **Questionnaires:** Culture questionnaires are often attitude questionnaires (see Chapter 4). Asking about employee attitudes can reveal a lot about the culture of an organisation.

✔ **Interviews:** Talking to people about the culture of their organisation is an obvious way of gathering information. You must be careful, though, as people may be reluctant to give honest views, especially to their managers!

Involving people in the change process and the decisions that underpin change can help to promote employee buy-in and should increase the chances of successful change.

Sometimes organisations employ change consultants who investigate and manage cultural change – a good approach as employees may be more honest with an external consultant. The consultant is also better able to take an unbiased view of the organisation than the leader or managers.

You should ideally gather information on the existing organisational culture prior to introducing the change by doing the following:

✔ Uncover and understand the existing values and attitudes in an organisation.

✔ Uncover any assumptions that influence how people feel and react at work.

✔ Understand how values, attitudes, and behaviours are shared among workers.

You can use this information to devise a change plan that can fit into the existing culture or provide reinforcement for new behaviours that can help to build a new culture. For example, if people are highly motivated as team workers, you can use team-based projects to implement change. Or, if dramatic cultural changes are desirable, if you think about what people value at work and make sure that the rewards in the new system take these into account, the cultural change is more likely to succeed.

A good understanding of the existing culture and a clear idea of what new culture is required can help in the production of a change process that won't conflict with the old culture too much. At the same time, it promotes those aspects of the new culture that are highly valued.

Managing change

Change will be unsuccessful if old and inappropriate behaviours are still being reinforced – for example, the organisation claims to be changing to a performance-based promotion culture and yet continues to promote long-serving rather than high-performing employees.

Here are a few other tips for managing cultural change:

- ✔ **Have a clear vision of what change is needed.** If you want people to accept change, you have to be able to clearly explain what change is needed and why.

- ✔ **Be committed to the change.** Everyone within the organisation must embrace culture change. The leader and senior managers especially should accept and promote the change in order to get employee agreement.

- ✔ **Ensure that leaders and senior managers exhibit behaviours that are consistent with the new culture.** Employees will interpret these behaviours and be guided by them. If the behaviours are contrary to the cultural values you're trying to promote, you've more of a risk of unsuccessful change.

- ✔ **Make changes to the organisation that support the culture change.** Change rules, policies, and recruitment and reward structures to match the new culture.

Handling big cultural changes: Merging and acquiring

Sometimes organisations merge, acquire another company, or are bought out by another organisation. These types of major events often result in the need for cultural change. Research into mergers and acquisitions reveals that although most companies plan these situations, many fail because they don't pay attention to cultural issues. Cultural incompatibility in these situations can cause major problems and even result in heavy financial losses.

We recommend that organisations do a culture audit before a merger or acquisition so they can proactively identify and address any culture clashes.

When their organisations are changing and they're imposing a new culture, employees worry about many of the following issues:

- ✔ Changes in colleagues and bosses
- ✔ Changes in power and status
- ✔ Disrupted career path
- ✔ New rules and regulations
- ✔ Increased workload
- ✔ Job loss or demotion
- ✔ Loss of existing work identity

Employees may be reluctant to give up on their old work culture where they knew where they stood on these issues. Embracing a new culture where these things are unknown can be a scary prospect.

Some organisational cultures are easier to change than others. Harrison laid down four culture types: power, role, task, and person/support (see Table 13-1), and believed that power and role are the easiest to change.

If you want to change a power culture into a task culture, you can promote many benefits to gain employee support (increased autonomy at work, for example; see Chapter 12 where we discuss job design). However, if you consider moving in the other direction from task to power, you may have difficulty thinking of positive ways of promoting a power culture to employees used to working in a task culture. Imagine an acquisition where an organisation with a power culture buys out one with a task culture. If the power culture organisation tries to implement workplace changes to the task culture, it will probably face resistance from employees. If you're an expert at your job working in a task culture, you're used to having the autonomy to make your own decisions and manage your work and won't like your new boss exercising so much control, which is a work style more typical of a power culture.

Employees typically consider two main aspects about an organisational culture when they're faced with a merger or acquisition:

✔ How attractive is the other culture to me?

✔ How willing am I to abandon my old culture?

Table 13-2 shows a model developed by Afsaneh Nahavandi and Ali Malekzadeh, both Professors of Management in the Arizona State University, US. This model predicts employees' likely responses to change when they take these two questions into account.

Table 13-2		Cultural Considerations During Mergers and Acquisitions	
		How Willing Am I to Abandon My Old Culture?	
		Very willing	**Not at all willing**
How Attractive Is the Other Culture to Me?	**Very attractive**	Assimilation	Integration
	Not at all attractive	Deculturation	Separation

As Table 13-2 shows, there are four different potential reactions based on cultural considerations following a merger or acquisition. These are:

✔ **Assimilation:** People are happy to give up their existing culture and willingly embrace the new culture.

✔ **Deculturation:** People don't like their existing culture but also don't like the look of the new culture. Employees can become confused and alienated.

✔ **Integration:** People like their old culture but also like the new culture. Ideally, in this situation, you'd end up with the best bits from both organisations. Integration isn't easy, though, and you risk culture collision as people vie to keep the things they value.

✔ **Separation:** People don't like the new culture and resist changes and try to hold on to their old culture.

If your organisation is involved in a merger or acquisition, consider how your employees are likely to view the change and whether or not there will be culture clash and potential problems. If you do identify problems, tackle them head-on rather than ignore them altogether. You may be able to reduce people's concerns and fears by explaining what changes are happening and why. You can also put emphasis on culture similarity and talk to people about how you're going to manage any difficulties arising from differences between the organisations. All these things should help to ease the transition and keep your employees happier.

Ensuring Safety at Work

The best way to understand organisational culture is to look at an example of culture in action. In this section, we explain what safety culture is and why it's important.

Safety culture – the safety ethic of an organisation – is a specific aspect of an organisation's culture. The attitudes to safety in the organisation can underpin the way in which people behave in relation to safety (for example, does everyone always use the safety equipment provided or is it seen as acceptable not to?). Research has shown that safety culture relates to accident and error rates. Consequently, many organisations at a high risk of accidents or where an accident would be disastrous, such as at a nuclear fuel plant, now look carefully at their safety culture in order to reduce the risk of accidents occurring.

Safety at work is a good example to use because it affects everybody. In addition to needing the places where you work to be safe environments, you also need places you visit where other people work to be safe. Next time you get on a train or an aeroplane, ask yourself how important it is that the workforce has a positive safety culture!

Safety culture in the nuclear industry

The nuclear industry in the UK and the US is credited with having a positive safety culture where safety is seen as paramount to operations. This approach to safety is believed to be one of the reasons why accident rates are, thankfully, so low. The attention paid to safety culture followed the Three Mile Island partial meltdown in 1979, which was partly blamed on poor safety training and human errors. Paying attention to safety culture in a pro-active way is seen now as best practice for many high-risk industries in developed countries, although less so in developing countries.

We focus here on safety in terms of accidents at work, but other types of organisations, such as healthcare and financial institutions, are looking at safety culture – which you can also call *risk culture*. Studies are starting to show that attitudes toward risk and safety are important in those types of organisations, too. Error rates in hospitals and financial losses have both being linked to the culture of the organisation in which they occur.

Knowing why poor safety culture develops

Interest in the culture of an organisation and how it affects safety at work began when psychologists noted that despite numerous safety improvements to workplaces, accidents continued to happen. These accidents often occurred because of human errors and people engaging in unsafe behaviour. These accidents and errors didn't occur because the equipment wasn't working or a safety system failed, but rather because people sometimes did things wrong.

Of course, everybody makes mistakes, and you can't really blame someone for making an honest error. Perhaps more worryingly, though, is the fact that sometimes an investigation reveals that an accident or errors were deliberate actions.

So why would somebody do something that wasn't safe? Perhaps that person didn't realise how important the job was, or perhaps some aspects of their workplace encouraged them to take risks – to cut corners to save time or meet a quota, for example. People's attitudes toward safety at work are important. Sometimes a manager even overlooks safety checks. An organisation's safety culture is made up of the attitudes people hold toward safety at work and the way in which people behave toward safety.

An organisation may have a poor safety culture for several reasons:

- ✔ **Production comes before safety.** The organisation focuses so much on production and high performance that aspects of safety are overlooked. Employees may feel that they don't get rewarded for working safely and sometimes report that they're encouraged to pay less attention to safety when high production is needed.

- ✔ **Breaking safety rules is the norm.** This problem particularly occurs if the rules slow work down. An accident hasn't happened yet, so why should it now? Of course, maybe all the other times, pure luck meant that an accident didn't happen. An example is a train disaster where a technician mended wires using tape instead of doing a proper repair. Signalling errors then caused the train to crash. Investigators discovered that taping wires, although officially against the rules, was common. It had become accepted as *normal practice*.

- ✔ **Management are weak or lazy.** The punishments and rewards used in the workplace can support or undermine safety. Managers may know that shortcuts are occurring, but turn a blind eye to it. Or they may actively encourage the breaking of minor safety rules to meet production targets. This approach sends the message to the workforce that safety isn't a priority, so employees are likely to act accordingly and pay less attention to safety issues.

- ✔ **People are overloaded with work.** Too much work can encourage unsafe acts and the practice of taking shortcuts. Overload is also linked to stress, and workers under stress are more prone to accidents and injury.

Promoting a positive safety culture

Finding out about the safety culture of a workplace can help identify problem areas, such as whether employees are following all the safety rules and what messages they receive about safety issues from their managers. You can use this information to take steps to encourage a more positive safety culture and a safer workplace. (The earlier section 'Investigating Organisational Culture Change' discusses how you can change culture.) In this section, we provide more detail on how to promote a positive safety culture.

The safety culture of a workplace is fairly stable and can be resistant to change. Changing culture and attitudes (see Chapter 4) takes time and effort. Research shows though that taking steps to improve safety attitudes and encouraging a positive safety culture can reduce the number of accidents that occur. People report taking fewer shortcuts at work, paying more attention to safety, and making fewer errors.

If you're a manager, you can help encourage a positive safety culture by following a few basic guidelines:

✔ **Be careful how you incentivise safe working.** If you reward people for not having accidents, they may be tempted to not report incidents.

✔ **Encourage people to report incidents and errors.** This way, other employees can benefit from the information, and you can take steps to prevent a reoccurrence. If people are encouraged not to report problems or are scared they'll be in trouble if they do report them, then incidents and errors are more likely to be repeated.

✔ **Promote communication between different levels in the organisation.** Make sure that people know how to report safety concerns and who they should report them to. Holding specific safety meetings can be useful.

✔ **Provide safety training and keep it up to date.** In addition to ensuring that your workforce has the required skills, current safety training is another way to send a message to your workforce that safety is important to the organisation.

✔ **See safety as the most important thing.** You need to make sure that employees know that a safety issue takes precedence over everything else. You should promote this message actively and continuously to ensure that it gets through and is heeded.

✔ **Show your commitment to safety in both your words and actions.** This advice is true for all positions of authority in your company, from the CEO to the most junior supervisor.

Paying attention to the preceding points can help improve safety attitudes at work and allow a more positive safety culture to develop. A more positive safety culture should in turn reduce the risk of accidents.

Instilling a safety culture in an organisation is an ongoing and continuous process. You can't just do it once and then forget about it. Organisations with the best safety culture and good safety records tend to address the points in the bulleted list as part of their normal way of working.

Chapter 14

Changing Organisations

. . . .

. . . .

*P*eople often say that organisations need to change to survive. This advice is especially true today because organisations need to adapt – for example, by downsizing or restructuring – to the ever-changing economic conditions to remain competitive and successful.

In this chapter, we discuss organisational change and consider the different types of change an organisation can face. Because we're work psychologists, we focus on the way in which people are affected by change rather than the change itself.

Understanding How and Why Organisations Change

Organisations can change in many ways and for many reasons. Sometimes change can be a minor thing that makes little difference to the way an organisation works and has limited impact on employees. At other times though, organisational change is a major event that has a big impact on employees. The type of change and the reasons for the change influences the ways in which people react to the change, which can often be negative.

Knowing the types of organisational change

Change within organisations can take many forms; so many that we can't hope to list them all here. Here are some examples:

✔ **Changing policy:** Making changes to organisational policies, such as changing pension entitlement or introducing flexible working.

✔ **Changing strategy:** Changing the goals and aims of the organisation and so changing the direction in which the organisation is moving. Strategy change can lead to changes in other areas to facilitate the new goals such as deciding to expand or outsource.

✔ **Downsizing:** Reducing the number of employees, often as a result of economic downturn or poor organisational performance.

✔ **Expanding:** Growing the business often by increasing the number of sites (especially in retail) or employees.

✔ **Outsourcing:** Deciding to contract out some of the work that was previously done within your organisation.

✔ **Restructuring:** Making changes in the way in which the organisation is structured – for example, by removing or merging departments or altering the chain of management to create a different reporting structure in your company.

Change terminology

The following table explains terms that work psychologists use to describe the different types of change in organisations.

Change Term	Definition	Example of Change Type
Continuous	Ongoing change often done for developmental reasons; can be consciously planned or be partly unplanned	Training
Episodic	Usually a one-off change event; can be caused by external challenges or be instigated by a senior person in the organisation who wants to make their presence known	Downsizing
Incremental	Small changes designed to improve organisational effectiveness	Introducing new technology
Planned	Change that's decided upon by an organisation	Expanding the business
Reactive	Change that occurs because of external events such as a recession	Implementing reduced working hours
Transformational	Change designed to have a big impact and to *transform* an organisation	Mergers

Exploring the causes of change

Workplaces have changed a lot over recent years, and much of the change is a result of the challenges that organisations are facing due to the economic downturn. Organisations have had to make difficult decisions and changes as they try to prevent organisational failure. Consider some of the news stories about redundancies, pay cuts, and recruitment freezes. Organisations typically don't make these types of changes by choice but as a necessary step to improve efficiency and profits at a time when every penny counts.

Responding to economic pressures is one reason for change. Here are some others:

- ✔ **Responding to the actions of competitors:** If your competitors are offering new services or products that may tempt your customers away from you, it can prompt you to make similar changes yourself.

- ✔ **Implementing government legislation:** Sometimes changes in laws have an impact on organisations. For example, when tobacco advertising was banned, tobacco manufacturers had to rethink their marketing strategy.

- ✔ **Listening to customers:** Feedback from customers about what they like and dislike about your organisation can lead to doing less (or differently) the things they don't like and doing even more of the things they do like.

- ✔ **Embracing technology:** The major advances in technology over the last few decades have resulted in many changes to how organisations do business, such as the increased use of virtual technology (see Chapter 16). Technology advances are likely to continue, and so is the need for organisations to understand and use this technology.

- ✔ **Reacting to changes in demographic factors:** Changing demographics in your customers or your employees can mean that you need to make changes to your organisation. For example, to serve an ageing population, you may need to change the way you market your goods to your customers or change the support you offer your employees.

Change doesn't happen on its own: Someone (usually high up in your organisation's hierarchy) needs to initiate a change before it can happen.

Change is a lot easier to implement in your organisation if it has the support of senior management. Likewise, change is less likely to be successful if people think that not everyone in the organisation agrees that the change is necessary – for example, management disagrees about the nature of the change. So if senior management support a change, make sure that everyone in the organisation knows this.

Reacting to Change

Of course, no matter what the cause (see preceding section) of change, employees can view them negatively. How would you react if you felt that your job was threatened or you had to watch colleagues being made redundant? These changes don't lead to a positive work environment, and the reactions of employees can make a huge difference as to whether or not steps such as these work in the long run. Think about it: if you alienate your employees because they feel that you're badly managing a situation and not showing any compassion for employees who are negatively affected by the changes you're making, then your employees aren't going to buy in to the new situation, which makes success even more unlikely! An unhappy employee is less likely to actively try to make change work, and may reduce their effort and goodwill towards the organisation. (Check out Chapter 4 for more on why negative attitudes from employees can be bad for your business.)

As a manager, taking time to explain to employees why you need to make changes that they see as negative can help to decrease the amount of negativity felt toward a change. Check out the 'Managing Change' section, later in this chapter, for more information.

Two factors affect how you or your employees react to change – your personal makeup and the circumstances in which the change take place. In the following sections, we look at change from the individual and situational angles.

Seeing how an individual copes with change

So how do people react to organisational change? Well, think about how you react to change in your life. If you see a change as positive, then you're likely to react in a positive way. For example, if your boss offers you a pay raise or a promotion, you probably aren't going to complain about this sort of change!

However, you may see some changes as negative. Imagine that you find out that your company is considering layoffs. How would that make you feel? Probably nervous about whether you'll still have a job in a few months' time and worried about the potential impact on you and your family.

Studies have shown that a change in your environment affects you. In a 1950 study, people sat in a room where they could hear the sound of a metronome going tick-tock. After a while, the sound of the metronome changed to a single tick. What was the reaction of the people in the room? Well, for such a small change, you may be surprised to hear that their heart rates shot up! If such a small change has this effect on people, then what are the likely results of big changes at work?

Reactions to change at work are often negative and may include:

- Changing productivity and quality levels

- Increasing anxiety and worry in employees

- Increasing stress levels and poorer health in employees

- Absenteeism or presenteeism, both of which are bad for the organisation (see Chapter 6)

- A desire for revenge if people feel badly treated (for more on what we call *equity theory,* see Chapter 11).

Appraising and reacting to change

When faced with a change, you appraise it and decide how it affects you personally. This appraisal then affects how you react to the change. Take a look at Table 14-1, which shows the different ways in which people can view change.

Table 14-1	Appraising and Reacting to Change	
Appraisal Outcome	*How You View Change*	*Example Change Event*
Change is irrelevant.	The change has no impact on you, so is unimportant.	Changes are being made to management pay levels. You aren't a manager, so it doesn't affect you.
Change is positive.	You view the change as an opportunity and something to embrace.	Your company is expanding, and promotion opportunities are being made available to you.
Change is negative.	The change has harmed you or is likely to harm you in some way.	Your company is making pay cuts to reduce the risk of bankruptcy. You're worried about how you'll manage to pay your bills next month.

In Chapter 10, we detail the psychological contract and talk about how important it can be in terms of the expectations that you have at work, both as an employee and a manager. You use the psychological contract, and in particular the breaking or violation of the psychological contract, as a framework to understand the way in which people react to change at work. You may want to take a look at Chapter 10 for more information.

Following the change-reaction cycle

Psychologists often talk about reactions to perceived negative change in terms of a *cycle,* and some have even likened the change cycle to bereavement models where people go through a number of stages before accepting the change that's happened to them. Typical stages in a change (and bereavement) model are shown in Figure 14-1 and include:

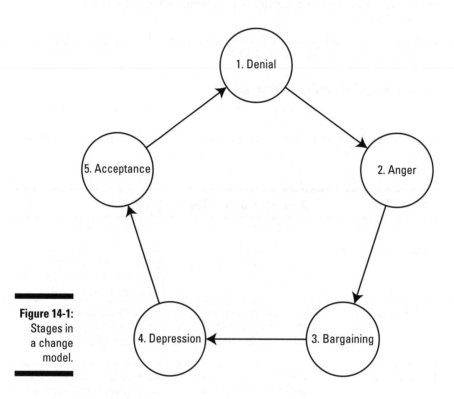

Figure 14-1:
Stages in
a change
model.

1. **Denial:** You refuse to believe that the change is happening.

2. **Anger:** You start to get angry at the people who are forcing the change on you.

3. **Bargaining:** You try to find ways of limiting the impact the change will have on you.

4. **Depression:** You resign yourself to the change but don't feel good about it.

5. **Acceptance:** You begin to accept the change and may start to see some of the positive things the change can bring you.

Managers: it takes time for people to work through the cycle, so don't expect to get immediate acceptance of a change you announce.

Individuals may be reluctant to change because they think that they'll have to work harder, especially during the change period where effort is needed to understand and adapt to change.

Making changes can mean changing familiar habits, which takes effort.

You're likely to feel comfortable when you think that you understand and have some control over the things that happen to you. Change at work that plunges you into the change-reaction cycle can reduce the feelings of control you have. People are generally reluctant to lose control, which leads to resistance. When you understand the change and how it will affect you, feelings of control can increase, and you see the change as less threatening.

Giving people some control over change events can help to increase satisfaction with planned changes, which in turn makes them more likely to succeed. Don't underestimate the importance of employee involvement and participation.

Factoring in personality and attitudes

You respond to change differently depending on the type of person you are. So things like your personality (see Chapter 3) and attitude toward work (see Chapter 4) affect how you react to change.

If you think about the people you know, either at work or family and friends, you can probably identify a person who you think would find change unsettling and a bit scary, and another person who would be more likely to embrace change and find it motivating. Imagine these people being told their job role is going to change and that they need to take on some new tasks. They may react differently to this mandate and be either worried or excited about the future. That's because the same change can affect people in different ways.

People may be different in several ways, which helps explain the different reactions they have to change:

- ✔ **Coping style:** People have different ways of coping with problems. One distinction made in coping styles is between having a *problem-focused* coping style where you actively try to solve problems, and an *emotion-focused* coping style where you cope by dealing successfully with your emotional reaction to a problem.

  Which coping style is appropriate to use in a change situation depends on the type of change. For example, being given new tasks may require problem-focused coping, whereas losing your job may need emotion-focused coping. How good you are at the different types of coping influences how well you react to the changes that happen to you. Imagine, for example, two employees – John, who is problem-focused, and Bill, who is emotion-focused. When faced with potential redundancies, Bill may handle the situation better because he can successfully deal with his emotional reaction to the potential change. John, on the other hand, may find it harder because his coping style relies on actively solving the problem, something he is powerless to do in a redundancy situation.

- ✔ **Locus of control:** Locus of control is all about whether you feel that you're in control of the events that happen to you and believe that you can influence the environment around you. If you believe that you have influence, you've an *internal locus of control*. If you think you've no control over the things happening, you're likely to have an *external locus of control*. Generally, having an internal locus of control is better and means that you feel positive about your influence when taking on the changes that are happening. But, if major change happens and you've an internal locus of control, you can experience high levels of stress because you realise that in such a case you really do have little control over what is happening to you and you're not comfortable with this. For more on locus of control, flip to Chapter 3.

- ✔ **Negative affectivity:** This term describes a general tendency to have a negative mood and to see things in a negative manner. If you've a tendency to be like this, you probably see change as a bad thing.

- ✔ **Neuroticism:** This Big 5 personality factor (see Chapter 3) relates to how anxious you're likely to feel about things. The more anxious you are, the less likely you are to embrace change.

- ✔ **Openness:** One of the Big 5 personality factors (which we explain in Chapter 3), *openness to experience* relates to how imaginative you are and how open you are to new experiences. The higher you are on this personality trait, the more likely you are to enjoy change.

- ✔ **Self-efficacy:** High feelings of self-efficacy mean that you have belief in yourself in being able to attain a goal. So if you believe you can manage the changes that are happening to you (such as taking on new tasks at work), you're more positive about the change. On the other hand, if you've low levels of self efficacy, you've less belief in yourself and are less positive about the change.

In addition to these elements of personality and attitude that affect reactions to change, life stage also plays a part. Your age and where you are in your career affects how you react to change. For example, being made redundant at the age of 55 may be harder to cope with than at age 25 because you may be worried about how hard it will be to find work as an older worker. (Check out Chapter 11 for more on age discrimination.)

Realising that the situation affects reaction to change

The way in which change is introduced and managed has an impact on how you react to it. So how you react is not all about the type of person you are (see preceding section), but also about the situation and environment you're in.

Two things have a big impact on your likely reactions to change:

- **Type of change:** We talk about positive and negative change and how you appraise change in the earlier section 'Seeing how an individual copes with change'. The type of change and whether or not you think that it will be good or bad for you is one of the biggest factors in how you react. You generally resist negative change, which we discuss more in the later 'Resisting Change' section.

- **Support available:** When a change happens at work, the support offered to help people manage the change has a big influence on how successful the change is likely to be. Think about things like the following:

  - Paying lots of attention to communication so that people know what is going on

  - Providing training so that people have the skills they need

  - Being an effective leader because the way in which you lead change affects how people react to it (skip to Chapter 8 for more on leadership)

If you're a manager, remember that even if you've no control of the type of change you have to introduce, you *do* have control over the support you offer your employees while the change is happening. Providing support, and taking the time and effort to ensure that employees trust you to do the best you can for them, can make change more successful. We discuss types of support in the 'Managing Change' section, later in this chapter.

Resisting Change

Changes in organisations aren't always welcomed, even when the change is necessary or important. Understanding that people can be resistant to change can help you successfully manage possible negative reactions to change. Although change can be difficult to manage, change is important to the survival and continued success of an organisation.

Lots of research into organisational behaviour has shown that people are generally resistant to change in the workplace, especially if they see it as negative or potentially threatening.

Two main types of resistance exist:

- **Resisting the change itself:** This resistance happens if you disagree with the content of the change – for example, a new pay structure means that you lose the automatic right to future pay increments.

- **Resisting the process of change:** Sometimes you can agree with the change itself, but be unhappy about the way in which this change is being introduced. For example, you may think that a new pay structure isn't so bad an idea because you'll be able to earn increments relating to your good performance. But you may be unhappy that the change is being imposed on you and that nobody has asked you how you feel about the change.

TIP

Managers can lessen resistance that happens because of dissatisfaction with the process of change by offering good support to employees. And good communication and interpersonal skills can help you introduce change more successfully.

Here are some reasons why employees resist change:

- **Fear of the unknown:** You probably fear the unknown; most people do. Not knowing what is going to happen creates uncertainty and worry.

- **Habit:** When you've been in a job for a while, you start to form habits about how you do your work. These habits become more and more familiar over time. When something happens (a change event) that threatens these habits, you see it as unsettling and may resent the effort that's required from you while you change your habits and adopt new ones.

- **Inconvenience:** You may view change as an inconvenience to you. Imagine changes that occur at work that require you to take on more workload. You're busy enough already, you may respond! Trying to manage change while doing all your work can be a major hassle.

- **Lack of trust:** If you don't believe that you're being told the truth about change, the reasons behind the change, or what plans are in store for the future, you may resist it. Being confident that changes are being done in the best way and with your interests taken into account make you more accepting of change.

- **Loss of security:** A big worry for you when change happens may be how it affects your security. You can go from feeling confident that you've a secure job and future to worrying about where you'll be in six months rather quickly! Security is important, and losing it can be a major blow. We discuss the importance of job security in Chapter 6.

- **Money:** One of the main things you'll worry about is how changes are going to affect you financially. You may worry about loss of pay if layoffs are mentioned or if you've concerns about future promotion prospects. You may also think that you're taking on more work but are not being fairly rewarded because you're still getting the same pay. Change can make people think about equity issues (see Chapter 9) more than ever.

✔ **No need for change:** A big factor influencing whether you resist change or not is the extent to which you think that the change is needed. If you believe that the change is wrong or unnecessary, you're less likely to react positively than if you think that the change is sensible and needed. Think about a time when you've been asked to do something that you thought was pointless. Did you want to do it?

Researchers measured resistance to change using a questionnaire, and they found that respondents who were higher on the resistance to change scale were more likely to react negatively to changes and find it harder to work effectively following changes at work.

Resistance to change makes change less likely to be successful and can affect your work performance and productivity. So, as a manager, proactively dealing with change resistance can increase the chances of success and increase performance and productivity.

Managing Change

How can change best be managed in organisations? We talk in this chapter all about the types of change that can happen and the way in which you may react to change. Now we think about the ways in which you can introduce and manage change in order to keep negative reactions at a minimum.

Consider these important principles to managing and introducing change:

✔ **Agreeing aims:** Make sure that you, and the people around you, have a shared understanding of where you're heading. Knowing what the aim of a change is can help the change be planned in a way that moves you toward that aim.

✔ **Communicating fully:** Pay careful attention to communicating with the people around you. You can use many methods of communicating to keep people up-to-date quite easily.

Giving bad news remotely (for example, through email) doesn't help you manage people's reactions, and you won't really know whether people have understood the message correctly. Meeting face-to-face with people can be challenging, but at least you can talk about your reasons for making the change and answer any questions people have.

✔ **Considering the impact:** Throughout the change process, think about who's affected by the change and what it means to them.

✔ **Involving people:** Wherever you can, involve people in change decisions and get their support for the change.

Change that's imposed on people is more likely to fail than if you involve people in deciding on change and the way in which change will be introduced.

✔ **Planning steps:** Consider what needs to be done and plan achievable steps that can move you along as you introduce the change. Think about the aims of the change and the people affected as you plan these steps.

✔ **Understanding where you are:** Think about the situation that you and your organisation are in at the moment so that you understand the need for change and where change is needed.

People are wary of the unknown; you can reduce their worries by communication and involvement. And the more people that are involved with a change, the more help you get with the things that need to be done. You can share tasks and increase involvement at the same time.

As a manager or leader, people look to you for guidance during a change process. The leadership style you adopt during change can affect the success of the change. Take a look at Chapter 8 to find out more about how your leadership style affects the people around you.

Table 14-2 shows techniques you can use to help you manage change in relation to the people you work with. Some are more positive than others, but the methods you use don't just depend on how nice you want to be but also on what the change is (and how you expect people to react to it) and how quickly you need to make the change.

Culture change: Unfreezing, changing, refreezing

Quite often with major change events, you don't need to change the culture of the organisation and the attitudes and behaviours of employees in order to make the change successfully. A lot of the research into organisational change has looked at culture change as essential to the change process. We talk about organisational culture and culture change in Chapter 13.

Kurt Lewin, an esteemed psychologist often described as the founder of social psychology, proposes that successful change needs three main steps to help ensure that the change is supported by the organisations culture:

1. **Unfreeze the present level.**

   Understand the need for change and prepare for the change. If you're a manager,

try to make sure that your employees also understand and are prepared for change.

2. **Move to the next level.**

   This step is where the change takes place and when people are getting used to the changes. Lewin describes this step as the transition stage. As a manager, you can offer support to your employees during this transition to ensure that change is being implemented and embraced effectively.

3. **Freeze the new level.**

   Sometimes known as *refreezing,* this stage is where stability can set in after changes have been implemented and where the change can be reinforced and accepted.

Table 14-2	Change-Management Techniques	
Technique	*Is It Positive or Negative?*	*When May You Use It?*
Education	Positive	When people need information about the change – so all the time.
Forced change	Negative	When you've no choice but to make the change and to make it quickly. (This approach makes change happen, but it also means that people will be most resistant to it.)
Help	Positive	When people are negatively affected by change and need training or support to help them adapt to the change.
Involvement	Positive	When you need other people on your side to help you get agreement to the change.
		When you want help with the tasks that the change brings.
		When you want to reduce other people's concerns about the change.
Manipulation of the facts	Negative	When you want to make change quickly. (Although you can manipulate people into agreeing to change by putting a positive spin on the changes and not focusing on the drawbacks, be careful; when people realise they've been manipulated, problems are likely to follow in the future.)
Agreements	Positive	When you recognise that people will be negatively affected by the change. Talking to people affected by change and negotiating some of the terms of the change can help reduce resistance.

Chapter 15

Keeping Pace with the Global Workplace

· ·

In This Chapter

▶ Defining international culture

▶ Appreciating cultural differences

▶ Behaving appropriately across cultures

· ·

*Y*ou may have noticed the growing number of people you meet who are from different countries. If you're attending college, many of your lecturers and fellow students may be working and studying a long way from their home country. If you're working in a multinational organisation, you may have an opportunity to visit, or transfer, to a site in a different country or be part of a virtual team scattered across the globe. Or you may be part of a team responsible for expanding your business into a growing market, such as China or India.

We could go on to discuss the opportunities available to meet and work with people from different cultures, but the purpose of this chapter is to explain *how* cultural differences are relevant in the world of work. Take, for example, an Englishman trying to do business in Japan. The Englishman asks the Japanese purchasing manager whether he agrees with the price and wants to proceed with the order, and the answer is 'yes'. The Englishman returns home and waits for the order, but it never happens. The Japanese manager wanted to avoid conflict, so he didn't say 'no', but he had no intention of placing the order. These incidents can be frustrating. Being aware of cultural differences can go a long way to anticipating people's behaviour and avoiding mistakes and misunderstandings.

Work psychologists are interested in understanding why people from different cultures behave differently. This knowledge helps to explain cross-cultural variations in attitudes and behaviours, which helps international managers to manage effectively and fairly and cope with their experiences. In this chapter, we introduce you to the meaning of international culture and explain in what ways countries are different. Throughout the chapter, we offer tips on how to behave and what to expect from different cultures. We generalise these differences in this chapter, but of course, not everybody follows the norm.

Recognising the Worldwide Workforce

Advancements in communication, technology, and transportation are opening up global opportunities for organisations at a rapid rate. As a result, the number of organisations prepared to expand to different countries and continents is increasing. In addition, people can easily move from country to country because traditional borders are almost outdated. The result is a global society where you're as likely to work alongside someone whose family has lived in the area for generations as someone from, for example, Latin America, Asia or Eastern Europe. For example, we work with small groups of postgraduate students, and a typical group consists of students from Uruguay, Turkey, China, Japan, and Pakistan, all of whom want to stay and work in the UK when they finish their studies.

Even though the workforce is mobile, employees bring with them their own cultures. People don't usually lose all their culture, and as such can have their own distinct customs, values, beliefs, and way of life. Many distinct differences exist between cultures, and you can no doubt think of a few. In our postgraduate group, which is made up of people from many nationalities, they've experienced problems understanding and appreciating each other's behaviour. The Chinese and Japanese students have been frustrated by the lack of punctuality of the Uruguayan student, and the Pakistani student can't understand the lack of flexibility to new ideas by the Chinese and Japanese. And these challenges exist in a small group of five – imagine what challenges exist in a multinational organisation!

Defining culture

Culture, like many concepts, is a bit woolly and therefore difficult to define. Basically, culture is about sharing patterns of behaviour that have evolved over time and that you probably don't even think about now. Culture is about how a community decides how to survive and stay together, and these ideas are passed down through generations.

Values, attitudes, and meanings are shared, and passed around by members of the community.

However, culture doesn't mean that all members of the community have to think in the same way, or have the same attitudes and values. If you travel outside your country, you notice that the locals do things differently from you. For example, the British are happy to get in line to wait for their turn, but if they try to do this in most other countries, even as close (geographically) as Poland, they end up being elbowed out of the way.

Cultural difference is a major issue facing a manager of a multinational work-force. The culture that you belong to influences your basic assumptions, values, and behaviour, which brings variety to a multicultural team. Cultural difference isn't an issue only for the manager, but also for the employee working in a foreign country. The cultural differences can affect how a manager interprets an employee's work performance and how the manager gets the best out of the employee.

International managers, both working abroad and managing diverse work-forces, need to understand different cultural perspectives. To be effective, managers need to know how to work with people from many cultures and, often more importantly, how others may interpret their own behaviour.

Bringing Worlds Apart Closer Together

Transferring to a job abroad can involve being confronted with a totally new world of cultural patterns that are at odds, to a greater or lesser amount, with your own values and how you live. Even if you're just moving from the UK to Spain, you may find it difficult to come to terms with taking a siesta in the afternoon and eating dinner at midnight! A big problem for managers, though, is being aware of different values and assumptions and not jumping to conclusions about why locals behave how they do.

Even if you're not moving to another country, as a manager or employee today you're likely to work with many people from different ethnic back-grounds. This diversity makes it really important to appreciate that people from other countries and cultures are different in a number of ways, such as the way they look at things, express themselves, and even dress.

In Chapter 13, you can read about organisational culture and why this culture is key to making sense of what goes on in an organisation. But what happens when an employee joins your organisation and comes from a totally diverse background, or perhaps you're transferred to the Timbuktu office? Being aware of cultural differences gives you a head start.

Recognising, and moving beyond cultural stereotypes

What makes a typical Brit? If you're British, you may find answering that question difficult, but if you're American, you can no doubt come up with ideas about the characteristics of Brits easily. *Stereotyping* (a fixed way of thinking about people where you classify people into specific categories) other people comes naturally.

A problem with stereotypes is that they can often be wrong and highly generalised. For example, a misguided British manager meets an American manager, and recalls experiences of the individual Americans he's previously met (friendly, a bit loud, optimistic, patriotic, and lacking cultural empathy). He compares his new acquaintance against his previous experiences and thinks, 'He's okay for an American.' Similarly, the American manager, who is also misguided, holds stereotypical views based on his experiences of the British people he's met (grumpy, smart, snobby, and cultured)!

In a work situation, problems can happen when managers deny having stereotypes. A manager may decide that the new employee from India is going to be lazy – because he holds a stereotype that all Indians are – and that view then taints the employee's actions. As a manager, you need to be aware of possible risks and missed opportunities if you ignore the impact of culture. You need to anticipate any possible impact of cultural differences and think about different ways to manage them. (Check out Chapter 8 on leadership styles.)

If you're a manager and think that you're guilty of having stereotypes, the best thing you can do is to admit it to yourself. Use it as a starting point and revise it as you get to know the employee.

Looking at the visible face of culture

Understanding a culture isn't as simple as visiting an organisation in a different country, but doing so is a great start. The picture you often take away is based on the superficial impression given by the behaviour of the people and the external signs (called *artefacts* – see Chapter 13), but a number of obvious artefacts and behaviour in an organisation tell you a lot about a culture:

- **Architecture and design:** In Japan, where teamwork is important, organisations often have large, but crowded, open offices that everyone (including the boss) shares, wearing the same company-issued uniform. In the US, the open offices tend to have space partitioned off with half walls, called cubicles, to give a sense of privacy and allow opportunity for employees to personalise their space. In Germany, employees tend to expect private offices with their title on the door. Just imagine how out of his comfort zone a German would feel working in a typical Japanese organisation.

- **Greeting rituals:** In the US, a quick, firm handshake tends to show self-confidence and masculinity, and a limp handshake from a man may be interpreted as a sign of weakness. But in most of Africa, a limp handshake, often lasting several minutes, is the right way to go. In Japan, the exchange of business cards isn't a case of taking it and putting it in your pocket; you have to carefully inspect it. And body contact is a whole different planet – Latin Americans are likely to hug, the French are inclined to kiss, but don't try any of this in Asia because people there often find physical contact when meeting a business colleague uncomfortable.

Don't be tempted to use your business card as a coffee mat – we know someone who was seriously told off by a Japanese manager for not respecting his position in the organisation!

✔ **Physical space and contact:** A popular stereotype of the British is that they're aloof and cold, but this appearance can often be explained by the amount of physical space (or their protective bubble) that they need to feel comfortable. The British tend to need to be at least an arm's length from people (unless they're in a relationship, and even then men sometimes aren't so sure!) as opposed to Latin Americans who are more likely to be happy being closer together. Different cultures also determine the amount of 'looking intensity' allowed. For example, in the Western world, eye contact usually shows that you're paying attention and indicates honesty – you don't always trust people who don't look you in the eye. But if you do make eye contact in Asia and Latin America, people can interpret it as a sign of disrespect, as status is linked to the quantity of eye contact, and hostility.

✔ **Dress code:** Northern Europeans are inclined to dress more formally than Southern Europeans (although in the UK, this dress code is usually because it keeps you warmer!). Rolling your sleeves up at work can show that you're getting down to business in the US, but you're unlikely to find a German doing the same.

✔ **Written or verbal contract:** The Chinese and Thais tend to rely on verbal agreements as they believe that the spirit of the agreement is more important than the letter of agreement. A written contract may be seen as offensive by indicating a lack of trust. On the other hand, Western organisations are inclined to put things in writing and often bring in their lawyers.

Knowing, and being aware of, cultural differences is half the battle. At least these signs and behaviours are reasonably obvious and easy to pick up on. Understanding beliefs, values, and assumptions gets more difficult, which we discuss in the next section.

Considering beliefs, values, and assumptions

Different cultures – and, as a result, organisations – tend to share similar beliefs, values, and assumptions about how you behave in organisations and when doing business.

Chapter 13 talks about the difference between beliefs, values, and assumptions.

How an organisation defines success, views the role of a manager, or selects potential employees determines its strategy and overall attitude to its employees. For example, a strategy of 'the customer is always right' affects how employees behave toward customers and may increase their emotional labour and stress levels (see Chapter 7). On the other hand, if the business strategy is to hand over large dividends to shareholders, the culture may be target-driven and ruthless.

A number of countries have different beliefs and values. For example:

- **Criteria for success:** In the US, the company often exists for the shareholders. In Japan, the customer tends to always be right. And in Germany, the employees are usually the most important.

- **Employee selection:** Selection practices differ around the world. If a global American organisation attempted to convince all subsidiaries to use the same selection methods, they would receive objections. For example, Germans, Americans, and the British regularly rely on references and résumés, whereas Italians tend to prefer traditional interviews and the French widely use *graphology* (handwriting analysis).

As you can see, these beliefs and values are quite obvious, open, and simple for an outsider to pick up. However, the underlying assumptions are a lot more difficult to grasp and easily misunderstood. How on earth do you know whether employees from different cultures are comfortable with making quick decisions or prefer to focus on analysis of data rather than abstract ideas in presentations? This example shows how difficult the task of being a manager of a multicultural team, or in a different country, can be. In the later section 'Managing Internationally', we provide useful tips, but here are a few examples of basic assumptions to be aware of:

- **Managing relationship with nature:** Do managers feel that they've control over nature? In the US, they tend to have a can-do culture, which suggests control over nature. In Islamic countries, religion plays more of a role, and the approach is more 'If God wills'.

- **Providing evidence:** The British tend to like facts and figures; the French often prefer to use logic, but Americans can see this approach as too analytical and abstract.

- **Respecting the boss:** In France, the boss is generally the boss, but in the rest of Northern Europe, status and power is often downplayed.

- **Taking action:** Americans and British people are inclined to take quick decisions and make things happen because they're willing to take risks and maybe even make mistakes. But French and Japanese people usually prefer to take time reflecting and planning.

- **Taking care:** In Nordic countries, the priority tends to be the quality of working life, so extensive social programs exist. In the US and Japan, the emphasis at work is more on earnings and company profits.

Exploring Value Dimensions

If you read anything about business and cultural differences, you certainly come across Geert Hofstede, a Dutch social psychologist and anthropologist. Hofstede looks at national and organisational cultures and how national culture influences values in the workplace.

Hofstede identified four value dimensions that countries differ on:

- Power distance
- Uncertainty avoidance
- Individualism/collectivism
- Masculinity/femininity
- Long-term orientation

Yes, we know that's five and not four, but another psychologist added the last dimension at a later point in the 1980s!

The following sections look at these dimensions and explain how they affect values and behaviours in different countries. Being aware of these underlying cultural aspects can help you to understand employee behaviour, as well as help you to know how to behave.

You can't use these dimensions to predict what *will* happen, but they can help you predict a little about what *may* happen.

Exploring cultural differences

In the 1960s, Geert Hofstede carried out an employee opinion survey asking about preferences in terms of management style and work environment. He compared work-related values and attitudes of 116,000 employees across 72 countries.

He found that if a multinational organisation tries to impose the same values across all foreign sites, it won't work, because the national values persist. The local values determine how the rules are interpreted and the policies implemented.

For example, if an American organisation sends around a memo to say that all vacancies must be advertised externally, their sites in Asia are likely to ignore the missive and continue to employ members of their family and people they know and trust.

We recommend having a look at Hofstede's website (www.geert-hofstede.com) because he provides lots of interesting comparisons between countries.

Weighing up equality

The first value dimension is called *power distance* and is all about whether power and influence are equal in a society. Power distance can be low or high.

Low power distance

In a *low* power country, everyone tends to have equal rights and opportunities to change their position in society. Low power countries are typically those where a manager works closely with and is happy to consult their employees when making decisions. To give you examples of scores, Britain scores 35 on the cultural scale (from 1 to 120) and the US 40. Arab countries are high on power and score 80. In the US, managers and employees often get together socially, but this would rarely happen in a high power society.

If you work with an organisation in a low power distance country, you need to

- ✔ Treat all employees with respect.
- ✔ Delegate important assignments to employees.
- ✔ Accept blame personally for things that go wrong.

High power distance

If a country is high on the power distance index, then everyone typically has their rightful place. High power distance countries (predominantly the less developed countries, such as India and China) tend to be those who value rural society above urban societies. China has one of the highest scores on this index, which is strange because the China you tend to see on the news is an urban, high-technology metropolis, but established values are difficult to change. In these typical countries, you don't tend to question superiors (although they can bully you!), and as a rule you need to be conscious of your position in society.

If you work with an organisation in a high power distance country, you need to

- ✔ Show respect and admiration to people in more senior positions.
- ✔ Be directive and use a more autocratic management style (see Chapter 8).
- ✔ Not expect employees to show initiative; give clear directions and stress deadlines.

In a high power country, going over your boss's head with an idea, for example, isn't always a good idea. This approach can be seen as subordination. But you can usually get away with it in low power countries.

Avoiding uncertainty

Uncertainty avoidance is about the level of concern a society has for certainty and security. A country can be high or low in uncertainty avoidance.

High uncertainty avoidance

If a country is *high* on the uncertainty avoidance index, it prefers stability and predictability and tends to be resistant to change, consequently imposing rules to maintain the status quo. Countries high on uncertainty avoidance include Greece, Japan, France, and Korea.

If you work with an organisation in a high uncertainty avoidance country, you need to

- ✔ Be patient when proposing new ways and methods, and wait for people to get used to the ideas.
- ✔ Be prepared for a more defeatist view as people tend not to feel in control and so avoid making decisions.
- ✔ Back everything up with facts and figures as anything risky is avoided.

Low uncertainty avoidance

A *low* country is inclined to be comfortable with uncertainty, seeing it as providing excitement and a chance for new ideas and change. Examples include Singapore, Denmark, India, the US, and the UK.

Both the US and Britain don't usually like having rules applied to them, so it's no surprise that they feel comfortable with each other's approach to work. On the other hand, France typically wants to know where it stands and is less amenable to ideas that deviate.

If you're working with an organisation in a country with low uncertainty avoidance, you need to

- ✔ Be flexible and open to new ideas.
- ✔ Put new plans into operation as soon as possible.
- ✔ Give employees guidelines, but let them have control over what they do and how they go about it.

Combining power distance and uncertainty avoidance indexes

In Table 15-1, we combine the power distance and uncertainty avoidance indexes (see the previous two sections) to give you a better picture of national cultures.

Table 15-1	Examples of Power Distance and Uncertainty Avoidance Index
(1) Small Power Distance + Weak Uncertainty Avoidance	**(2) Large Power Distance + Weak Uncertainty Avoidance**
Australia	China
Britain	Hong Kong
Canada	India
Denmark	Indonesia
US	Countries of West and East Africa
(3) Small Power Distance + Strong Uncertainty Avoidance	**(4) Large Power Distance + Strong Uncertainty Avoidance**
Austria	Greece
France	Italy
Finland	Japan
Germany	Korea
Israel	Mexico
	Venezuela

The countries we list aren't the most extreme in any of the indexes because our aim is to provide an overview of typical countries. If you want to know the exact scores and rankings, refer to the Hofstede website (www.geert-hofstede.com).

Here's a breakdown of what the table means in practice:

- ✔ Countries high on both indexes (4) tend to be bureaucratic.

- ✔ Countries low on both indexes (1) are less hierarchical and have fewer formalised rules.

- ✔ Countries low on power distance and high on uncertainty avoidance (3) have cultures typically based on equal rights and opportunities for all, but they tend to be concerned about stability. These cultures have less of a need for a manager as the organisation usually follows routines and keeps running as it always has done.

- ✔ Countries high on power distance and low on uncertainty avoidance (2) tend to believe everyone has their place in society, but they're comfortable with uncertainty as it can offer opportunity for innovation and change.

Looking out for number one or all in this together

Individualistic societies are those where people have loose ties and tend to look after themselves and immediate family, such as the US, UK, and Italy. Societies where people belong to groups and look after each other are called *collectivist* and include Asian and Latin American countries.

Individualistic cultures

As you can probably guess, individualistic cultures, such as the US, UK, Europe and Australia, tend to be more self-centred and think about their own goals than collectivist cultures. When they talk in business, people in an individualistic culture usually get to the point quickly. In the US the aim is often to get to the top of an organisation, and sometimes it doesn't matter who you tread on, on the way up. Business relationships are often made for what you can get out of them, and it's up to you to promote yourself whenever possible. If you ask an American office to conduct a survey and get back with the results, the task is likely to be given to one person, and you probably receive the results back reasonably quickly, as the employee wants to get on with it to show how efficient and effective he is.

If you're working with an organisation in a country with a high individualistic culture, you need to

- ✔ Allow employees to work by themselves and use their own initiative without seeming like an intrusive manager.

- ✔ Work by yourself and use your own initiative rather than relying on other group members for answers.

- ✔ Be aware that employees are likely to promote their achievements whenever possible, as their sights are often set on climbing up the career ladder.

Collectivist cultures

In *collectivist* cultures, such as China, Guatemala, Indonesia, and Pakistan, the team is generally all important, and they can see individualistic cultures as cold and unsupportive. They would rarely dream of disagreeing with someone in public, and saying 'no' is unlikely to happen – they're more likely to use alternative negative phrases and say, 'That may be difficult'. Relationships between managers and employees and other organisations are commonly based on trust. If you ask an Asian office to conduct a survey and get back with the results, the response may take months because the task may be given to the whole department to work on, and no one person takes responsibility.

If you work in a country based on a collectivist culture, don't get frustrated by long and rambling meetings. The business isn't moving forward, but the relationships are. Cultivating relationships is more important than doing business.

If you work in an organisation in a country with a collectivist culture, you need to

- Praise the team, not an individual.
- Recognise that any decision-making is going to be slow because many team members need to be consulted.
- Understand that promotion is based on experience and seniority.

Thinking about masculinity and femininity

Women's values are more likely to be similar in all cultures – focusing on caring for others and quality of life – but male values can differ to a greater degree. In some countries, men are assertive and competitive and are more interested in money and things, but in other countries, they're more modest and caring.

In *feminine* countries, both females and males have the same caring values and are more interested in quality of life and relationship building. In *masculine* countries, both males and females show more competitive and assertive qualities, although women a lot less so than men, and tend to focus on values such as getting rich.

Feminine countries

Typically, feminine countries include the Netherlands, Denmark, and France where people tend towards a more caring and nurturing approach to society.

As a manager in a masculine culture (see the next section), you need to be decisive and assertive. However, in a feminine culture, you need to rely more on your intuition and do all you can to get your employees to agree with your plans.

If you work in an organisation in a highly feminine country, you need to remember

- Family time is important, so working overtime is not usually a normal practice.
- Trust in business relationships is often more important than making the biggest profit margin.
- Conversations at business functions tend to focus on people's life and interests rather than business.

Masculine countries

The UK, Japan, and Mexico are high on the masculinity index, while the US is only moderately so. Despite the perception that the US has a culture focused on goals, results, and efficiency, the research by Hofstede suggests that Americans are more inclined toward equality and balance at work than the Brits.

If you work in an organisation in a highly masculine country, you need to remember to

- ✔ Never ask personal questions, but you can talk about business anywhere, even at social occasions.
- ✔ Not expect people to show interest in developing closer relationships.
- ✔ Be direct, concise, and unemotional in what you say.

Looking to the future or living in the past

Long-term oriented societies, such as China, Japan, and Korea, don't tend to expect instant results in business and patiently wait for future rewards, such as growing their market position. As a result, managers aren't usually expected to show immediate results and are given time and resources.

In *short-term oriented* cultures, such as in Western societies, the bottom line (profits!) is generally the major concern, and managers are judged by it regularly.

If you work in a highly long-term culture, you often need to be patient! And if you work in a relatively short-term culture, the focus is generally on the 'here and now' and on a need for more instant results.

Managing Internationally

Work psychologists have discovered a lot about managing cultural differences at an individual level from expatriates, but many organisations don't listen to feedback. Even countries that are close neighbours can have different perceptions.

For example, a German manager who came to the UK was surprised by the behaviour of his management team. Every Friday, the team went off to a local pub for lunch, something that's common in the UK. The German manager stopped the Friday lunch outing because it wouldn't be acceptable in Germany and refused to let staff leave the premises during working hours. It wasn't a popular decision and resulted in some employees looking for alternative employment.

In this section, we provide guidance for managers working outside of their own countries or working with foreign people.

Adjusting to working abroad

If your organisation sends you on an assignment to a different country, you go though stages of cultural adjustment, which follow a U-curve:

- ✔ Initial elation
- ✔ Optimism (a honeymoon period)
- ✔ Irritability, frustration (called the *morning after*)
- ✔ Gradual adjustment (a feeling of happy-ever-after)

The morning-after period is when the assignment is at risk of failing. You experience a type of culture shock where even minor events can make you feel depressed. You're trying to understand the differences, but sometimes the culture shock is just too much, and you stop learning.

One dilemma facing expatriates (or *Euromanagers,* if you're European and work across borders in Europe) is whether to go native or stay within the expat community.

The more you interact with local people, and get to know more about the local culture, the more you adjust to the new environment. But if contact just reinforces your existing stereotypes, your frustration intensifies.

If you're from the UK, you're less likely to have cultural interactions as a Euromanager than managers who go to Asia or America. You tend to think that back home is much closer and that you don't see much difference between cultures. But that attitude can be a mistake: see the example of the German manager banning the pub lunch in the introduction to this section.

Working with people from all nationalities

Whether you're considering working abroad, or you need to hire someone to work in an overseas location, you must have (or look for) the right skills and attitude. The competencies needed include

- ✔ **Having a laugh:** Knowing how to laugh at your mistakes and misunderstandings is good as a coping mechanism and for breaking down barriers.

  Be careful with sarcasm because many cultures don't get it.

✔ **Relating to people:** The ability to form relationships is absolutely crucial. Going into an unfamiliar situation, maybe with an agenda set by someone from a different culture, is stressful. The ability to establish trust and share knowledge helps minimise stressful uncertainties. But even more important is making sure that you (or the manager you're looking for) have the technical expertise; otherwise, the assignment won't get done, but you will have a good time making new friends!

✔ **Respecting culture:** You may find it quite tempting to compare the new culture with back home, but a better way is to find out why people in the culture do things the way they do. Having the ability to show understanding and empathy toward others is important.

✔ **Speaking the lingo:** Even today, when English is so widely spoken, speaking the local language can help make contact and shows a willingness to join in.

If you're living in your own country, you may be interested in how to manage virtual teams based in a number of different locations and countries. If so, have a look at Chapter 16 where we focus on managing virtual teams.

Whether you're working abroad, in your home country managing, or working alongside employees from different cultures, it helps to have a *global mindset* (in other words, an openness to, and awareness of, cultural diversity and the opportunities that follow) and to be open and not fixed in your opinions – be able to see things your way and their way.

Chapter 16

Working Virtually

*T*he rapid growth of more affordable communication technologies is changing the structure of organisations. Easy access to the Internet and computers is transforming the communication of information and the development of organisational systems and processes. As a result, the traditional workplace is evolving and is no longer restricted by geographic locations. You can live in the UK, but effectively work in the United States. Your fellow team members may live in Mumbai, Paris, and Hong Kong, instead of all working from the same building. And on a less dramatic note, more employees are working from home instead of commuting to an office on a daily basis.

But what impact does remote working have on the employees involved? Do these employees work as effectively? How does a manager manage an employee who's 10,000 miles away on another continent or 10 miles away working from a spare bedroom?

In this chapter, we introduce the issues for the virtual organisation. In particular, we look at how virtual teams work together and discuss potential problems for employees working away from the workplace. We look in detail at the most popular type of virtual worker – the teleworker. And if you're a virtual employee, or a virtual manager, we offer hints and tips to cope with the situation.

Shaping the Future of the Workplace

The increasing sophistication of information technology is making it easier for organisations to create structures that ignore time zones and traditional geographic restrictions. As a result, more and more organisations are introducing flexible working practices, such as teleworking (working away from the office), that take advantage of new technology or outsourcing operational functions to distant countries, in order to benefit from the potential cost reductions.

Working on projects with virtual work teams spread around the globe is no longer unusual. Resources such as Skype and video conferencing allow employees to collaborate across distances.

One of the downsides is that the opening up of location means more competition for jobs. It's no longer good enough to live within commuting distance of an organisation because plenty of people are out there with knowledge and skills who are able to work for less pay, due to exchange rates and lower living costs.

Not all types of jobs can be virtual, though; for example, hairdressing, child care, and dentistry are impossible (unless you know otherwise!), to name a few. However, the general move away from production to service-related businesses has produced more knowledge workers who aren't stuck to specific physical locations. For example, you can do technical jobs, such as website design and software programming, and non-technical jobs, such as customer service, accounting, and project management, from any location. You may contact a virtual worker when you call about your mobile phone contract or your telephone services. And we know someone who writes the cheesy rhymes for greeting cards for a UK organisation. He moved from the UK to Australia, and still does the same job with the same company.

Going virtual

A *virtual organisation* is one where the employees of a company work in different locations and mainly use computer-related communication, such as email. Although not all organisations or employees are suitable for working virtually, some organisations ignore this logic and go virtual purely for financial gain. Organisations may not be suitable because of the following:

- ✔ **Culture of organisation:** In bureaucratic-control-based organisations, clerical and non-professional employees are unlikely to be seen as trustworthy enough to be offsite. Organisations benefit most when they already have a culture of flexibility, trust, and openness.

- ✔ **Limited availability of suitable jobs:** Not all jobs can be part of the virtual organisation, restricting the number of employees who can benefit from this lifestyle. This fact may create feelings of unfairness between employees who can and can't work virtually (see Chapter 11 for more on fairness in the organisation).

✔ **Morale:** Creating virtual jobs is often done as a way of saving money, especially if the organisation is being relocated. This fact can have a negative impact on the employee's view of virtual working and she may leave the organisation, as not everyone wants to work away from the office.

As you can see, organisations becoming virtual isn't always a straightforward decision.

Managing a virtual team

Many organisations form *virtual teams,* where employees dotted around the world (or around a country) combine their knowledge and skills to collaborate using computer-mediated-communication (CMC) to work on workplace tasks. The benefits are increased flexibility and responsiveness for the business. Technologically, virtual teams can work, but what can a manager do to make things go smoothly from an organisational behaviour point of view? Cultural differences (have a look at Chapter 15 to understand more), relationship problems, and issues with trust and team cohesion (see Chapter 5) can all occur.

When the virtual team is first formed, we suggest that you as a manager do the following:

✔ Where feasible, get the team members to meet at the beginning. These early meetings need to focus on getting to know each other.

✔ Encourage the team members to spend time on social emails, phone calls, and video conferencing, if physical meetings aren't possible.

✔ Arrange online chat sessions with all members and use humour to lighten the mood.

The main emphasis is on communication. If you take just one idea from this section, make it encouraging your virtual team to communicate in a variety of different ways, and not just to rely on email. Relying solely on email can be a bad idea as the new team are less likely to bond together, build a relationship based on trust, or pick up on non-verbal cues, which can lead to misunderstood communication. (The later section 'Recognising the drawbacks of technology' describes the negative side of CMC in more detail and Chapter 5 explains why team members must be cohesive and trust each other.)

Female-only virtual teams are better at getting to know each other and developing a trusting relationship through social communication, and enjoy the team experience more than mixed or male-only teams. In fact, men find creating relationships in virtual teams more difficult, and in mixed teams they're less able to dominate the proceedings than in non-virtual teams.

As a manager, you have to remember that not everyone is suited to working in the virtual world as it creates more uncertainty and a feeling of increased accountability. You need to choose your virtual team members carefully and look for certain personality qualities:

- ✔ Dependable
- ✔ Independent
- ✔ Responsible
- ✔ Self-sufficient

These qualities are useful in traditional, face-to-face teams, but are even more essential in virtual teams. (Check out Chapter 3 for information on selecting employees for personality types.)

Virtual work arrangements aren't really suitable for new employees or those new to a position, as they need more direct support and guidance until they gain enough experience and knowledge about the job.

Working remotely

Teleworking (or *telecommuting* in US terminology) is the practice of working away from the office, at home, in another remote location, or out in the field. Teleworkers are most often in sales or service jobs, but teleworking is becoming more common in other roles as part of a set of flexible working practices. One of the main reasons teleworking is so popular is that it gives the employee a better balance between home and work. (See Chapter 6 for how this balance helps to improve employee health and wellbeing.)

You may think teleworking means working away from the office all the time, but in fact the average is two days at home and three days at the office.

In 2007, more than 44 per cent of UK and US firms offered their employees the opportunity to telework. In the UK, the number of people working mainly at home, or using their home as a base, is on an upward trend from 3.2 million in 2007 to 3.7 million in 2011. However, trends in the US suggest that teleworking's popularity may begin to tumble as the recession takes hold. For example, from 33.7 million teleworkers in the US in 2008, the number in 2011 is now about 26.2 million. During times of uncertainty, employees may prefer to stay close to the office and make themselves more visible and less dispensable – wouldn't you?

Teleworking is recognised as benefitting employees, employers, and society as a whole, as Table 16-1 illustrates.

Table 16-1	Advantages of Telework	
Organisation	*Individual*	*Society*
Improved productivity	Flexible working hours	Reduction of pollution (fewer journeys)
Improved employee retention	Better work/life balance	Less consumption of energy resources
Better staff flexibility	Increased morale	Increase in community stability (no need to move home for work)
Attractive as part of a benefit package	Reduced commuting and costs	
Increased skill base	Reduced costs for work clothes	
Efficient use of office space	Better job autonomy	
Reduced utilities costs	Less disruption while working	

Of course, a downside to teleworking exists, too; see the later section 'Realising the Downsides of Virtual Working.'

Although teleworkers don't feel that they're working harder, productivity records and supervisor ratings tend to show that they are. You only have to think about typical office interruptions (discussions about TV programs, sport results, and world news to name a few!) to realise how much time you can waste at work.

However, not all employees are suited to telework. For example, if working from home in your pyjamas, without your boss breathing down your neck, is your dream, have you thought about whether you're suitable for it? Ask yourself the following:

- ✔ **Do you have a positive outlook?** Our own research suggests that teleworkers may experience more loneliness, irritation, guilt, and worry. These negative emotions are all tied to the lack of social relationships.

- ✔ **Are you happy in your own company?** Our research suggests that working around other people has a positive impact on you and your health, and as a teleworker, you may feel unhappier in the long term. The loneliness can result in increased psychological ill health and physical symptoms of stress (see Chapter 6 for more details), especially for men, who seem to be more vulnerable to feeling a loss of status, through being invisible to other organisational employees, and the effect on their social position.

✔ **Are you well-organised and self-motivated?** When working by yourself, you can find it easy to lose focus (and we've experienced this loss of focus a lot while writing this book!), and it can be difficult to stay productive.

Existing teleworkers say that the personal qualities they find most important in teleworking are self-motivation, organisational skills, self-confidence, time management skills, computer literacy, and trust in others in the organisation.

Working virtually isn't right for everyone, but if you're aware of the drawbacks, you find it easier to cope. What you need is an understanding and supportive manager. (We tell you how to be one in the next section.)

As a virtual worker, send your manager more emails and voicemails than you would in a traditional job, to keep them informed.

Managing Virtually

Admit it: as a manager, you're apprehensive about letting employees work from home, or remotely. It's only natural not to trust employees to pull their weight when they're not in the office.

Donna, a friend of ours, used to work as a sales manager with a team of sales representatives covering an area close to the head office. She did so many years before mobile phones and computers, so the team would visit potential customers and then come into the office to process orders. One team member, Joy, would turn up at the office at the same time every day, without fail. Donna began to think it was strange because staff found it impossible to plan meetings with clients so precisely every day. So, one day, during working hours, Donna drove to Joy's house, and sure enough, her car was parked outside. She waited for two hours until Joy got in her car and drove to the office for her normal time. They had an interesting discussion about trust and Joy's commitment to work when she arrived at the office!

Overseeing virtual teams

Virtual teams don't perform any better or worse than traditional face-to-face teams, but they encounter a number of different issues. Although communication is technically as effective, virtual teams feel less satisfied with team relationships, and this dissatisfaction affects the way information is exchanged. This dissatisfaction is more likely to be the case where virtual communications are used to do more than simply report or inform.

As a manager, you can reduce the chance of dissatisfaction with team relationships by following these tips:

✔ Organise a number of face-to-face meetings at the beginning of a project (where feasible).

✔ Establish who's the team leader and encourage that person to involve the more silent members, look after the weaker members, and encourage alternative views. (Go to Chapter 5 for more details on effective teamwork.)

✔ Encourage the team members to communicate regularly with each other and not leave out some members.

You can see from these tips that the idea is to create the feeling of unity and being close to each other.

Using technology, such as video conferencing or Skype, offers even greater opportunities for team communication. Even using smiley faces (emoticons) in e-mails and web conferencing can make the team feel closer.

If you read Chapter 8 on leadership, you can pick up more detailed tips. However, you need to be even more careful and precise about what you want from virtual teams than face-to-face teams because it can be more difficult to keep on top of what they're doing.

Keeping an eye on them while you're not there

You're likely thinking, 'If I can't see them, how do I know what they're doing?' Research by Wayne Cascio, a psychologist, suggests that you can put your mind at rest about their performance by making sure that you do the following:

✔ Outline the team's performance:
  • Tell them what's expected of them.
  • Explain their responsibilities.
  • Detail how far their authority goes.
  • Set specific, challenging goals (see Chapter 9).
  • Develop clear assessment criteria.

✔ Help the team's performance:
  • Anticipate and reduce potential difficulties.
  • Carefully select suitable employees (see earlier tips and Chapter 17).

✔ Encourage the team's performance:

  • Provide sufficient rewards.

  • Ensure that the rewards are valued and fair.

  • Reward in a timely manner so that the employee knows she's receiving the award.

Look at Chapter 9 on motivation for more details on why this approach works and how to do it.

Managing from afar

To manage the distance between you and your team and to establish trust, you may want to

✔ **Manage productivity:** Ask employees to provide a progress report to prove how much work is completed. Include details on how much time is spent on each task.

✔ **Expect contact:** Ask to be kept informed by regular email, text, or calls, for example.

Managing the teleworker

Although much about teleworking is positive – for example, less travel-related stress and fewer irritating interruptions – a number of drawbacks exist. Negative aspects of teleworking include more frustration with the lack of technical support, feeling even guiltier when you phone in sick, greater resentment toward the impact on home life, and increased loneliness working away from the office. In this section, we look at these issues in more detail and explain what help you can give as a manager.

Knowing the key considerations

As a manager, you can't just ask employees to start working from home, or remotely, next week. These tips can set you on the road to effective teleworking:

✔ Assess the level of secure and reliable Internet connections.

✔ Ensure provision of appropriate technological equipment.

✔ Prioritise the technical support for teleworkers to reduce a key source of stress – technological breakdown.

✔ Establish a clear policy and directions for teleworking that offers these workers the same rights as their office-based colleagues, including aspects like core hours to be worked and sick leave.

- Decide how to handle meetings and conference calls.

- Agree on the number of days away from the office.

- Reduce potential issues of isolation (see the following section for more details).

- Offer support and advice to employees considering teleworking in the following areas:

  - Dealing with stress (Chapter 6 has more information)

  - Work and family boundaries

  - Work–family conflict that can arise (see the following section 'Realising the Downsides of Virtual Working for more details)

An idea is to offer benefits in the form of equipment needed to work from home to reduce the resentment teleworkers may feel about the blurring of work and home life. You may also find it useful to consider a pilot program, or trial periods, if teleworking is a new practice, to work through any possible problems.

Keeping in contact

To create and maintain a committed workforce, employees need to understand the culture of the organisation they work for. Culture influences the behaviour of people within an organisation because it affects the way they think about work, their work tasks, and their coworkers. (You can read more about culture in Chapter 13.)

Teleworkers don't have the same opportunities for social contact and aren't as immersed in the company culture as traditional workers, although if they communicate by phone, as opposed to e-mail, this issue is less of a problem. Teleworkers can also miss out on support networks, such as those provided by trade unions and counselling services that a traditional office worker takes for granted.

As a manager, you can introduce your teleworkers into the culture of the organisation by

- Organising regular meetings at the work site.

- Ensuring minimum requirements for office attendance – for example two days a week.

- Including teleworkers in social programs and events.

- Including teleworker's coworkers in meetings as well (when possible) to maintain a team contact.

- Using video conferencing to replace face-to-face communication.

✔ Including virtual workers in departmental organisation charts and in company telephone directories.

✔ Introducing *health circles* (usually a group of employees with a trained professional who acts as moderator) to openly discuss the issues that virtual workers face and come up with solutions.

You need to develop different ways to manage teleworkers effectively. No right way exists, but if you focus on the social aspects, by setting up support networks, creating different ways of communicating, and showing you trust them, you can go a long way.

Realising the Downsides of Virtual Working

Teleworking can raise a number of issues for employees, such as feeling like they're being overlooked for promotion and missing out on the benefits of working as part of a team. Not getting enough face-time with their manager may make virtual employees feel like they don't have a strong employee–manager relationship. Also, the close friendship and trust you get from working in a team is less likely to happen in a telework situation.

The selection process is critical to hiring teleworkers. Chapter 17 gives you the best process to follow, but remember that teleworkers need to be able to self-manage and use their time effectively in order to do their job without their manager watching them.

One of the main disadvantages for teleworkers is the greater conflict between work and home life; being able to manage time well is an essential skill!

As a manager, it helps to understand the increased challenges to work–life balance that can happen with the blurring of the physical boundaries between work and home. A teleworker can easily work past normal hours when the workplace is next to the kitchen. Strong evidence, though, shows that working long hours can not only damage your health and family life but also productivity. (See Chapter 6 for more information on how stressful this situation can be.) As a manager, you need to be aware of the dangers of working long hours.

To create an environment where opportunities for development and promotion are available for virtual workers, you need to

✔ **Be aware of workers' need for recognition.** Just because the virtual employee is out of sight (of you and the rest of the organisation), you still need to offer praise and acknowledgement of her achievements.

To do this, you need to focus on the task itself, rather than the way she achieved it. You can't see how she's approached the task, but you can see the end result.

✔ **Initiate an open communication policy.** Make sure that virtual workers don't feel they're overlooked for promotion. You can easily forget about people if they're not physically present.

Selecting the right type of people to telework, giving them the appropriate tools to do the job, and offering support and training to overcome the challenges can lead to happier, and more productive, employees.

Don't fall into the trap of thinking 'out of sight, out of mind' for your virtual workers. Be aware of the challenges faced by virtual workers and use the techniques we suggest to motivate them.

For teleworking to be more efficient than traditional working, you need the following elements:

✔ Telework needs to be used for the right type of job.

✔ The employee needs the right skills.

✔ You're implement teleworking for the right reason (not just to save money).

✔ You need to be the right type of manager.

Often, the best managers of teleworkers are those who've worked as teleworkers – they know what skills and support are needed.

Recognising the drawbacks of technology

When you communicate with someone through computer-mediated technology, you can't hear, see, or feel each other, and you don't pick up on any feedback, such as nods, gestures, and tone of voice that you do face to face, or even over the phone. In other words, you're in a sort of social vacuum. The fact that you can't see each other also dehumanises the interaction – can you tell the gender, race, or age, for example, of the other person in an email conversation? This lack of info can have advantages – for example, people find it more difficult to dominate a situation via email and it can prevent sexual and racial discrimination (see Chapter 11). But overall, lack of person-to-person contact over a long period of time is a negative.

And email can be problematic as well:

✔ A study by psychologists Justin Kruger and Nicholas Epley found that people overestimate their ability to communicate by email and to interpret the tone of other people's messages. Unlike face-to-face communication, sarcasm and humour are more difficult to pick up.

- Negotiating by email has a number of pitfalls. People tend to be less inhibited, and as a result often more negative by email, and as email is shorter and snappier, they've less time to build up a relationship.

- Psychologist Charles Naquin and colleagues found that you're 50 per cent more likely to lie in an email than on paper. Email is seen as chattier than a letter and more like a conversation, so you're more likely to act without inhibitions online. And, as you feel less rapport with the other person, you don't feel a personal connection with them. This lack of connection is called *moral disengagement theory* in social psychology.

Lack of social contact can make some people more insensitive and rude.

Extracting yourself from email overload

Over the last 20 years, information technology and emails at work has grown phenomenally. Email is now the most popular means of communication. Can you imagine what work (or your personal life) would be like without it? However, email is also said to be the number one productivity killer in the workplace. When the pop-up 'You've got mail' (or flashing icon) appears at the bottom of your computer screen, how long do you wait before you click it? We bet you wait no more than 6 seconds! And so, your work, and train of thought, is interrupted as you rush to respond.

Email overload is a recognised cause of stress, with work emails creeping into personal time, and working hours increasing to cope. Organisational psychology goes some way to observe and explain behaviour:

- Checking for email is an addictive behaviour, like gambling. Most of the messages you get are boring, but now and again, an exciting one appears, so you keep checking. Psychologists call it a *variable interval reinforcement schedule*. This principle is used to train strong habits by providing unpredictable rewards.

- Twenty-three per cent of your working day is likely to be spent dealing with email. You open 70 per cent of your emails within 6 seconds and you take 64 seconds to get back to your previous train of thought.

- Your brain can only juggle seven things at a time. So, when emails arrive in groups, it can overload your judgement. But some good news: this growing stimulus is increasing IQ rates around the world.

Most of the above list is enough to put you off emails totally! Maybe the best thing to do is to take the advice of another psychologist Michael Morris and pick up the phone – a single phone call can create enough rapport to overcome many of these problems.

Practical steps you can take to avoid email traps involve checking emails less often to control any addiction and loss of concentration. Try turning off the 'You've got mail' facility, and keep emails concise.

If you want a drastic way to deal with your overflowing inbox, you can always go for email bankruptcy: deleting every email in your inbox, hoping the important ones turn up again, and starting over again – if you dare!

Avoiding creating a company of loners

Research by us and other organisational psychologists has shown that one of the main problems of working virtually is loneliness. However, some teleworkers, particularly women, can have a different problem. Working at home, for example, isn't always seen as real work by friends and neighbours who feel that they can call round when the teleworker is actually working. The problem isn't as bad for men, though, as most of their friends are office-based, and not around during the day.

But though some workers may be overloaded with company, many others struggle with loneliness. Relying on computer-related, rather than face-to-face, communication, without the support of coworkers, decreases many virtual workers' emotional well-being. For many employees, the social banter and buzz of the workplace is extremely important.

Teleworkers need some sort of social contact. As a manager, you can take action to reduce the potential negative impact of loneliness; see the earlier section 'Keeping in contact' for suggestions.

A recent study points out that less than half the companies that have introduced teleworking in the UK have actually taken any steps to counter the possible effects of isolation.

Part V

All About Hiring and Developing People

The 5th Wave   By Rich Tennant

"Bob, I want to tap into that part of your brain that wants to lead, that wants to inspire, that wants to stop leaning against my desk,..."

In this part . . .

The success of an organisation boils down to the caliber of its staff. So, in Part V, we focus on bringing the right people into an organisation and then helping them to develop. We look at recruitment and selection and discuss what works, what doesn't, and why. Then we consider ways in which you can assess and appraise employees to get the best results both for the organisation and the individual. We also take you through common kinds of training and development initiatives, such as mentoring, and show you which ones work and how you can improve success rates.

Chapter 17

Hiring the Right People

. . . .

In This Chapter

▶ Figuring out the skills that the job requires

▶ Pinpointing desirable traits and skills

▶ Exploring hiring methods

▶ Using technology in the hiring process

. . . .

*A*lmost all companies have to recruit and select new employees at some point. Whether you're a small company that replaces staff occasionally or a large organisation that is constantly managing the recruitment and induction of new employees, getting selection right is advantageous for your organisation; getting it wrong can be disastrous. The scale and importance of recruitment and selection activity makes it a topic of huge interest to managers, organisational behaviourists, and work psychologists.

Hiring the right person for a vacancy can result in huge benefits for both the new employee and your organisation, including high performance for your company and a satisfied and committed employee. The main aim of the hiring process is to match the skills and abilities of applicants to the job responsibilities because it increases the odds of your new staff member performing well at work. You may also want to look at the personality profile of a candidate to see how well he's likely to perform and whether he'll fit into your organisation. (Check out Chapter 3 for more on this topic.)

In this chapter, we discuss the importance of job analysis and person specification. Paying attention to these early steps of the selection process allows you to choose selection methods that inform you about the skills and abilities you're looking for in a candidate and makes the comparison of candidates easier and fairer.

We introduce a number of different selection methods in the chapter and detail their advantages and disadvantages. We compare effective selection methods (such as psychometric tests) to less effective selection methods (such as unstructured interviews) and discuss what you should consider when deciding which method to use. We also look at how technology is changing recruitment and selection.

Analysing the Job

If you were given the task of hiring a brain surgeon, how would you go about it? Well, unless you already have some knowledge of the skills, qualifications, and experience of brain surgeons, your first move would probably be to find out more about the job so that you know what to put in the job listing.

The investigation and understanding of job content is what recruitment and selection specialists call *job analysis*. If you don't do any kind of job analysis and just run off to hire a brain surgeon, you run the high risk of not getting the best people applying for your job vacancy. Without understanding the job you're recruiting for, how do you know who'll do the job well and who'll do it poorly?

If you don't know what you want, you're unlikely to get it! You may hire a poorly performing employee or someone who leaves quickly because they're not well matched to the job. This mistake costs the organisation because it has to recruit again. And, of course, if you're hiring an expert such as a brain surgeon, you face wider risks. (Would you want to be operated on by somebody who'd been hired through a badly designed selection process that didn't check key skills and experience?)

Job analysis should be the first step of a well-designed selection procedure.

Benefitting from job analysis

So why is doing job analysis an important first step in a good selection procedure? Well, it allows you to do the following:

- ✔ **Understand the job.** Job analysis provides detailed information on the job and its related tasks. After completing a job analysis, you know the duties and requirements of the job, and you understand the relative importance of these responsibilities.

- ✔ **Identify skills and abilities that you want to see in job applicants that indicate they can do the job well.** You use the information you gather during job analysis to prepare a person specification, which details the competencies needed in an applicant. (See the next section 'Creating the Person Specification' for more on this topic.)

- ✔ **Produce clear job listings.** After you understand the job and identify the necessary skills and abilities, you can design a job listing that targets the people you want to attract to work for you – those people who have the skills and experience you need.

- ✔ **Choose appropriate selection methods.** Knowing the skills and abilities you need from a job analysis means that you can pick the best selection methods to assess these skills in your candidates. (For more on the different types of selection methods, see the later section 'Choosing Effective Selection Methods.')

✔ **Select the right candidate.** Recruitment and selection is expensive, so you want to do it as well as possible. This way, you can maximise the return on your investment in recruitment and selection by attracting and hiring the best candidates.

✔ **Follow regulations.** Being able to demonstrate that any skills or abilities you're advertising for in applicants are needed to do the job can protect you from claims of unfairness in selection. (We discuss fairness in detail in Chapter 11.)

Performing job analysis

Job analysis is all about gathering information. Here are some things you may want to find out about as you analyse the job:

✔ **Colleagues:** Who is the new person to work with and report to? Is he to work alone or as part of a group? Who'll be his manager? Or, conversely, how large is the team that he's to manage?

✔ **Equipment:** What equipment will the new person use as part of his work? Knowing what equipment he needs to use in the new job (such as a waiter using a till and electronic payment machine) can help you assess whether a candidate already has the skills he needs to use the equipment or whether you need to provide training.

✔ **Performance expectations:** What level of performance is expected in the job? For example, if you were working as a waiter, how many tables would you be expected to wait on in a typical evening shift?

✔ **Skills and abilities:** What knowledge and abilities does the new person need to do the job? This answer depends on the job (a brain surgeon needs more existing skills and abilities than a waiter, for example). Also consider how much training you're prepared to offer candidates. For example, you may decide to advertise only for trained waiters if you don't want or don't have the time to train somebody with no experience at all.

✔ **Tasks:** What tasks is the new person expected to do as part of his job? A waiter, for example, needs to take orders from customers, serve food and collect payment. A simple job may require only a fairly small number of tasks, while a more complex job, such as a teacher or dentist, includes a much longer list of tasks.

✔ **Work environment:** Where is the new person to be working? This consideration is especially important if the working environment has any risks, such as working with dangerous chemicals or aggressive customers.

✔ **Work output:** What is the output of the job? A waiter's output is to provide a service to the customers of the restaurant. Other work outputs may include making products. A growing trend in the UK and US is for people to work in the service industry.

Tracking down the information

So how do you find out all this information? Well, in many cases you may already know a lot of the information already. Your knowledge depends on how close you are to the job role. If the job is one you've done yourself, you should have a good idea of all the details. If you're a manager, you may have a good understanding of many of the jobs in your section, although probably not in as much detail as the job holder. After all, sometimes managers know how a job should be done whereas the people doing the job know how the job is actually done. The author Sheena once had the tricky job of training the manager's son to do her job, which entailed a lot of her saying, 'This is the procedure, but we do it this way. Don't tell your dad!'

Even if you think that you already know a lot about a job, talk to other people (especially people who are already doing the job) to ensure that your understanding is correct.

Here are a few ways of gathering information about a job:

- ✔ **Chatting to people:** Talk to the employees who actually do the job to find out exactly what they do and how they do it. Also, talk to supervisors and managers to establish their understanding of the job and what their performance expectations are of the post holder.

  Sometimes people are untruthful about their tasks, responsibilities and day-to-day activities at work – often because they want to be seen as more productive than perhaps they actually are.

- ✔ **Task inventories:** You can ask your current employee to tick off the tasks they complete on from a list of tasks. Task inventories are quick to complete but are limited in detail and so may not capture everything you need to know.

  Use rating scales alongside checklists to provide more information, such as how important a task is and how much time is spent on it.

- ✔ **Diary studies:** Ask people to keep a record of what they do at work. Such diaries typically record the tasks completed in a particular day or week, and how much time is spent completing each task. This level of detail, especially if completed by numerous people, can quickly provide lots of job and task information.

- ✔ **Documentation:** Review any job-relevant documents and procedures, such as training material, induction guides, procedure handbook.

- ✔ **Observation:** As well as asking people about the job, observe what people do at work. Observing is easier to do with some jobs than others: observing a waiter gives you a reasonable idea of the job, but observing a teacher marking essays doesn't tell you in any detail what the teacher is doing other than sitting with her head down for hours and hours. Such *mental work* isn't suitable for observation. Asking employees or other experts is the best way to approach this *cognitive task analysis* because the focus is more on what people are thinking and not what they're doing.

Figuring out how much time and effort to put into job analysis

The different approaches to job analysis are numerous. If you used all of these techniques, your job analysis would become expensive and time consuming. So be selective in the approach you use, perhaps choosing one or two of the methods that fit your organisation and the type of job you're investigating.

The following factors affect your decision about how much time and effort you put into job analysis (and recruitment and selection more generally):

- ✔ **Cost:** How much do you want to spend?

- ✔ **Importance of getting it right:** If you're hiring for a simple job, you can probably provide the training needed quite easily, so getting the right applicants with the relevant skills to apply is less important. If, however, you're hiring for a complex job, then it may be more important that you select an applicant with the skills to do the job. Salary costs can also dictate the amount of effort put into job analysis. You probably need to spend more on hiring for a $100,000 ($64,000) per year position than you would for a $25,000 ($16,000) per year job.

- ✔ **Time:** How much time do you have? Do you need to hire somebody immediately, or are you planning a recruitment strategy to hire your managers over the next few years?

Creating the Person Specification

After you complete a job analysis (see previous section), you can use this information to create a *person specification* – a description of the competencies (skills, abilities, and qualities) you'd like candidates to have. Think of a person specification as a description of your ideal employee – the person who would best be able to complete the work because he has all the skills needed and fits perfectly into your organisation.

Seeing the benefits of a good person specification

After you analyse the job (see the earlier section 'Analysing the Job'), you can draw up the person specification. This process can seem long, and some hiring managers even argue that the process is unnecessary. Indeed, many managers rush into hiring decisions without paying attention to such details, so why shouldn't you do the same? Is the person specification really necessary?

The short answer is, yes! Here's why:

- ✔ **Accurate job advertisements:** You can use the person specification to draft accurate job listings and application forms to help you attract and identify the best candidates.

- ✔ **Comparison of candidates:** Knowing the essential and desirable characteristics of job applicants helps you compare candidates on these criteria and select the applicant who best fits the job.

- ✔ **Fairness:** Using informed criteria to attract and compare job applicants helps ensure that you're being fair to applicants and that you're making hiring decisions based on relevant information.

- ✔ **Identification of training needs:** You can use the information gathered during selection to identify any training and development needs of your new employee.

- ✔ **Informed applicants:** The information contained in the person specification enables job applicants to review the requirements of the post and decide whether they meet them. The person specification can reduce the number of applications you get because only those who fit the person specification are likely to apply. Candidates weeding themselves out before applying can save you time and money because you don't have to sort through many unsuitable applications.

- ✔ **Informed employers:** Going through the process of job analysis and drafting a person specification gives employers a good idea of what skills and abilities candidates need to possess to perform well in the job.

Knowing what to include

Here are some areas to include in your person specification:

- ✔ **Experience:** Do you want applicants to have prior experience of the work, or are you going to provide any training needed?

- ✔ **Individual characteristics:** Do you need job applicants to have particular characteristics (such as an outgoing personality) or circumstances (such as the ability to travel)?

- ✔ **Qualifications and education:** What level of qualifications do you need to see in applicants?

- ✔ **Skills and knowledge:** What skills and knowledge does an applicant need to have to be able to do the job?

If you ask for qualifications in your person specification that aren't relevant to the job, you may be accused of discrimination. (Check out Chapter 11 for more on direct and indirect discrimination.) Take care to ensure that the person specification is fair.

Splitting the specification into essential and desirable elements

You can further develop your person specification by referring to the job analysis and noting the personal characteristics required to complete each task. Then consider how important each item is to the overall job.

Try listing the characteristics you desire under two headings, *essential* and *desirable*. Making the distinction between these two categories helps you focus on those things that are most important to successful job completion and helps you to compare candidates.

Here's how to determine what goes into each category:

- ✔ **Essential criteria:** A candidate must have these attributes to do the job. If a candidate doesn't meet the essential criteria (for example, having a medical degree in the case of a doctor), you can exclude the person from the process because he clearly is not suited to the job.

    Try to use the essential category sparingly. Otherwise, you run the risk of being so specific in your requirements that no one applies for the job.

- ✔ **Desirable criteria:** These characteristics are useful but not essential to do the job. An example of a desirable characteristic is asking for prior experience of the job role. Somebody without experience may be able to do the job, but an experienced person would probably perform better, at least at first.

    Having desirable criteria can help you select between candidates who all meet the essential criteria. So if five doctors apply for your post, but only one has experience, you may decide that the experienced person is the best candidate.

The best way to illustrate how the essential and desirable elements of a person specification work is with an example. Sheena recently had to hire a researcher to work on a project with her. She determined what skills and abilities the researcher needed to successfully complete her project. Table 17-1 lists the essential and desirable characteristics Sheena used in the person specification and job advertisement. Notice how the essential characteristics are more general than the desirable. Sheena used these characteristics to compare the applications she received, allowing her to interview only those candidates who best matched her needs. She found a fantastic researcher through this process who completed her project very successfully. (Thanks, Sara!)

Table 17-1	Essential and Desirable Characteristics of a Researcher	
Essential	**Desirable**
Ability to manage multiple strands of research	Ability to conduct hierarchical and cognitive task analysis
Good communication skills and high standards of oral and written English	Ability to use qualitative research computer packages
Strong teamwork and interpersonal skills	Experience working within NHS/clinical environments
Ability to interact with a wide range of people at different levels	Experience working with a team of researchers
Willingness to travel in order to conduct research in a variety of clinical sites	Experience preparing and submitting research funding bids
Availability to start work on the project immediately	Publications in peer-reviewed journals

Choosing Effective Selection Methods

You can use a job analysis and person specification to help you choose the selection methods that provide you with the information you need to make the right decision about who to hire. Choosing the right selection methods can help you assess applicants' abilities and compare them to find the best person for the job.

If you know that you need to hire somebody who's very good with figures because they'll be doing calculations as part of their job, you should test for this aptitude during selection. While you can look for this skill by looking at their qualifications, you can also use a test of numeric ability during the selection procedure to see which candidates perform best.

You can use several effective methods to recruit and select your candidates: structured interviews, work samples, tests, and assessment centres. We describe these methods in this section. (We cover the less effective methods – unstructured interviews, references, and graphology – in the later section 'Avoiding Less Effective Selection Methods'.)

A good selection method is

> ✔ **Affordable:** The amount you're willing to spend on selection depends on the amount of money you have and the job you're recruiting to. You can find out more about this topic in 'Counting the cost', later in this chapter.

✔ **Fair to candidates:** Don't discriminate against people because of the type of selection method you use. (We talk about discrimination in Chapter 11.)

✔ **Popular with candidates:** Don't forget that candidates are also assessing you and your company to see whether they want to accept a job, if offered. The way people are treated during recruitment and selection influences how they feel about a job offer and influences whether or not they accept it.

✔ **Practical:** Making good decisions in selection doesn't just mean using the best methods but also knowing when they're practically needed. In theory, you can use all methods every time you recruit for a new post. In reality, though, this approach is time consuming and expensive. You have to balance the practicalities, such as the time you have to recruit, against the selection choices available.

✔ **Reliable and valid:** *Reliable* means that if you use the same method again, it will give you the same information. *Valid* means that the method measures what it is meant to be measuring (such as a numerical test that measures numerical ability).

Structured interviews

Interviews are one of the most popular selection methods. Most people have attended an interview. And if you're a manager, you've probably interviewed candidates yourself.

Despite the popularity of interviews, they're not always a good method to use because if they're unstructured they can be unreliable. Structuring the interview so that you know exactly what you're going to cover can make an interview much more informative and useful.

You can use two types of structured interviews:

✔ **Completely structured:** You determine before the interview exactly what questions you're going to ask.

✔ **Semi-structured:** You determine the general topics you want to cover in an interview. You may include specific questions, but you also allow some flexibility to include other questions during the interview.

The pros of structured interviews

The advantages of using a structured interview over just using an interview as an opportunity to chat to an applicant are many. A structured interview is

✔ **Comparison friendly:** Comparing candidates is easier if you've asked similar questions to each person.

✔ **Comprehensive:** Pre-planning the interview content ensures that you don't accidently forget to cover some important points.

✔ **Consistent:** Structuring the interview means that all candidates are asked the same questions so that you find out the same relevant information about each candidate.

✔ **Fair:** Every candidate is treated the same way and asked the same questions during an interview. This means that people are being treated fairly and the legal standing of using interviews as a selection method improves.

✔ **Predictive of performance:** Because you're asking relevant questions, the information you gather helps you more accurately assess how well a person is likely to perform in the job.

✔ **Relevant:** Deciding in advance the content of an interview means that you can ensure that you include questions relevant to the position. (You can use the job analysis and person specification to prepare relevant questions.)

The cons of structured interviews

If you think that a structured interview is clearly the best way to select people, you should be aware of a few issues with interviews:

✔ **Interviewee dishonesty:** Sometimes candidates don't give an accurate response to a question or embellish the truth. A candidate wants to look as good as possible to increase their chances of being offered the job, so they may stretch the truth a little. This reason is an example of why using more than one selection method is a good tactic. For example, a candidate may tell you in an interview he's an excellent team leader and provide examples from previous jobs. You may want to assess this assertion in other ways, though (such as during an assessment centre exercise – see the later section on this method) to ensure that he really has the skills he claims to have.

✔ **Interviewer error:** Remembering all the relevant information obtained during an interview can be very difficult, although a well-structured interview can help. Bias can also enter into the interview process with research showing that sometimes interviewers make a decision on a candidate before an interview is completed. (See Chapter 11 to find out more about selection bias.)

Training interviewers in interview methods, techniques, and interviewer bias can help to reduce interviewer error.

Liar, liar

Surveys done by recruitment firms in both the UK and US suggest that around a quarter (and sometimes more) of people reported that they had or would lie when asked about things like their existing job title and pay level – presumably to make a current job role seem more important and to increase the chances of receiving a higher pay offer. Lying about things like this is often seen by candidates as necessary as 'everyone does it', and 'it is expected that you enhance the truth a little'. You need to be careful though as lies can catch up with you and people have been fired and prosecuted for lies they told when applying for a job.

Work samples

When using *work samples* as a selection method, you ask candidates to do a piece of work similar to what they'll be doing in the job. Their performance on the work sample is a good indicator of how they would perform in the job.

You can choose between four different types of work sample test:

- ✔ **Group decision-making:** You put people into groups to work on tasks so that you can assess their contribution to the group.

- ✔ **Individual decision-making:** You ask the candidate to make decisions similar to the decisions you'd need to make in the job. An example is *in-tray exercises,* which are commonly used in management selection. Candidates are given a typical in-tray consisting of emails, reports, memos, and so on. The candidate then has to work through the in-tray, prioritising tasks and completing work.

- ✔ **Job-related information:** You test job-related knowledge that affects performance. You can administer a written test in which all the questions relate to specific aspects of the job and test applicant knowledge in those areas that affects job performance.

- ✔ **Psychomotor:** You look at hands-on skills, such as using machinery. An example of a psychomotor test is a typing test where you ask candidates to complete a piece of typing (word processing) so that you can see how quickly and accurately they work.

Work sample tests have standardised instructions and give candidates a specified amount of time to complete the work. Not only is everyone treated the same way (ensuring fairness), but you can easily compare performances as well.

As with most selection methods, work sample tests have both advantages and disadvantages (see Table 17-2).

Table 17-2	Advantages and Disadvantages of Work Sample Tests
Advantages	**Disadvantages**
Realistic tasks: Candidates like them because they're realistic and resemble actual work tasks. This type of test gives candidates a good idea of what the job involves and helps them to decide whether they even want the job.	**Job specific:** Work sample tests tend to be highly job specific. The usability of this test is limited to that job.
Fair selection: Because you're testing actual job skills, you've less chance of candidates feeling unfairly treated during selection. You're basing your selection decision on who performs best on job-related tasks.	**Expensive** Depending on the complexity of the work sample, these tests can be expensive to develop. Consider preparing an in-tray exercise and how long it would take you to develop all the different pieces of information.
Predictive of work performance: Because work samples so closely resemble the work done in the job, performance on the test is a fair indication of performance on the job.	**Time consuming:** Work samples can be time consuming both in their development and in the time it takes to deliver a test. Imagine that a work sample test takes 1 hour to complete, and you've 20 candidates – it means almost 20 hours of almost continual testing! And then you have to interpret the results and compare candidates.

Psychometric tests

A *psychometric test* measures psychological attributes and includes measures of knowledge, ability, intelligence, and personality.

Organisations commonly use psychometric tests in selection, and you may have been asked to complete an ability test or a personality test when you've applied for a job. A good selection process makes sure that you know exactly why you're being asked to take a test and why the test is relevant to the job you're applying for. Otherwise, you may wonder why you're taking a test and feel that the test is not relevant.

Explaining why a test is relevant means candidates are more favourable toward the test and less likely to complain of unfair treatment.

Table 17-3 details advantages and disadvantages of psychometric tests.

Table 17-3	Advantages and Disadvantages of Psychometric Tests
Advantages	**Disadvantages**
Standardised: Having standard content, administration, and scoring of tests means tests are reliable, and every candidate is tested in the same way.	**Not always applicable:** Although tests are useful and can provide quite detailed information, they're not appropriate to every situation. Job-specific skills can be tested by psychometric tests, but occasions exist where bespoke tests would be better predictors of job performance.
Quick: Tests are usually quick and easy to score and administer (after you're trained to do so).	**Negative applicant reactions:** Some people don't like taking tests, especially when applying for jobs. You may not care much about this reaction, but imagine if you put off the best person to do your job because he hates taking tests.
Predictive: Tests have been shown to be good at predicting job performance. As long as you pick appropriate tests, they should be very informative.	**Adverse impact:** Some tests can discriminate against groups of applicants (such as a written English test discriminating against non-English speakers). Be careful to choose appropriate tests that relate to the job in question to ensure that you're not inadvertently discriminating against some applicants.
	Costly: Well-designed and predictive psychometric tests aren't always cheap. (Prices vary.) You may also need to employ or hire somebody to do the testing for you because people are required to have appropriate training and certification to administer and interpret some tests.
	Can be faked: Faking this type of test isn't easy, but candidates can fake results of some psychometric tests such as personality tests. These tests are harder to fake than many other selection methods, though.

In this section, we look at psychometric tests in general. You may also want to take a look at Chapter 3 where we discuss personality and intelligence in more detail.

Assessment centres

Assessment centres use a combination of selection methods that are typically administrated over one to three days, making them a fairly expensive, but very useful, selection tool. Because of the cost and time involved, most organisations usually use assessment centres only when filling higher-end jobs, such as management recruitment.

Assessment centres may use a combination of psychometric tests, interviews, and work-sample tests, which we cover in the preceding sections. Assessment centres may also use group discussions and exercises to understand how candidates act in group situations. Skills they may be looking for in group exercises include

✓ Initiating behaviours, such as making proposals to the group

✓ Reacting behaviours, such as supporting or disagreeing with the group

✓ Clarifying behaviours, such as seeking and sharing behaviours.

A typical assessment centre has between 6 and 12 candidates and a number (as many as one for every two candidates) of trained assessors who run the assessments and evaluate the results.

The different tests and methods used in an assessment centre assess different competencies relevant to the post. (The earlier sections on the job analysis and person specification detail how you identify these competencies.)

Table 17-4 shows the advantages and disadvantages of using assessment centres in selection.

Table 17-4	Advantages and Disadvantages of Assessment Centres	
Advantages	*Disadvantages*
Test multiple competencies: You can include selection methods in your assessment centre that measures all the skills, abilities, and qualities important to the job.	**Costly:** Because of the time they take to develop and run, assessment centres are often used only for filling senior roles and by large organisations.

Advantages	Disadvantages
Candidates reactions: Although assessment centres are demanding for applicants, they're usually well received because candidates have the opportunity to demonstrate their competencies.	**Assessor error:** As with interviews, assessor errors can affect the validity of assessment centres (for example, where candidate performance on one task affects ratings on another task). Use well-trained assessors to minimise the risk of error.
Predict performance: Because of the detail they include and the different selection methods used, assessment centres are a good way to assess and predict performance on the job.	**Arguably, don't offer much more than other good selection methods:** Although assessment centres are predictive of performance to a higher degree than, say, interviews or cognitive tests, the increase in performance prediction may not be balanced by the significantly higher cost of using an assessment centre compared to using simpler methods.

Avoiding Less Effective Selection Methods

The purpose of using selection methods is to find out more about candidates and predict how well they'll perform at work. If a method doesn't tell you anything useful about a candidate or fails to predict their performance accurately, the method is pretty useless.

In this section, we focus on three less effective selection methods (ones that don't work well): unstructured interviews, references, and graphology. (For more on the ones that work well, see the section 'Choosing Effective Selection Methods,' earlier in this chapter.)

Unstructured interviews

An unstructured interview runs a high risk of failing to gather relevant information, which makes it a much less useful method of selection. If you've ever gone to an interview and wondered what the point of half the questions were, or you left feeling confused about the job, then you've likely been to an unstructured interview.

Sheena attended an interview once and ended up chatting to the interviewer about their shared interest in psychology (she was studying at the time), barely discussing the job, which had nothing to do with psychology. At the time, she was fine with it – a nice easy interview, after all. Now, though, she wonders what the interviewer was thinking to not discuss the job more, and what did he talk to the other candidates about? (In case you're interested, she didn't get offered the job.)

References

Everyone uses references in selection, right? Well, you may be surprised to discover that references are actually a pretty bad selection tool. Their reliability and validity is poor because they often don't give consistent or relevant information about candidates.

References do allow you to verify that a candidate is telling the truth about a previous job they've held. References are commonly used in this way just prior to making a job offer to check a candidate is representing themselves honestly.

Although most references ask people to report on other issues, such as the candidate's productivity, timekeeping, and motivation, this information is generally not very reliable. Here are two reasons that references don't work very well:

- **Reference honesty:** How sure can you be that a reference is giving an honest appraisal of the candidate's abilities? People are wary of writing bad references partly because they generally don't like to bad mouth people and partly for legal reasons. (See the sidebar 'Legal issues surrounding references'.) Someone may even give a person a good reference because he wants that person to leave – and this does not mean you gain a valuable employee!

- **Selective references:** Would you ask someone to provide a reference for you if you knew they would say bad things about you, or would you choose someone who would sing your praises? Yeah, thought so. You choose a referee who maximises your chances of a job offer. So does everyone else. The information you gather from a reference is therefore likely to be positively skewed in favour of the candidate.

Graphology

Graphology is the analysis of handwriting. Organisations don't commonly use graphology in the US and UK as a selection method, but graphology is much more common in European countries like France and Italy.

WARNING!

Legal issues surrounding references

Know the law when it comes to references:

✔ **Checking references:** In the UK and in many states in the US, you need written permission from a candidate before you can contact their references. This request is reasonable, of course, because you wouldn't want a potential new employer to approach your current employer if they don't know that you're considering leaving them.

✔ **Writing references:** Laws designed to prevent people giving untruthful or malicious references have resulted in people being reluctant to provide more than the most basic information for fear of being prosecuted. Legally, people are permitted to provide facts and opinions about candidates in a reference, but they may not want to do so, particularly if it puts the candidate in a negative light.

Graphology has many supporters (do an Internet search, and you'll find many sites telling you how fantastic it is), but very little evidence supports its use in selection. Quite simply, most studies have shown that graphology isn't reliable or valid, so as a method graphology is not that useful. Indeed, the British Psychological Society ranks graphology as having zero validity, the same rating as astrology. Would you offer someone a job on the basis of their star sign? No? Well, don't do it on the basis of their handwriting either!

Weighing the Options

So how do you decide which selection method to use? In this section, we discuss matching the type of job to the appropriate methods and the importance of the cost of different methods. We also discuss the importance of knowing which methods work best, meaning that they actually predict performance in employment.

Considering the type of job

The main consideration in relation to the job is to understand the type of job you're recruiting for and then use this information to design a selection procedure that works well for your organisation. You want to use the right selection methods to inform you of the candidates' abilities in relation to the skills you're looking for. Usually, a few different selection methods give you the information you need. How well the method works and how much it costs (see the following section) influence which method you choose.

If your new employee must be able to word-process documents quickly and accurately, add a work-sample test of their work-processing skills to the selection process. Or you may ask in an interview (structured hopefully!) about previous experiences where they used these skills.

Counting the cost

A key consideration when recruiting is to decide how much money you want to spend. You need to consider the level of job you're recruiting for because you're probably willing to spend more money when you're recruiting for a high-end job. Other criteria, such as the length of the job (for example, is it permanent, full time, or a short-term contract?) also influence how much money you're prepared to pay on recruitment.

Clearly, some methods are more expensive than others. An assessment centre, for example, can be expensive to set up, so even though this selection method is a good one in terms of performance prediction, you may decide that it's too costly and instead choose a cheaper option, such as a structured interview. (See the section 'Assessment centres' earlier in this chapter.)

Of the good methods we discuss in this chapter, the cheapest is probably structured interviews, then (in order of rising costs) psychometric tests, work samples, and assessment centres.

Using information from more than one selection method during recruitment is a good way of increasing the reliability of the information you get.

One final cost consideration is who does the recruitment. Do you have employees trained to recruit? (Remember that for some psychometric tests, training is a legal requirement.) Or do you need to hire somebody to manage your recruitment?

Don't scrimp too much on costs, or you run the risk of having a poor selection process. When you hire a poorly performing employee or someone who quickly leaves, you have to repeat the recruitment exercise, which increases your cost.

Using Technology in Selection

The use of technology in selection has led to changes in the way organisations recruit. For example, posting a listing on the Internet is likely to increase the number of people who see it. Online testing during the recruitment process is also increasingly popular.

Using technology in selection has undoubtedly offered many benefits to organisations, and investment in such technology has been steadily increasing. However, we do offer points of caution.

Increasing the pool of applicants

When you're looking for a new job, you probably use one or more of the many job search sites available on the Internet. (If you don't, you probably should!) If you're recruiting for a job, advertising on the Internet can help you reach many more people than traditional methods of advertising (such as through job centres and in newspapers).

WARNING!

Advertising on the Internet may allow you to reach more people, but keep in mind that you may not reach the people you want, such as older candidates who may not be as technologically savvy as younger candidates.

Consider how you can best reach your target audience with a job advertisement. You may want to list your add on general job search sites or through more specific websites that you know people visit.

As a psychologist and an academic, for example, if Sheena were looking for a new job, she would look at psychology associations (BPS or APA) job postings on their websites and also specific academic job search websites (such as www.jobs.ac.uk). Would something similar reach your target audience? Also consider non-web-based methods, such as advertising in specific papers or magazines.

Testing online

Online tests can be *screening tests* – specific tests designed for the job in question that allow you to screen applications and identify the applicants who have the particular skills you need. For example, a well-designed online application form can let you find out about past experience and knowledge of the job. You can then use this information to select those candidates you want to see in an interview. Doing this step online can speed up the process and allow the inclusion of many more applications than if the screening were done by hand.

In addition to screening tests, some psychometric tests (see the earlier section on these tests) can also be completed online.

Table 17-5 outlines some of the advantages and disadvantages of online testing.

Table 17-5	Advantages and Disadvantages of Online Testing
Advantages	**Disadvantages**
Candidate reactions: Online testing can be convenient to candidates who can complete them at a time and location that suits them.	**Deterring candidates:** Some people aren't comfortable with online tests. People who are less comfortable with IT may be put off.
Cost: Although setup costs can be high, especially if you're designing a new test, the running costs are usually fairly low.	**No, or poor, connections:** If you don't have easy access to the Internet or your Internet connections are slow, you may be at a disadvantage when you take online tests.
Time: Online testing is quick.	**Cheating:** You can't be sure that people are answering honestly – or even that the actual candidate is taking the test! To counter this issue, check references or tell candidates they will be retested if they make it to the next selection stage.

Chapter 18

Assessing and Appraising

. . . .

In This Chapter

▶ Understanding attributions in appraisal

▶ Exploring the advantages of appraisal

▶ Choosing methods of appraisal

▶ Improving appraisals

. . . .

Assessment and appraisal within organisations allows you to understand performance in the workplace, both in terms of performance levels (such as whether targets are being met) and those things that may be affecting performance (such as the need for training). Why is understanding performance important? Well, information on performance is essential if an organisation wants to be able to analyse successes and failures and maintain success or make improvements to performance. Without some form of appraisal in a workplace, determining the influences on performance is difficult, and thus so is making any improvements needed.

And in addition to understanding past performance, appraisals are an opportunity to make plans for the future – for example, by setting performance targets to match individual and organisational goals.

In this chapter, we detail the importance of attribution theory to the appraisal process. We also outline the advantages of appraisals and discuss the different types of appraisal that organisations use. Finally, we offer suggestions for how to improve appraisals.

Interpreting Employee Behaviour Correctly

Appraisals help you understand behaviour and performance at work. However, you can incorrectly interpret, or *attribute,* another person's behaviour. You may believe that you understand why people behave the way they do and what influences their behaviour, but you can interpret this behaviour incorrectly because of your own assumptions about the way people behave. Research in social psychology explains these incorrect attributions using *attribution theory*.

Looking at internal and external factors and dimensions

One of the first things to consider when attributing behaviour is whether internal or external factors are influencing behaviour:

- ✔ **Internal factors** are personal characteristics, such as personality (see Chapter 3) or attitudes (see Chapter 4).

- ✔ **External factors** are things in the situation that are external to the individual and out of their control, such as faulty equipment or an aggressive customer.

Generally speaking, when assessing a person's behaviour, if you decide that most people would act in the same way, you're probably attributing behaviour to external factors. If, however, you decide that other people would act differently, you're probably attributing behaviour to internal factors.

Problems can arise in appraisal when you attribute behaviour to internal factors (you blame the person for their poor performance) when in fact external factors are to blame. This mistake can lead to perceptions of unfair appraisal. (For more on this topic, see the section 'Being fair,' later in this chapter.)

Before you read about the main attribution errors in the following sections, consider the following three dimensions that are important when determining causes of behaviour:

- ✔ **Consensus:** How do other people behave? Does the behaviour generalise to other people?

- ✔ **Distinctiveness:** How does the person behave in other situations?

- ✔ **Consistency:** Is the behaviour always the same for this person and this situation? Or is it a rare occurrence?

Take a quick look at Table 18-1. In this table, we use the example of an employee being late for work and indicate how you can use the three dimensions to determine whether lateness relates to internal or external factors.

Table 18-1	Determining the Causes of Behaviour: Being Late for Work		
Dimension	*Considering Dimension in Relation to Being Late*	*Level of Dimension*	*External or Internal Attribution?*
Consensus	Lots of people were late.	High consensus	External
	Only one person was late.	Low consensus	Internal
Distinctiveness	Person isn't usually late for meetings or team briefings. This late behaviour is therefore distinctive.	High distinctiveness	External
	Person is regularly late for other meetings or team briefings. The behaviour is common and not distinctive.	Low distinctiveness	Internal
Consistency	Person is never or rarely late.	Low consistency	External
	Person is always or regularly late.	High consistency	Internal

 Next time a person you know behaves in an unexpected way and you're trying to figure out why, consider the three dimensions and how they can help you determine the causes of behaviour. You may discover that you're considering these things anyway but have probably just never seen it labelled *attribution theory*.

Attribution theories

Attribution theory encompasses a number of different theories that help explain how people try to understand behaviour, and the mistakes you can make when interpreting another person's behaviour. In the next few sections, we briefly detail the four main attribution theories:

✔ Fundamental attribution error

✔ Actor/observer divergence

✔ Self-serving bias

✔ False consensus effect

The two key triggers that cause you to make attributions about people's behaviour are unexpected outcomes and failure to achieve goals. So, for example, if you're reviewing an employee's progress and they've had customer complaints or not achieved the targets you set them, you look for explanations for why these things have happened. It's no surprise then that attributions occur during the appraisal process as this is when you're most likely to try to understand why an employee is behaving and performing in a certain way!

Fundamental attribution error

The *fundamental attribution error* relates to how you generally underestimate the influence of external factors and overestimate the influence of internal factors on other people's behaviour.

Cultural differences exist in people's propensity to commit the fundamental attribution error. In Western cultures, such as the United States and UK, people tend to look for internal explanations for behaviour, whereas in non-Western cultures, people tend to look at the situations and possible causes of behaviour.

You can see an example of cultural differences in the investigation into the Baring Bank crisis in the 1990s, where Nick Leeson's unauthorised trading activity led to the collapse of one of Britain's oldest merchant banks. In the UK, the focus was on the individual involved (internal focus), whereas investigators in Japan and Hong Kong placed more emphasis on the organisational culture of Barings and the influence of senior management (external focus).

As a manager, in an appraisal situation, you're more likely to blame a person for poor performance than to recognise that factors within the situation influence someone's behaviour.

Actor/observer divergence

As well as having a tendency to blame internal factors for other people's behaviour (see the previous section), you're likely to overemphasise the role of external factors when explaining your own behaviour. This theory is *actor/observer divergence*.

Do you drive? A good example of actor/observer divergence most people can identify with relates to driving behaviour. If you make a mistake while driving – for example, you brake hard suddenly – you likely blame other drivers or poor weather conditions (an external explanation for your behaviour). If you see another driver make a mistake, though, you probably don't think that she has a reason other than she's an idiot (an internal explanation for the behaviour).

Imagine one of your employees makes a mistake at work. You may attribute this error to internal factors and see her as being slipshod or not working hard enough. Your employee, though, may believe the behaviour is due to external factors, such as being too busy or not having support available.

As a manager, actor/observer divergence can result in you unfairly blaming employees for poor performance. This assumption is more likely if you feel that an employee's poor performance reflects badly on you if that performance is due to external factors (which you, as a manager, have some control over) rather than the employee's internal factors (which you've no control over).

Self-serving bias

Self-serving bias comes into play because you want to be seen in the best possible light. When you're practising self-serving bias, you're taking credit for your successes (attributing success to internal factors) and blaming other things for your failures (attributing failure to external factors).

You may use the self-serving bias to explain your performance in an exam. If you perform badly, you may blame external factors, such as poorly designed questions or not being taught the material you need. If you perform well, you're more likely to give yourself credit and put the success down to your ability and hard work.

As a manager, you're more likely to try to take credit for successes (internal attribution) and blame your employees for failures (external attribution).

False-consensus effect

People tend to assume that their own behaviour is normal and expect other people to behave in a similar way. This theory is known as the *false-consensus effect*.

You may be motivated to work long hours to improve your performance and expect other people to do likewise. If you've colleagues who don't work long hours, you may see them as less motivated, whereas they may just have other demands on their time.

Some evidence suggests that managers are more likely to employ people who are like them because of the false-consensus effect. We explore fairness at work in Chapter 11.

Assessing performance and attribution

The previous sections describe the main attribution errors you may make when assessing performance at work. You can easily see how such errors can have a negative impact during employee appraisals and more widely in the workplace. For example, if your manager blames you for mistakes and doesn't accept that external factors play a part, then you don't feel that the appraisal is fair. You feel worse still if the outcome of your appraisal affects other things, such as a promotion or a pay rise, and your boss keeps you from promotion because she doesn't understand the reality of a situation.

Managers should be aware of

- **Their own attribution style:** Understanding the different attribution errors and the risks attached to attributing behaviour at work incorrectly helps reduce the risk of bias. Training managers in appraisal techniques improves the quality of appraisals; see the later section 'Training assessors'.

- **Employee attribution style:** The attributional style of employees can influence their future behaviour. If an employee has low self-esteem, they may inaccurately blame internal factors for failures. Understanding and correcting this belief can help improve future performance.

- **Unfairness:** Reducing attributional bias at work can make appraisals (and workplaces) fairer. See Chapter 11 for why unfairness matters.

Appraising at Work

The majority of organisations use appraisals in some form in the UK and United States. (Estimates vary, but we reckon over 90 per cent). Non-Western countries, such as China, Japan, and India, also use appraisals (but not as widely), although their popularity is increasing.

Appraisals are usually conducted face to face and consist of a meeting between manager and employee. You generally use appraisals to

- Assess and compare employees
- Develop and motivate employees

You're an *appraiser* if you're conducting an appraisal. You're an *appraisee* if you're receiving an appraisal.

An appraisal should consist of a review of past achievements and the setting of objectives for future performance. The way in which you assess performance and set objectives depends on the type of job. (Some jobs, such as sales roles, are easier to quantify than others.) Appraisals are often linked to rewards.

Appraisals versus assessment

Appraisals are different than assessments. For example, one of the earliest known assessment and rating methods consisted of a UK mill owner placing wooden cubes over employee workbenches. He used different coloured cubes to designate different performance levels and changed the cubes when performance changed.

Although fairly crude, this method is an *assessment* process because it monitors and rates performance. For it to be an appraisal process, the owner needed to discuss the performance with the employees and devise a plan for how to improve performance. (We don't know whether this appraisal eventually happened, or whether the mill owner just showed employees their varying performance using the cubes.)

What's the point of appraisals for employees?

The main thing that you, as an employee, get from an appraisal is feedback on your performance and an indication of how your performance is viewed within your organisation. This feedback can have a huge influence on your future performance, your satisfaction at work, and the likelihood that you stay in your job. Receiving feedback on your performance at work can be highly motivating, especially if this feedback is linked (fairly) to rewards, and plans are made for the improvement of performance in the future.

Appraisals also fulfil these functions for employees:

- ✔ **Communicating:** Communication is a good thing, particularly if constructive. Appraisals give time for discussion with your manager that may not otherwise occur.

- ✔ **Considering performance:** Assessing and reviewing performance in an appraisal can identify problem areas that may be negatively impacting performance. You often discuss training needs within an appraisal, and you can tell your manager what training you feel that you need to improve your performance.

- ✔ **Securing fairness:** You need to feel fairly treated both during the appraisal and by any reward or promotion decisions that are made. (Chapter 11 covers fairness.)

The quality of your relationship with your manager and how much you trust her to appraise you fairly and accurately influences your appraisal experience.

What's the point of appraisals for organisations?

The key thing that organisations get from appraisals is information. A good appraisal process tells you how well or how badly your employees are performing. It gives you time to discuss things with employees and uncover any problems or issues they have. It also allows time to plan future goals with your employees, and, of course, involving people in the setting of goals makes them more likely to be attained. (Head to Chapter 9 for details on motivation.)

When it comes to appraisals, organisations have the following concerns:

- **Decisions about rewards:** If performance and rewards are linked, then you must be able to monitor performance. Discussion of performance assessments forms a part of the appraisal process to allow a shared understanding of the things that may be affecting performance and to ensure that any reward decisions are seen as fair.

- **Happy employees:** A good appraisal system leads to higher employee motivation, satisfaction, and performance.

- **Knowledge:** Organisations use appraisals to gather detailed knowledge on employee (and organisational) performance.

- **Planning:** Knowing what's going on means that organisations can better plan for the future. For example, appraisals help you identify top performers. Managers can use this record of achievements when considering promotions.

- **Reacting to poor performance:** Assessing behaviour means that you notice and monitor poor performance. You can use evidence from an appraisal to create plans to deal with poor performers (such as disciplinary proceedings).

- **Record-keeping:** A systematic appraisal process results in documentation that supports the decisions made. If an employee claims that she has been unfairly dismissed, for example, an organisation can show that past appraisals and warnings have raised concerns about performance. These records help the organisation rebut the unfair dismissal claim.

Assessing Performance at Work

When you decide to assess employee performance at work, you need to consider these five aspects of appraisals:

- **Aims:** What's the aim of the appraisal? Is the goal to compare performance across employees or to develop and motivate employees? The aim should, of course, be both.

✔ **Content:** What do you intend to measure and how? This answer all depends on the type of jobs involved. You may find measuring some aspects of the job, such as number of calls answered in a customer service role, easy, while measuring quality, such as customer satisfaction, is more difficult. Think about the job roles you're appraising and the best way to measure performance.

✔ **Approach:** Appraisals are most commonly held between manager and employee; but other approaches exist. The following sections detail the different approaches.

✔ **Process:** Having a detailed appraisal process means that both you and your employees know what to expect during the appraisal. Consider the documentation you're going to use, how often you're going to hold appraisals, and how long they should last. This information should be freely available within your organisation.

✔ **Monitor:** After you've gone to the trouble of designing your appraisal, don't forget to monitor it to see whether it works! Things to consider include completion rates (does everyone get appraised?), satisfaction of managers and employees, and whether performance changes over time.

Organisations use a number of approaches in appraisal

✔ **Self:** You assess your own performance.

✔ **Downward:** Your manager assesses you – the most common method.

✔ **360 degree:** Everyone assesses everybody (well, not quite, but kind of; you can find more on this approach in the later '360 degree, and upward appraisal' section).

✔ **Upward:** You assess your manager.

The following sections detail the main approaches to appraisal.

Assessing yourself

Evaluating your own performance can be a tricky business. Clearly, you don't want to evaluate yourself as underperforming. On the other hand, you don't want to oversell yourself, especially if you know that you're overdoing it a bit.

Research by work psychologists has shown that if you appraise yourself, you're likely to inflate the appraisal a bit so that you look better. You emphasise your strengths and downplay your weaknesses. (For an explanation of why you slant your self-appraisal, check out the earlier section 'Interpreting Employee Behaviour Correctly')

Despite the inflation of positive points when self-appraising, sometimes employees are the best people to appraise their own behaviour. Employees know the job best and so have information readily at hand about their performance.

If you want to use self-reports in your appraisals, the following can help to ensure that self-reports are valid and not overinflated:

✔ **Match to external criteria.** If you know your report is to be checked against other records, you're less likely to report incorrect information.

✔ **Compare to others.** Ask employees to compare their performance to others, and they'll probably be more accurate in their assessment of their own performance.

✔ **Ensure anonymity.** If you ask people to compare to peers, guarantee that the process is anonymous.

Assessing others

If you're a manager, you probably have experience of assessing other people's work because the most common appraisal structure is for immediate managers to conduct an employees' appraisal *(downward appraisal)*.

Other types of appraisal exist, though. You can appraise your colleagues *(360 degree appraisal)* or manager *(upward appraisal)*.

Downward appraisal

The odds are that if you've been appraised at work, then your supervisor or manager conducted a downward appraisal.

Think about whether this appraisal was worthwhile. Did you get the opportunity to ask questions? Did you leave the appraisal knowing what your plans were for the following year? Did you have a clear idea of how well you were performing? If you answer yes to these questions, then you experienced a pretty good appraisal.

Managers are often required to conduct employee appraisals, but they may not like doing them. Perhaps they lack the skills and confidence to manage the appraisal situation. In addition, giving negative feedback to someone can be incredibly hard. If a manager is uncomfortable in the situation, then she may downplay any negative feedback to make the situation easier to handle. The result, though, is a less than optimal appraisal, an employee who doesn't receive accurate feedback, and a missed opportunity to take steps to improve that employee's performance.

Provide training to managers who conduct appraisals to make the appraisals more successful. (We provide tips in the later section 'Training assessors'.) A good appraisal system helps improve performance so that any investment in training pays off over the long term.

360 degree, and upward appraisal

Often used for developmental purposes, a *360-degree appraisal* (also called multi-rater appraisal) is where multiple people appraise you. Organisations commonly use this method to appraise management. Its strength is that it gives you an idea of how the people you work with see you.

This type of appraisal works on the premise that the people who observe your behaviour at work are the best people to evaluate it. You usually find large organisations use 360-degree appraisal; around 40 per cent of FTSE companies use it (the Financial Times and the London Stock Exchange includes the largest companies listed on the stock exchange in London).

If you're a manager, the people who may appraise you during 360-degree appraisal include

- ✔ Peers
- ✔ Subordinates
- ✔ Supervisors
- ✔ Customers
- ✔ Other managers/colleagues

Table 18-2 outlines the main advantages and disadvantages of 360-degree appraisals.

Table 18-2	**Pros and Cons of 360-Degree Appraisals**
Pros	*Cons*
Receiving information from numerous sources leads to a clearer overall picture of performance.	Office politics can lead to raters supplying inaccurate ratings.
Detailed feedback on performance from numerous sources raises awareness of strengths and weaknesses and how other people in the organisation view you.	Involving more people in the appraisal process makes the process more complex and time-consuming.

(continued)

Table 18-2 (continued)

Pros	Cons
Giving employees the opportunity to rate how they're managed gives them a voice, which they're likely to view positively.	This more complex appraisal process is more expensive than a simple downward assessment.
The detailed information provided during the appraisal and the raised awareness of your own strengths and weaknesses can help positive behaviour change and lead to improved managerial effectiveness and leadership.	Hearing criticism from your colleagues/subordinates can be difficult, and managers may not enjoy the process.

People can take criticism badly. Take care to sensitively provide assessment feedback to individuals.

Upward appraisal is where you're asked to appraise the performance of your manager or someone else in a senior position to you. If you're using 360-degree appraisal, you'll be asking some people to upwardly appraise.

If you want honest feedback from subordinates about a manager's performance, keep the process anonymous. After all, if you're worried that your manager will see your ratings because they've the potential to 'make you pay' for a negative evaluation, you may be tempted to say only nice things, even if they're not true.

Implementing or Improving the Appraisal Process

If you're thinking about improving your appraisal process (or implementing one), then you need to ask yourself whether the current appraisal process is

- ✔ Working well
- ✔ Fair
- ✔ Linked to the job under assessment
- ✔ Well structured
- ✔ Based on evidence
- ✔ Conducted by trained assessors

The following sections look at each aspect of the process in turn.

Appraising the appraisal process

How do you know if an appraisal system is working? Table 18-3 lists both short-term and long-term criteria that can inform on appraisal quality.

Monitoring your appraisal process to make sure that it's working well is important. If you identify problems, tackle them to make the appraisal process better.

Table 18-3	Appraisal Quality Indicators: Short and Long Term		
Short Term		**Long Term**	
Criteria	**Description**	**Criteria**	**Description**
Completion rate	If you aim to appraise all employees and appraise only 20 per cent, you have a problem. Find out why staff aren't completing appraisals. Perhaps they don't have time or are avoiding doing appraisals because they don't feel comfortable, in which case they may need training.	Organisation performance	Appraisals should link to organisational aims in terms of things like productivity, training plans, and customer satisfaction. Consider overall organisation performance and how appraisals can be designed to enable individuals to work toward both organisational and individual goals.
Action taken	If part of your appraisal involves setting aims for the next year, make sure that you review these goals to see whether staff are taking any required action. Aims from a previous appraisal can form the basis of the next year's appraisal.	Employee performance	Do you have good records of employee performance? Also, are training and aims set during appraisals resulting in improved employee performance? If they're not, you may have a problem that needs addressing.

(continued)

Table 18-3 (continued)

Short Term		Long Term	
Criteria	Description	Criteria	Description
Quality of appraisal reports	Is your appraisal documentation of good quality, giving you the information you need? Also consider whether managers are consistent in their appraisal reports. If you identify poor quality reports, investigate why and take action to improve the reporting.	Employee retention	High levels of employee turnover is a sure sign that something is wrong. Good appraisals should help you identify problems so that you can take steps to reduce turnover.
Attitudes toward appraisal	What do managers and employees think about appraisals? If attitudes are negative, then something may be wrong with your process.	Employee commitment	Less committed employees are more likely to leave, so employee commitment is linked to turnover. You can measure employee satisfaction and commitment (both in general and directly in relation to appraisals) through attitude surveys. See Chapter 4 for more on surveys.

Being fair

In the earlier section 'Interpreting Employee Behaviour Correctly', we discuss attribution biases and how these biases can make an appraisal unfair because your manager may interpret your behaviour incorrectly.

As well as unconscious attributional bias, other reasons can mean that you may deliberately inflate or deflate appraisal ratings.

Reasons for inflating appraisals include

- ✔ **Avoiding confrontation:** You don't want to have conflict with a problem employee, so you avoid it by giving a higher-than-deserved rating.

- ✔ **Denying problems:** Not wanting people outside your department to think that problems exist can prevent you from giving poor ratings.

- ✔ **Getting rid of poor performers:** Giving good ratings to poor employees can be a devious way to get them promoted away from you.

- ✔ **Protecting motivation and performance:** You protect an underperforming employee from a negative appraisal if you think that it's going to damage their motivation and performance.

- ✔ **Rewarding effort:** You know that an employee has worked really hard, so you give good ratings, even if the performance was poor, in order to reward their effort.

- ✔ **Securing a pay rise:** You like your employee and want to help them get a pay rise or promotion by giving a good appraisal rating.

Reasons for deflating appraisals include

- ✔ **Encouraging exit:** Rating people negatively (which may also affect pay and other rewards) is a way of encouraging someone to leave the organisation.

- ✔ **Punishing:** You use poor appraisal ratings as a way to punish people you have conflicts with.

- ✔ **Scaring:** We don't mean scaring people like in horror films, but scaring people with poor ratings into working harder.

If appraisals aren't accurate, then employees see them as unfair, which can negatively impact employee attitudes and performance. Research shows that satisfaction with the appraisal system leads to displaying helpful behaviours to the organisation.

People look at a number of things when determining the quality of their appraisal. If you want to ensure that employees see appraisals in a positive light, you need to keep the following in mind:

- ✔ **Clarity:** The clearer you are about the purpose and process of appraisal, the more positive the employee feels.

- ✔ **Communication:** The more communication and information flow that occurs between an appraisee and appraiser, the better.

- ✔ **Trust:** If you trust your appraiser, you see the process more positively than if you don't trust your appraiser.

- ✔ **Fair treatment:** Feeling fairly treated is essential to a successful appraisal process.

Relating to the job

Make sure that the things you appraise people on are actually related to the job and are relevant. How do you identify behaviours, skills, and abilities applicable to the job and applicable within an appraisal? We suggest that you take a look at Chapter 17 where we introduce job analysis. In that chapter, we relate job analysis to recruitment, but you can also use job analysis information to inform the content of your appraisals.

Using a rating scale

When you've identified the behaviours, skills, and abilities needed to perform the job effectively, you need to consider how you're going to measure them during appraisal. A common technique is to use rating scales.

You can choose from two main types of rating scale:

- ✔ **Ranking:** You rank employees in terms of performance, a technique most commonly used in the US. This rating scale forces managers to make tough decisions on best and worst performers. Employees don't always like this rating approach because someone always has to come last, even if everyone has performed well.

- ✔ **Absolute ratings:** Use rating scales with verbal (for example, is someone performing well, adequately, or poorly?) or numerical (for example, rating performance out of ten) intervals.

The advantage of using rating scales is that people easily understand them and therefore appraisers find the scales simple to complete. They're also good for comparing the performance of employees.

 Completion of rating scales can be subjective and open to bias. Appraisers may interpret scales differently and rate people in different ways, which reduces the fairness of the system. With any rating scale, people also tend to use the middle scores the most, which means the majority of people end up being rated as average, and comparing employees is harder.

Basing on evidence

Basing your appraisal process on evidence only, not subjective opinions or rating scales, is an option, but is only really suited to jobs where performance levels are obvious, such as number of sales made or number of products manufactured. Evidence-based appraisal can provide less information than rating scales because you're limited to looking only at measurable things.

Revisit the aims and targets set in previous appraisals to see whether performance is improving as planned.

Training assessors

If you don't feel confident or competent to perform appraisals, then you're probably going to do a poor job. Training people in the skills they need to conduct a good appraisal is important.

The type of training you offer depends on the type of appraisal system you have. Elements of training to cover include

✔ **Listening skills:** Appraisals are about listening to employees, but sometimes appraisers need reminding of this skill because they can tend to dominate appraisals by talking all the time!

✔ **Content and terminology:** Making sure that appraisers understand the appraisal process, content, and the terminology used can make it easier for people to conduct appraisals and improve the consistency of ratings.

✔ **Attributions:** If you understand the attribution errors you may make when appraising, you look out for them and are less likely to make them. Similarly, understanding the attributional style of employees can help you to manage the appraisal process successfully.

Chapter 19

Training and Developing People

. . . .

In This Chapter

▶ Taking a look at training

▶ Designing and evaluating training

▶ Investigating different types of training

▶ Ensuring that training applies to the workplace

▶ Thinking long term about development

. . . .

Training is an activity that occurs in most workplaces. In some organisations, employee training is very organised and a training program guides employees toward the training that is appropriate for them. In other organisations, training is more ad hoc. The approach that your organisation takes toward training sends a message to employees about how much the organisation cares about their career development.

Investing in training can be a wise move for organisations because they're likely to end up with better skilled and more satisfied employees. However, the value gained from training is linked to the quality and relevance of the training on offer. Paying for inadequate or irrelevant training is pointless, not least because employees recognise that the training isn't useful to them and won't be motivated to complete it. In this chapter, we explain how to design effective training that meets employee needs. We also discuss the advantages and costs of training and look at the different types of training an organisation can offer.

Talking about Training

A simple definition of *training* is gaining skills that improve performance at work. Organisations invest in training because they want to improve both individual and organisational performance.

While you'd like your employees to enjoy the training, enjoying it doesn't necessarily mean that the training worked or that the training is relevant to the job. If the training wasn't relevant – say you were sent to a class that focused on a piece of design software that you never use at work – why were you doing the training, and how did you feel about attending the course? Often, if training isn't relevant, people feel that they're wasting their time (which usually means a waste of money as well).

A better measure is whether any training provided helps someone perform their job. If it does, then the training worked! Unfortunately, though, lots of training isn't beneficial, and organisations waste money.

Many people think of training as a one-off event, such as a training course, and organisations have for many years provided this type of training to ensure that their employees have the skills they need to complete their work competently. More recently, though, some organisations are focusing more on overall employee development, particularly for higher-end jobs such as management. *Employee development* is different to one-off training because this development is concerned with continuous learning and the long-term development of people rather than the training of specific skills (although, of course, the training of such skills may form a part of overall employee development). More and more development training, such as coaching and mentoring, is available. (See the later section 'Considering Development'.)

Employees can see training as a job benefit or reward. If you make changes to the training you offer, think about how the changes may affect employees. Talk to your employees and find out what they think about any changes you're considering. That way, you know whether they're likely to view the change positively or negatively.

Probably the most important message in this chapter is the need to link training to performance on the job to ensure that the training transfers. After all, training is about improving performance, so if you're not seeing improvements, then something is wrong.

Training or learning?

Training and learning are clearly linked and are similar concepts. *Learning* is a more general concept, though, and although both terms relate to skill and knowledge acquisition, learning doesn't imply improved performance. *Training*, on the other hand, is linked to improved performance and so is a more specific term.

And while we're looking at terminology, keep in mind that if you're delivering training you're a *trainer*; if you're receiving training you're a *trainee*.

Knowing the advantages of training

Good training that transfers skills back to the workplace and helps improve performance offers numerous advantages, not only to individual employees but also to organisations. Table 19-1 outlines the benefits of training.

Table 19-1	The Advantages of Training
Individuals	*Organisations*
Skill and knowledge development	Improved performance and productivity
Increased variety of work	Safer workplace
Enhanced promotion opportunities	Improved employee wellbeing
Increased attractiveness to other organisations	Improved employee satisfaction
Performance and productivity improvements	Improved employee commitment
Reduced errors	Lower levels of absenteeism
Safer work environment	Reduced turnover

As well as offering benefits to individuals and organisations, society can benefit from having high numbers of trained people in the working population. The economic strength of a nation is linked to the skills and knowledge of its population. Think about it this way: an overseas company is going to invest in your country only if skilled workers are available for them to employ or if they can train workers cost effectively.

Appreciating the costs

In 2007, the National Employer Skills Survey estimated that the UK spent £38.6 billion on training. In the US the estimate was even higher, with Andrew Paradise (the research manager for the American Society for Training and Development) estimating that over $125 billion was spent on training. Clearly, then, training is big money. Worryingly, though, work psychologists have estimated that organisations have wasted a huge proportion of this money because training isn't resulting in improved performance.

Work psychologists who have studied the effectiveness of training estimate that at the low end only 10 per cent of money spent on training led to effective change in the workplace; at the high end, they estimated that a better (but still pretty rubbish) 50 per cent of the investment led to change. These figures are general ones, and some excellent training that produces better returns probably does take place out there, but overall the effectiveness of training estimates are believed to be pretty poor.

The quality of training and the value for money you receive from your investment in training is linked to well-designed and relevant training that ensures skills are transferred back to the workplace.

Following the Training Cycle

Think of training as a cycle. Training provision should be a continuous process, which means an organisation evaluates the success of a particular training event and uses the information from this evaluation to inform the next training event. Through this process, the organisation assesses training to ensure that it's achieving its aims, identifies any problems, and enables any necessary changes.

Figure 19-1 shows a training cycle that incorporates different stages of the training process. We expand on the different elements of this cycle in the following sections.

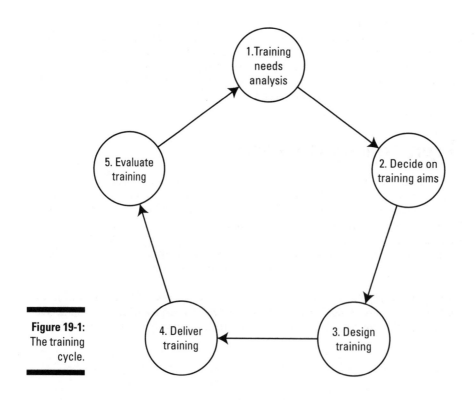

Figure 19-1:
The training cycle.

Assessing training needs and determining training aims

Training works best when well matched to the needs of the people being trained. The aim of training should be to meet people's needs. Training that isn't matched to needs can be worse than no training at all.

Conducting a *training needs analysis* is a formal approach to establishing the training requirements of your organisation. It involves finding out the details about the jobs that people do and establishing where skills or knowledge are lacking, in order to improve performance. You can then select training to meet your aim of ensuring that employees have the skills and knowledge they need.

You can start a training needs analysis by asking (and answering) these questions:

- ✔ **What training do we need?** For example, does the organisation have a problem with performance that training may help to solve?

- ✔ **Who needs training?** Do you want existing employees to develop new skills? Or do you have new employees who need training to develop the skills they need to perform their job successfully?

- ✔ **What training is currently in place?** Understanding what training employees have received, or expect to receive, can help you identify training that isn't working as it should be and enable you to design and implement training that complements what you currently offer.

Informal training needs analysis occurs all the time in organisations. Both employees and managers realise that a training need exists. Sometimes a problem in performance or during an appraisal assessment (see Chapter 18) brings to light the needs for training.

Although organisations rarely conduct a formal training needs analysis, you can take a more formal approach and conduct a full job analysis that provides you with detail about the jobs and the potential training needs of the people working in them. We detail job analysis in Chapter 17.

The key point to keep in mind is that you provide training in response to a need:

- ✔ Don't waste money by paying for training that isn't needed.

- ✔ Do improve individual and organisation performance by providing training that is needed.

Designing training

Some organisations have dedicated training departments, others outsource training, and some use an expert in the department – for example, a supervisor, manager, or experienced employee. In theory, then, anyone may find themselves being responsible for a training session.

After you know what training you need (see the section 'Assessing training needs and determining training aims', earlier in this chapter), you can start to think about the actual content of your training. To a large extent, the type of skills and knowledge you want people to develop determines the content of the training.

A manager, Jo, in a large organisation conducts a training needs analysis and identifies that her employee, Max, needs computer training because he's struggling to work with a database that plays an important part in his job. Jo needs to figure out exactly what skills Max needs to acquire so that she can then decide how to deliver the training. She writes a list of the key content required for Max's training:

✔ Segmenting data

✔ Running reports from the database

✔ Using the data cleansing function

Now that Jo knows what training Max needs, she can start to look at her options: who should train Max, where, and how much this training costs. She considers sending Max to a computer course or asking another computer-savvy employee to provide training. Finally, she decides to use an external training provider who specialises in intermediate computer skills. The later section 'Training location' explores different options.

You can often find more than one possible approach to training. We introduce many different types of training in the later section 'Exploring Types of Training'.

Delivering training

You've two main considerations when delivering training:

✔ The structure of training

✔ Where the training occurs

Training structure

The content of training has a strong influence on the structure of a training session, so, for example, a training session on computer skills is very different than a training session in first aid. You need to tailor training content and activities to match the type of training you're offering if you want to deliver it successfully.

Despite the differences in training structure in relation to content, the most effective training is based around three basic principles:

- **Clear information:** Trainees need to know exactly what knowledge and skills they are to take away from the training session.

- **Opportunity for trainees to practice skills:** By practicing what they discover, trainees consolidate their new knowledge.

- **Feedback to trainees:** You need to offer feedback so that trainees can monitor their progress. If a trainee receives no feedback as to how they're performing at work, knowing whether the effort they're putting into using newly trained skills is actually paying off can be difficult for them.

Lack of feedback makes acquiring knowledge less likely to occur, meaning that the training is less successful.

Training location

The choice of where training takes place is broadly split between *in-house training,* which occurs within your own organisation with an internal or external trainer, or *out-of-house training,* where employees receive training away from work from an external provider. Each type of training has advantages and disadvantages, as shown in Table 19-2.

Table 19-2	In-House and Out-of-House Training: Advantages and Disadvantages	
Area	*In-House Training*	*Out-of-House Training*
Cost	Can be the cheaper option because you provide your own premises.	Can be cost-effective if you're training a number of employees at once. Providing your own training in-house for one or two people may be more expensive than sending those people to an external course.
		Keep in mind that if trainees have to withdraw from training, fees are often non-refundable.
Equipment	You have to use what's available, which may not be geared to training.	You can outsource expensive training equipment (such as training simulators).

(continued)

Table 19-2 *(continued)*

Area	In-House Training	Out-of-House Training
Specificity	You can make courses specific to your organisation (e.g. using your own equipment and work procedures).	Training may be less specific to your organisation's needs because it's designed to be applicable to most organisations.
Interaction with others	Trainees meet people only from your own organisation, thus limiting interaction and development opportunities.	Trainees meet people from a variety of organisations, thus maximising interaction and development opportunities.
Ability to focus	The risk of being interrupted to deal with work issues is high because trainees remain at work during training.	Trainees can't be called away from training to tackle work issues because they're not at the office.
Openness of trainees	Trainees may be unwilling to discuss work problems because coworkers are present.	Trainees are more willing to discuss work problems because work colleagues aren't around them.
Timing	You've more choice about when you want to train.	Training providers determine the availability of external training courses and how often they run, leaving you less control over the timing of training.
Transferability	Transfer of training can be easier to achieve because the similarities between training and work are high.	Transfer of training can be harder to achieve because the training environment differs to the work one.

Consider the needs and aims of training when determining whether in-house or out-of-house training is the best approach to take. Both have their advantages and disadvantages, so considering your needs and aims alongside cost and timing issues can help you to make the best training choice.

Evaluating training

The evaluation of training is essential to good training, and organisations often build evaluation into training models or cycles. Unfortunately, organisations often *don't* evaluate training well in practice.

Considering technology in training

With the advances in technology over recent years, organisations have more and more choice in *remote training*, which involves accessing training from external providers via mediums, such as Internet courses and video conferencing. The increase in choice that technology brings to training may well be a good thing, but take care because the effectiveness of these types of newer training methods is less well understood than more traditional training methods. As with any type of training, evaluate the training's success to help decide which training method works best for your organisation. (See the section 'Evaluating training'.)

After your new training is up and running, you need to know whether the training is working. During the training's design stage (see the earlier section 'Designing training'), consider how you're going to evaluate training effectiveness. For example, does assessing performance tell you whether the training is working? Another option is to ask your employees whether they believe the training is worthwhile.

Joanne has recently sent her employee Tim on a computer training course Imagine that, after Tim's training, Joanne evaluates his progress and finds that error reports from the database have stayed at the same level. As a result, Joanne believes that the computer training hasn't worked because Tim is still making mistakes. So does Joanne then continue to pay the training provider to train other staff? Or does Joanne start to look around for a training provider who can reduce error rates by improving staff skills? We would hope the latter. Imagine that Joanne didn't evaluate the training, though. She may never have discovered that the training wasn't working.

When evaluating training, also consider how well your organisation sells training to employees. The culture of your organisation (see Chapter 13) and how committed management are to providing quality training influence how employees view training in your organisation. The view of training can influence attitudes and motivation toward training and ultimately how successful the training is.

For more on employee perceptions, see the upcoming section 'What influences training transfer?'

Exploring Types of Training

Training comes in many different forms, but you're probably most familiar with informal, hands-on training, where a colleague trains you how to complete a work task, or formal classroom training, where a trainer delivers information in lesson format to a group of people.

In the earlier 'Training location' section, we explain the difference between in-house and out-of-house training. The following tables detail the different types of training you may come across in either setting. We indicate whether each training method is formal or informal.

Think about the training content you need and consider which method is best to introduce that content to trainees. The method suitable for your training depends on the knowledge or skill that is being trained. For example, training that facilitates practice is probably best for motor skills where you need to discover how to use equipment, whereas a written format may be better for detailed information on procedures or rules.

Table 19-3 gives examples of types of in-house training.

Table 19-3	Types of In-house Training	
Training Method	*Description*	*Formal or Informal?*
'Sitting next to Nellie'	The trainee is placed with an experienced employee and finds information out by watching.	Informal
Training manuals	Training material appears in a written format. It provides structured training material to large numbers of employees. It can be a cheap method of training, but be careful as sometimes people don't like picking things up from manuals and can feel isolated and demotivated.	Formal
Delegation	A manager assigns tasks to employees, supporting and coaching them in task completion.	Informal
Projects or assignments	Employees receive specific projects or assignments to research and report on. These assignments may be individually or group based.	Informal
Training film	Similar to a training manual, a training film is delivered via video, DVD, or online instead of in written format. A training film cheaper than face-to-face training.	Formal
Job rotation	Trainees move between different jobs or tasks so that they can gain experience of different aspects of work.	Informal

Table 19-4 shows training methods that you can use both in-house and out-of-house.

Table 19-4	Types of In-House or Out-of-House Training	
Training Method	*Description*	*Formal or Informal?*
Experiential learning	Basically, learning by doing something: experience-based training. This can be done actually on-the-job (e.g. managing customer queries) or off-the-job (e.g. role play with 'difficult customers').	Can be both
Demonstrations	A trainer demonstrates how a task is completed (e.g. using a new computer system) and trainees practise to acquire the skills they need. Can be done face-to-face and online.	Can be both
Group briefings	Manager describes a new task or procedure to employees, who should then be given the opportunity to ask questions and discuss.	Informal
Computer-based training	Essentially similar to training manuals but where information is presented to trainees through a computer. The Internet has led to advances in this type of training. For example, you can now have computer-based training but also have help available online should it be needed. Done well, this can reduce feelings of isolation while completing a training program.	Formal
Action learning	Basically, learning by doing things. With action learning the trainee completes a given task (often as a group) and then reflects on the experience to learn from it (e.g. by identifying what worked and what went wrong).	Formal

Some training methods require specialist equipment or trainers with particular expertise who may not be available to you in-house. Out-of-house training is sometimes the only option. Table 19-5 details out-of house training methods.

Table 19-5	Types of Out-of-House Training	
Training Method	**Description**	**Formal or Informal?**
Simulation	Probably most widely known in the context of aviation where flight simulators are used within pilot training. Technology advances are resulting in increased simulation use in other sectors, too, such as in healthcare.	Formal
External training course	Attending a prepared training course on a relevant work topic.	Formal
Outdoor training	Commonly used as team-building exercises. Outdoor training is usually group-based and consists of groups being given challenging tasks (for example, crossing a river or climbing a high wall) that they can complete only by working together as a team.	Formal
Business games	Can be board games but probably now more likely to be computer-based. Most often used in management training, managers make decisions and take action in relation to work tasks and scenarios that are modelled in the game. The game provides feedback on the outcome of actions that can guide learning in the real world.	Formal

Transferring Training to Work

Training transfer refers to taking the knowledge and skills acquired during training and using them back on the job. After all, training isn't useful if none of the training content is used (or useful) back in the workplace.

The result of training is one of the following:

- **Positive transfer:** The knowledge or skills acquired during training have a positive influence on work performance.

- **Zero transfer:** The training has no effect on performance. In this situation, you need to think about whether your training is worthwhile.

- **Negative transfer:** Training is so bad that it makes performance at work worse! Clearly, this effect isn't what you want.

Your priority is to find out whether your training works. If you know that training is working, you've a reason to continue using it. Similarly, if you know that training isn't working, you can consider changing it to something that works.

As we explain in the earlier section 'Appreciating the costs', too many organisations waste money on ineffective training. The amount of money being wasted on training is directly related to the lack of training transfer.

As with all investments, you need to know what your return on investment is. Think about the value of your training in terms of the improved performance you receive in return for the money you invest.

Assessing training transfer

In the 1970s, Donald Kirkpatrick, professor and leading consultant in training evaluation, developed an evaluation framework to assess training. Organisations today still widely use this framework, which comprises four levels of evaluation:

- ✔ **Level 1 – reactions:** Trainee attitudes toward their training. Often measured using satisfaction questionnaires handed out at the end of a training session.

- ✔ **Level 2 – learning:** The increase in knowledge or skills following training. Can be assessed through tests or assessments.

- ✔ **Level 3 – behaviour:** Training transfer in terms of changed behaviour at work and individual performance. Assessed in the workplace, possibly by the supervisor or manager. Sometimes done formally during appraisals (see Chapter 18).

- ✔ **Level 4 – results:** Training transfer in terms of business performance, productivity, and profits.

The four types of evaluation are progressively harder to measure, with level 1 being the easiest to measure and level 4 the hardest.

Levels 3 and 4 are the most important because they relate to training transfer.

Evaluating training using Kirkpatrick's level 4 can be challenging because of problems in establishing clear links between training and business performance. So many other things can impact on business performance, so how can you be sure what the exact influence of training is?

Assessing individual behaviour and performance (Kirkpatrick's level 3) instead of overall organisational performance may be easier when deciding whether training is effective.

Research into training effectiveness

Researchers have examined which types of training are effective and have reported that the following tick the effectiveness boxes:

✔ Sales training

✔ Stress training

✔ Cross-cultural management training

✔ Leadership training

✔ Diversity training

But what's missing is information on training that doesn't work as well. Unfortunately, limited information is available on unsuccessful training. This scarcity of information is probably because of a tendency, known as *publication bias,* for scientific publications to publish successful rather than unsuccessful research.

Experts in training evaluation suggest that Kirkpatrick's model needs an additional level –return on investment. This level would consider the amount of money invested in training in terms of improved business performance.

What influences training transfer?

For positive training transfer to occur, you need to ensure that training content and delivery are well matched to the aims of training. (See the earlier section 'Following the Training Cycle'.)

All sorts of things can influence the effectiveness of training. Sometimes even the best training doesn't produce great results because of the influence of other factors.

Individual differences in trainees

Individual differences, such as personality and general mental ability, influence training success. General mental ability is believed to be the best predictor of success with higher ability linked to better training performance.

The personality traits of *extraversion* (being outgoing and enjoying interaction with other people) and anxiety are also linked to training performance with extraversion linked to training success and anxiety linked to lower performance. (See Chapter 3 for more on personality and general mental ability.)

Motivation is also linked to training success, with higher motivation linked to both training performance and training transfer. (You can read more on motivation in Chapter 9.)

Organisational culture

Having a positive training culture within your organisation is linked to training success. Think about things like whether trainees are given time off to attend training, the support they receive at work in relation to training, and whether training is presented as an opportunity for people or as something they have to do.

If people are forced to attend training, they may be resistant to it, and the training will be less successful. Studies have shown that people react more positively to training that they decide to attend themselves.

A positive training culture encourages good communication about training between managers and employees.

Putting training into practice

Receiving support is one of the most important factors influencing training transfer. Support from a manager or supervisor is most influential, but support from colleagues is also important.

Jenny works in a factory and needs to find out how to use a new piece of machinery. Jenny's supervisor, Jack, sends her to a training course. Then, the first week Jenny returns from training, Jack ensures that Jenny has plenty of opportunities to use the machinery. Jenny is able to use new skills straight away, which helps her retain the knowledge and skills she developed during training.

As well as the need for support, you need access to the right tools and equipment, as well as the time to practise new skills.

A friend of ours was trained to use a computer when computers were first introduced in her workplace. However, because she had no computer to use for over a year, she forgot all the training before she had chance to use it. She wasn't happy about it, and the organisation wasted money on the training!

If you're a manager, provide support and assistance to help people implement new skills and knowledge in the workplace following training to help with training transfer. For example, use task assignments that require the trainee to use her new skills. Be positive about training and show employees that you've confidence in their ability to transfer skills back to the workplace.

Pay and promotion policies

Employees need to feel that they're going to be positively affected by completing training. For example, you can give employees the chance to be involved in more interesting work that can help them work toward a promotion or pay raise.

If trainees believe that training won't lead to a positive outcome, the odds of training transfer are reduced.

Financial issues

The financial health of your organisation affects the amount of money invested in training. In times of financial hardship, organisations often reduce their training provision in order to save money.

In the long run, reducing training to save money isn't a good plan because you lose the benefits that training offers.

In the event of a labour shortage, increasing training activities is a way to retain good employees. Conversely, in times of high unemployment, training may reduce as more skilled workers are available, and organisations have less need to provide training.

Considering Development

Some organisations focus more on overall employee development rather than one-off specific training courses. Organisations that place emphasis on training and continuous learning are known as *learning organisations*.

Learning organisations

- ✔ View learning and training as essential to their overall organisational performance
- ✔ Have strategies surrounding learning and training that are linked to organisational development and organisational goals
- ✔ See learning and training as providing them with a competitive advantage

Developing managers

Management development is a form of training that is usually planned long term with the aim of producing good managers and facilitating the smooth running of the organisation. Management development

- ✔ Ensures that people with the required skills are available to meet the needs of the organisation
- ✔ Develops talent from within your organisation (as opposed to hiring in new managers)
- ✔ Helps encourage loyalty and commitment from employees, who can see the opportunities for career progression

Management development training helps individuals to develop the skills they need to hold down management roles. The training and development requirements of managers are related to the type of work they do. A definition of the tasks involved in management work includes four broad areas. Management training would covers aspects of each of the following areas, although specific training may be identified, dependent on the demands of a particular job:

✔ Controlling

✔ Motivating and coordinating

✔ Organising

✔ Planning

To make management development effective, follow these conditions:

✔ **Emphasise the importance of training.** Management development should be viewed as an important activity within your organisation.

✔ **Link to a business plan.** Match management development needs and the training you provide to your business plan.

✔ **Link to managerial work.** Design training to match the nature and content of the manager's role.

✔ **Link to the individual.** Make decisions about training in relation to the needs of individuals.

✔ **Make development a continual process.** See training and development as ongoing and necessary things rather than single, one-off events.

✔ **Review training regularly.** Assess the quality and value of managerial training regularly and make changes where needed.

Coaching and mentoring

Coaching and mentoring are increasingly popular types of training that are designed to provide individuals with help and advice to assist them in their job. Coaching is used most often with senior employees, and quite often the coach is external to the organisation. (For more on executive coaching, do an Internet search.)

Mentoring usually involves a relationship between a young or new employee and a more experienced person. Most commonly, a *mentor* is someone within the organisation who can assist with work-related queries, although occasionally the mentor may be external.

If you're doing the coaching or mentoring, you're known as a *coach* or *mentor.* If you're being coached, you are a *coachee* or *mentee.*

Both coaching and mentoring provide two areas of support:

- ✔ **Career:** A coach or mentor can assist you with your career planning, help increase your visibility within your organisation, and offer general advice about work problems and issues.

- ✔ **Social:** The support provided by coaches and mentors has been likened to counselling and friendship and is believed to be valuable in terms of your own career progress.

Part VI
The Part of Tens

The 5th Wave   By Rich Tennant

Don, you're obviously the nonconformist creative type in the group. Why don't you kick off this session?

In this part . . .

In Part VI, we offer a collection of interesting and helpful lists about hot organisational topics. We give tips on how to have good employee relations and look at the most stressed occupations. We also consider how you can successfully manage your manager and cover up-and-coming issues in organisation behaviour. We then explore how to encourage employee engagement.

Chapter 20

Ten Tips for Good Employee Relations

Managing other people isn't easy and requires good social and inter-personal skills. You probably know somebody who's not great at relationships and who manages to upset people without even realising it. Now think about how it would be if that person was your manager – not ideal, is it? Without good social and interpersonal skills you can easily end up offending employees, demotivating rather than motivating them, and generally reducing their performance.

In addition to social and interpersonal skills, knowledge and competencies in finance, human resource policies and practices, marketing, and the like are also important. A good manager is skilled in all these areas. A *great* manager excels in all these areas.

Think about one of your managers (past or present). Was she a good manager? What was it about that manager that made her good or bad at her job? We bet at least part of your answer relates to how well she knew her job and how friendly or sociable she was.

You can focus on several aspects of managing others to help creating good employee relations. To be a great manager read, remember, and, where possible, implement the list described in this chapter (and also check out Chapter 8 on leadership in the workplace).

Offering Praise and Rewards

The best way to get results is to manage people by praise and reward and not by fault-finding. At work, most people are told when they do something wrong, but surprisingly few managers understand the power of praise and of letting people know when they've done a good job.

Have you ever worked really hard at something that has gone unnoticed and unmentioned by your manager? Frustrating, isn't it? And it can be even worse if your manager picks up on any mistakes and yet doesn't notice your successes.

 An effective manager, like an effective parent, knows when to balance rewards and praise with negative feedback, which is key to motivating people. Unfortunately, though, managers tend to forget to reinforce the positive behaviours of their staff and often choose to focus on the negative things. (To find out how to improve motivation at work, head over to Chapter 9.)

Rewarding Effort Financially

The previous section explains the important of praise and rewards. Here, we want to take that idea one step further and suggest that you make sure that the people who are delivering the business or service have some stake in it. Effective employee relations come from individuals feeling that their efforts are valued and rewarded.

John Lewis Partnership, which is owned by its employees, is a great example of ultimate ownership, but other models of giving employees a stake in the enterprise exist – for example, having employee bonuses linked to organisational profits.

Allowing Autonomy and Control

To empower people and increase motivation and performance, strive to provide your employees with a great deal of autonomy and control over their jobs. Research has repeatedly found that people who feel in control at work, who don't feel micro-managed, and who are trusted to get the job done tend to be more productive, healthier, and job-satisfied. (Find out more in our discussion of job design in Chapter 12.)

If you're a manager who metaphorically 'looks over the shoulder' of your staff, undermines their self-confidence, and doesn't help create an open and meaningful relationship with the people you manage, you're going to have dissatisfied and unhealthy employees. Not only that, but also you create more work for yourself because you're trying to oversee everything that's going on.

Appropriately delegating tasks reduces your own workload and improves the work experience of your employees.

Engaging Your Employees

Try, wherever possible, to engage your employees in decisions that affect their jobs, directly or indirectly. The research evidence on engagement indicates that higher levels of engagement and involvement from employees not only enhances their wellbeing but also produces greater performance and more team-building.

Also, obtaining your employees' opinions about broader organisational issues makes people feel part of the wider work culture and helps them identify with the business.

And don't forget that by involving people more, you may get suggestions, help, or advice that you wouldn't have come up with alone, which can be a good thing!

Setting Achievable Workloads

The people you work with need to have reasonable and achievable workloads. Constantly giving people more and more work to do doesn't always lead to more work being done and may even cause the staff to complete less work and make more mistakes if they feel under too much pressure and experience work stress as a result. (Chapter 6 focuses on the subject of stress at work.)

Given the downsizing that has taken place in the UK and elsewhere, fewer people are now doing more work. This approach may save money in the short term, but in the end, if the workload on remaining individuals is too excessive, they won't produce quality output. Overloading your workers can adversely affect customer/client satisfaction as well as make people ill. So think carefully about the workload implications for staff when downsizing a team.

Encouraging Flexible Working

Ensure that you don't create a long-hours culture, where people feel they have to come in to work early and stay late even if they don't have much of value to do. Evidence shows that consistently working long hours can damage health and productivity and is counterproductive, and the National Institute for Health and Clinical Excellence in the UK makes flexible working a priority in its recommendations for improving psychological health at work. So, instead, try to create a culture that allows flexible working arrangements that meet the needs of the individual and the role they play in the organisation.

Employees generally react favourably to flexible working because it gives them some control over their work and home lives and can help create a good work–life balance. And sometimes personal commitments, such as child or elder care, can mean flexible working is essential to some people.

Flexible working is increasingly possible, with the option of working from home open to more and more people as technology allows people to work virtually (see Chapter 16 for details), so why not use it to your, and your employees', advantage?

Communicating Fully

Communicate, communicate, and communicate again! Let everybody know what's happening, not only in a particular part of a business or organisation, but also in the organisation as a whole.

Tell your employees about major events, such as restructurings, layoffs, mergers/acquisitions, or any planned technological innovations. Communicating with people can reduce resistance to change and means that your employees trust you more to tell them the truth about what's going on. (For more on change resistance, see Chapter 14.)

Basically, you can't communicate enough. Without communication, you end up with rumours, which frequently are inaccurate and cause worry and concern.

Ensuring Development Opportunities

Everyone in the workplace needs development opportunities. Most people value the opportunity to pick up new skills and develop themselves at work.

This development may involve further training, being given a new role, or helping to create a new product or service. Working with people on their training and development needs is a fundamental part of ultimate job satisfaction.

The right training and development is good for your employees and your business because it increases satisfaction and improves performance. Involving people in discussions and decisions about training development increases motivation and maximises your return on investment (ROI).

Getting Involved in Socially Responsible Work

Engage in socially responsible work with the community you work in. Employees like to feel that the organisation they work for is involved in and committed to the community in which they work.

You can get involved in a variety of ways, such as through local schools or sports clubs or helping with youth unemployment. The important thing is to enable the workforce to take part in representing the company to do something for others less fortunate than them.

Walking the Talk

This tip is a simple one, but so many managers fail to do it, and as a result, they become alienated from their employees. You need to 'walk the talk' and get out there, interacting with your employees. You should have regular contact with the people you're responsible for if you want to know exactly what's going on in your workplace.

If you walk the talk, you have a better understanding of your employees, their workloads, and what they do for the organisation. Crucially, you experience the problems and dilemmas faced by your staff. This knowledge and experience can help you plan for the future because if you want to know how to do things better, you need to know the problems before you can find the solutions.

Chapter 21

Ten Stressful Occupations

S ome jobs are more stressful than others because of the demands they place on the people working in them. Examples of these demands include a lack of control at work, excessive workloads, and the need for employees to engage in emotional work in order to perform their jobs successfully. Emotional labour (see Chapter 7) is a part of almost all the stressful occupations we list in this chapter, suggesting that emotional labour is an important component of what makes jobs stressful. In Chapter 7, we explain what makes emotional labour stressful and offer tips for managers to reduce employee stress. Also check out Chapter 6 for more on what can cause stress at work and for advice on monitoring and managing workplace stress.

Research carried out by Lancaster University and the Universities of Manchester and Liverpool, in the UK, studied more than 26 occupations for their psychological and physical stress levels. They found the following top ten occupations where people reported high levels of stress. All these occupations, rank highly on lack of physical wellbeing, lack of psychological wellbeing, and job dissatisfaction. The causes may be different, as you see in the following sections, but the outcomes are negative in that the employee's health and wellbeing are compromised, and stress levels are particularly high.

Teachers

Teachers lead the table with the highest reported stress levels. Reasons include the emotional demands of the job with teachers having to manage multiple relationships with pupils.

Other reasons for the high stress seen in teaching include

- ✔ Working long hours
- ✔ The interference in their jobs by central and local government
- ✔ Constant change
- ✔ Unruly pupils
- ✔ The naming and shaming of schools on league tables
- ✔ The demands of set curricula (which takes away teachers' autonomy, thus reducing control and increasing stress)

Care Providers in Social Services

Care providers working in social services are high up the league table of stressful jobs. Their clients place demands, meaning emotional work forms a large part of the job. Other causes of stress reported are excessive workloads often compounded by understaffing, the unsocial hours that care workers have to keep, and the potential negative consequences if they make the wrong decisions.

Ambulance Staff

Ambulance workers have to make life-or-death decisions each day. These demands plus interacting with ill and injured people mean that the emotional work required of ambulance workers is high. Added to this responsibility is the fact that ambulance workers are confronted by horrible scenes, such as severe motor accidents with maimed bodies or dead people, as well as people with life-threatening illnesses.

Prison Officers

Prison officers have to deal with disturbed and anti-social inmates, and work in some of the most unpleasant environments, so both their emotional job stress and basic working conditions lead to high stress levels. Prison officers also work in a severe hierarchy-based organisation, meaning that their job control is limited and bullying, by other prison staff, is particularly widespread. Their job dissatisfaction levels are the highest of all occupations.

Managers (Private Sector)

Managers are increasingly working longer and longer hours, are contactable 24/7, and have to work to a bottom line that's becoming more difficult to achieve, particularly in challenging economic conditions. In addition, managers often don't feel valued by their organisation, have excessive and sometimes unachievable workloads, and have poor work–life balance. And the plight of the manager is likely to get harder before it gets easier – employees becoming more concerned about their future means that managers will have a harder job of keeping their workforce motivated and productive.

Customer Service Workers

Customer service workers, such as those manning the phones in call centres, don't usually suffer from some of the basic work stressors. For example, they don't often have to work long hours, and they don't usually have responsibility for people. However, they commonly report high stress levels because customer service workers have constant demands on them throughout the day with often little control over how they manage their work. For example, having to follow a script while talking to customers contributes to reduced control and increases emotional labour (see Chapter 7). If you've ever worked in a customer-facing role, you know how stressful interacting with the public, face-to-face or over the phone, can be – especially if you're dealing with difficult customers who may get angry or upset.

Other stressors resulting from customer service work include little career progression and not much interpersonal time to spend with colleagues while at work.

Support at work is a good way of reducing and managing stress, so a lack of interpersonal time can be a big problem.

Clerical and Administration Staff

In most organisations, the numbers of clerical and administrative staff have dramatically declined due to reduced staffing or combined administration departments. Often, this cost-saving effort has left those remaining with heavy workloads and less available support, both of which increase feelings of stress. Employees can also feel less valued by the organisation as a result of changes and may feel their own jobs are at risk. Other stress factors include being underpaid, frequently doing menial work and having little prospect of career development and training.

Police Officers

Police officers do a difficult job, often with little thanks. Fewer police are on the frontline, and they're doing more work while facing potential danger every day. Police officers are unhappy with the mountains of paperwork they have to do and about wasting time in court during prosecutions. The work they do involves high emotional demands, and they deal with both the perpetrators and victims of crime. In addition, police officers are concerned about career progression, with promotion to higher ranks taking a long time, unless they're on a fast-track scheme. The work hours are also often long and lonely, meaning that police officers report having less family time than they want and find that the job interferes with family life.

Firefighters

The stress factors for firefighters are clear. They do a potentially dangerous job and have to work offbeat hours and spend long periods away from their family. Putting yourself in danger as part of your day-to-day working life is extremely stressful, although it can also be highly rewarding when such efforts save lives. Despite the potential rewards, firefighters are regularly exposed to human tragedy. In addition to their own personal reactions to such devastating scenes, firefighters often have to deal with the reactions of family and friends in dangerous and unpredictable situations.

University Lecturers

You wouldn't expect university lecturers to be highly stressed, but they come up high on the list of low levels of psychological wellbeing (and also report poor physical wellbeing and job dissatisfaction). These findings are supported by another survey of university lecturers that found over 50 per cent of lecturers reported high levels of psychological strain. This result is because of the changing nature of their job, which is no longer just about lecturing but about raising research funding, being managed by people who aren't trained, being expected to work long hours and producing scholarly outputs to meet government-sponsored assessment of research output. Add to this scenario the emotional work involved with student interactions, and you end up with another highly stressful occupation!

Chapter 22

Ten Tips for Managing Your Manager

In This Chapter
▶ Knowing what makes your manager tick
▶ Offering solutions, rather than complaints
▶ Being a good listener

*T*he boss–subordinate relationship is one of the most important workplace relationships in terms of your career, wellbeing, and performance. Building a good relationship with your manager makes sense. After all, if your manager knows you and your work, she's more likely to notice how good you are and what you bring to the organisation. Building a good, honest, and trustworthy relationship with your manager is fundamental to achieving your objectives at work and to enjoying your job.

Managers are taught a great deal about how to manage people at work, particularly their subordinates, but little advice helps you manage your manager. In this chapter, we offer tips for working well with your boss.

Understand Your Boss

Different types of managers exist:

✔ **Bureaucratic:** If your boss is a bureaucrat, she wants to do everything 'by the book', to follow organisational procedures and policies. If you want to influence this type of person, you need to follow the rules.

✔ **Charismatic:** If your boss isn't a detail person but is instead a big-picture type who's charismatic and not into detail or bureaucracy, then you probably have more leeway about how you can do your job. In this case, she probably wants to bask in the glory of your achievements, so you're likely to have a freer hand.

✔ **Political:** If your boss is highly political, then you have to check with her about everything you do so that you don't embarrass or undermine her political strategy.

You must understand the type of person your boss is, so assess her and think through the appropriate strategy to get what you want from her.

Never say, 'It can't be done.'

If you want to develop a good working relationship with your boss, be positive about the tasks you're presented with and find ways to get the job done. If you can complete a task, then do so and make sure that your boss knows you've done it.

If you're given a task that you doubt you can complete, instead of just saying that you can't do it, talk to your boss and provide explanations. Look at it as your job to get her to discover the problems in completing the task for herself with the help of your expertise.

Get your boss to explore the options you provide her with and ask her which approach she'd rather you took. This way, rather than looking obstructive and simply stating that you can't do something, you offer solutions and information and involve your boss in decisions.

Offer Solutions to Problems

If you've a problem at work, whether a technical one or a people one, the worst thing you can do is to whine about it to your boss without saying what you think can be done to make things better. So, in line with our suggested approach to an unachievable task (see the previous section), adopt the rule of never going to your manager with a problem for her to solve without offering a solution.

The best thing to do is to think through a few options to deal with the problem and then go to your boss to say you've had this particular issue but think that you've come up with possible solutions. This way, you're bringing a problem to her but also helping to resolve the issue – much less stress for the boss and you look like a proactive problem solver!

Tell the Boss about Your Successes

For the sake of your career, you need to make sure that your boss knows when you've successfully achieved a task. Your boss won't always know when you've done something unless you tell her, so make sure that your boss knows about your successes via a brief email or conversation.

Unfortunately, women don't tend to do communicate successes as much as men because, in general, women are much worse than man at talking about what they're good at and what they've achieved. Consequently, the boss doesn't always know as much about the achievements of female employees compared to male employees when considering people for a new project or promotion. So if you're a woman, remember to talk about your achievements as much as your male counterparts do.

Develop a Personal Relationship with Your Manager

When your boss knows you as person and you know her, it makes it easier to relate on a wide range of issues, particularly ones where other people and personalities are involved. Building a good relationship with your boss should make working together easier because you'll be able to predict each other's attitudes, behaviours, and responses to events.

Don't underestimate the social cement of a meaningful relationship between you and your boss, particularly when you need her support with a potentially risky decision, work, or a personal problem. Invest time and effort into creating social space and developing this relationship.

Go Beyond Your Job Description to Achieve Your Objectives

If your manager sees you as being committed to achieving organisational aims as well as your own, she appreciates even more the effort you put in. And by taking on roles and tasks that help your boss achieve her objectives as well as your own, your boss will rely on you more. Managers at all levels appreciate value and ultimately respect people who want to do an excellent job and take the initiative to get it done.

Give your all; don't be a nine-to-five drone. We're not saying you should work excessive hours, but do make sure that your boss realises you do more in your day than wait for 5 p.m. so that you can head home and forget about work (although, of course, everyone has days like that!).

Refrain from Bad-Mouthing

Whatever you do, don't bad-mouth your boss with anybody in the organisation because ultimately this negativity gets back to them and adversely affects your relationship. Nobody likes being talked about negatively, after all! Think about how you would feel if someone was bad-mouthing you behind your back.

Even if you feel that your boss has made a wrong decision, forget about it and be sure to support her in making different and more effective decisions in the future. Calling names and moaning about a bad decision won't change the decision and can create problems for you when the boss finds out what you've been saying.

Be Loyal

Loyalty can be difficult to find in the workplace these days because of job insecurity and frequent turnover of staff in organisations, but nothing influences a manager more than a subordinate who's loyal. Trust and loyalty are essential to developing a good relationship with your boss to enable you to achieve your objectives and goals; they're the bedrocks of an effective boss–subordinate relationship. Your boss should know that she can trust you and that you're loyal to her.

Listen Carefully

If you want to influence your manager, listen carefully when she explains what she'd like you to achieve. Sometimes you need to read between the lines to understand what a boss really wants. If you're still unsure, then check with your boss and listen carefully to explanations. Asking for your manager's advice on how she would go about it can appeal to her sense of status. Better that than press ahead and make mistakes.

Just as you like to be listened to and not ignored or misunderstood, so does your boss. Most people like other people who are prepared to invest time and effort to listen to their issues and problems.

Be Clear about What You Want

Before trying to manage your manager, think about what you want to get out of a course of action. Each time you interact with your boss in an effort to achieve one of your objectives, ask yourself, 'What do I want to get out of this meeting? What outcome would make me happy?' After you know what you want, you can plan how to get it. Think about it: if *you* don't know what you want, how can your boss? And if nobody knows, what you want isn't likely to happen, is it?

Chapter 23

Ten Up and Coming Issues in Organisational Behaviour

*I*n this chapter, we introduce some of the major recent and future issues for organisations. Many of these issues are due to the changing world of work; for example, what do organisations need to pay attention to as they enter the post-recession era and try to survive in increasingly difficult economic conditions and times of great change?

The world of work is changing dramatically, with more and more restructurings, downsizings, delayerings, mergers and acquisitions, outsourcings, and the use of temporary freelance workers. These changes have brought with them a range of contemporary issues that need exploring.

Indeed, as Machiavelli wrote in *The Prince*:

> *It should be borne in mind that there is nothing more difficult to arrange, more doubtful of success, and more dangerous to carry through than initiating change. . . . The innovator makes enemies of all those who prospered under the old order, and only lukewarm support is forthcoming from those who would prosper under the new.*

To help, here we highlight what we feel are the main challenges facing organisations today and offer a number of tips to help organisations focus on the relevant issues.

Managing Post-Recession

One immediate challenge facing organisations is managing a workforce concerned about the effect of the recession and post-recession economic conditions on their jobs. Many organisations have had to make changes at work that affect employees, causing them to feel less secure, motivated, and satisfied at work.

Paying attention to how change affects employees and communicating about change clearly and in a timely manner helps decrease resistance to change, something we discuss in Chapter 14.

The way in which organisations react to poor economic conditions and the subsequent impact on the workforce is an area that is receiving increasing attention from organisational behaviourists.

Handling Constant Change

What can organisations do to manage rapid change, in a constantly changing world of work? Change management has been in the curriculum of most business schools and management training programmes for many years, and we detail some of the theory in Chapter 14.

A lot of change management theory looks at single change events, but given the speed of change facing organisations at the moment, a need to manage constant and unremitting change exists, not just as a result of a new CEO or merger or acquisition but as a result of global competition, government or European Directives, financial crises, and the like.

Organisations need a new paradigm in understanding change management that goes beyond predictable or traditional events. Successfully managing constant change will receive increasing attention in organisational behaviour theory in coming years.

Engaging the Workforce

Engagement has been the mantra of the last few years in the human resource literature because those who study organisational behaviour increasingly understand that an engaged workforce is better than a disengaged workforce. But how do you engage a workforce where organisational loyalty has disappeared? Take a look at our top ten engagement factors in Chapter 24 for tips.

Organisations now carry out regular engagement surveys, exploring different aspects of engagement through salaries, benefits, training and development, employee involvement in decision-making, internal communications within organisations, and so on.

Organisations need to do more to unpack other factors than the traditional ones in terms of engagement, though. For example, recent work has indicated that organisations should consider flexible working arrangements to help increase engagement levels from employees. Because engagement plays a positive role in organisational performance, research into attaining employee engagement will continue for the foreseeable future.

Changing Jobs and Career Development

With the decline of jobs for life over recent decades, people have increasingly moved between organisations as they try to manage their next career move. Research in this area has brought insight into how people view their careers and what influences their career plans. For example, employees look at long-term prospects and training opportunities when considering whether or not to remain in a job or move elsewhere.

Although the current economic conditions may mean less movement overall, organisations still need to pay attention to helping people manage their careers successfully if they want to retain the best workers. One of the challenges facing organisational behaviourists and organisations is how to achieve this goal in times of reduced resources and increasing uncertainty.

Achieving Work–Life Balance

Employees are now often working longer and longer hours because fewer people are doing more work and because they're scared of losing their jobs (job insecurity). As we explain in Chapter 6, increased hours have a negative impact on the health and performance of people at work. Because flexible working has been shown to improve work–life imbalance, organisations now need to explore further the concept of flexible working arrangements, not only for women but for men as well.

Organisations need more evidence about what type of flexible working contributes to the bottom line, as well as the health and wellbeing and job satisfaction of the employee.

A number of years ago, Lloyds-TSB introduced their Work Options scheme, which enabled their employees to discuss with their human resource department an idiosyncratic flexible working arrangement scheme that suited their specific circumstance as long as there was also a business case to do so. The data collected showed that it increased employees' satisfaction and self-perceived performance.

Maintaining Health and Wellbeing

How do you enhance the health and wellbeing of people at work? What strategies are necessary to ensure a healthy and motivated workforce? Organisations need more than gyms, healthy staff lounges, and an apple a day! They need to create a people-friendly working environment that takes seriously the health and overall wellbeing of their staff.

A number of years ago, Volkswagen created their *health circles,* where groups of employees who work together gathered to discuss over lunch how their working environment could be made healthier. They would then action these ideas, with the consequence that health and team-building both improved.

Continued research into these types of initiatives will provide information and advice to organisations on how to successfully manage the health and wellbeing of the workforce.

Considering New Industrial Relations

Organisations are moving toward a new approach to industrial relations. For the last couple of decades, where economic growth was high, the industrial relations confrontation of the 1970s hasn't recurred. Times are now changing dramatically, with more redundancies, outsourcing, and the like, altering the psychological contract between employee and employer (which we explore in Chapter 10). As a result, more industrial relations disputes are likely to occur, as well as the 'them versus us' mentality of the 1970s.

The old-fashioned industrial relations model isn't working in the context of constant change, so one of the challenges of the next decade is how to protect the rights of workers but allow organisations to adapt to these rapid changes in technology, competition, and so on. Organisations need greater dialogue and a different approach to union-management negotiations; they need a new relationship between industrial/commercial partners for the future.

One approach that may gain popularity in the future is *pendulum bargaining,* where disputes are settled by independent bodies on the best case-presented basis. No negotiations take place; each side simply puts their case forward, with their wage demands or offers, and then the panel decides the winner. Both sides think carefully about what they're demanding or offering because the decision is win-or-lose.

Being Happy at Work

A growing movement is looking to create a happier workforce: people who are self-motivated, feel part of the workplace culture, who are job satisfied, and who commit fully to the organisation. The happy worker phenomenon has been around a while, but has now extended to the happy workplace, with research into this idea trying to unwrap what makes a self-sustaining, contented, and flourishing workplace.

You can find plenty of research from positive psychology about hope, optimism, and resilience in respect of individual characteristics of a happy worker, but less research exists on how to create these same constructs in the DNA of the organisation. Many companies, such as Ben & Jerry's, created happy workplaces in the start-up years, but the key is to sustain that happiness as the organisation grows and develops. Ben & Jerry's seem to have been successful, winning a number of accolades under 'Best Companies' to work for.

Psychologists need to do more research to highlight the approaches to creating a happier workforce and to ensure that the benefits of having a happier workforce are communicated to organisations.

Understanding Management Style

Recent research shows that the way a manager behaves, whatever level they are in the organisation, has positive or negative consequences for those they manage. What we need to know now is more about what kind of management style, whether transformational or transactional or bureaucratic, in particular circumstances and during growth and downturns, produces positive outcomes for the organisation in terms of greater productivity, higher levels of job satisfaction, minimal absenteeism/presenteeism, and so on.

Management coaching is a growing trend used to support managers during times of organisational change. Managers are expected to be adaptable, competent, and effective in social skills, and leadership now requires managers to reflect on their feelings and principles. So coaches, who support and maximise a leader's performance, are becoming more necessary.

Leadership is critical for the success of any business or organisation, but the interface between a particular style in a particular context and at a particular time is less understood and requires further research. To find out more about leadership, skip to Chapter 8.

Managing the Ageing Workforce

The workforce is getting older for numerous reasons, such as people living longer, retiring later, and the baby boomers entering the older worker age bracket. As a result, organisations are going to have to adapt to manage this older workforce. For example, they may need to approach training differently to ensure that older workers are engaged, and to provide health and wellbeing advice and support suitable to the age range of the workforce.

Research is increasingly recognising the need to understand and actively manage the needs of the workforce while taking age into consideration. Already the advice available to organisations is acknowledging the importance of age. As research in the area continues, more understanding and advice will follow in years to come.

Chapter 24

Ten Engagement Factors for Employees

In This Chapter

▶ Knowing the importance of engagement

▶ Considering respect, pay, benefits, and progression potential

*F*rom an organisational perspective, having an engaged workforce is good news because it means that employees are more likely to work hard and produce good results. In this chapter, we summarise some of the things that can help keep you feeling engaged with your job, meaning that you feel motivated and satisfied at work.

The well-respected Mercer group has developed a table of engagement factors through a survey conducted in seven large countries (China, France, Germany, India, Japan, the UK, and the USA). This group explored a range of engagement factors; we list their top ten, in order of preference, in this chapter. These factors are the aspects of your job that make you feel the most engaged, and the areas you should pay attention to if you're a manager who wants to increase engagement levels in your workforce.

All these ten engagement factors are important in different configurations for different sectors as well as different countries. If employers invest in these areas, they get the returns of enhanced wellbeing, health, and job satisfaction, which ultimately translates into better performance.

Respect

You like to feel respected and valued by the people you interact with, right? Well, the same is true in the workplace. Respect at work is about the emotional relationship an organisation has with its employees. Employees who feel that their organisation respects and values them are more likely to feel engaged. If you feel that your organisation doesn't value your input at work, you're less likely to work hard to achieve organisational goals and more likely to want to leave the organisation. (Take a look at Chapter 11 to find out more about how a lack of respect at work can affect feelings of fairness and what problems this problem can cause.)

Of the countries in the survey, the UK comes out on top on this factor.

Type of Work

If you do interesting and stimulating work, you feel engaged and job satisfied. If you find your job repetitive and unchallenging, however, you're likely to be bored and dissatisfied at work. The best kind of work includes variety and makes you feel like you're making a contribution to the product or service. (Job design can have a big influence on the type of work you do day to day and on your satisfaction levels, something we discuss in Chapter 12.)

France comes out on top on this factor.

Work–Life Balance

Having a good balance between the time and effort you spend at work and at home positively affects job satisfaction and limits the stress experienced at work. As we explain in Chapter 6, poor work–life balance is a work stressor.

Organisations that create a long-hours culture and ensure that work spills over into an individual's private life come out low on this engagement factor. But organisations that recognise the importance of good work–life balance, keep control of working hours, and provide working arrangements where employees can work partly from home and partly from a work environment are the most engaged (see the later section 'Flexible working').

France comes out on top of the list on this factor.

Good Service to Customers

A business culture that respects customers or clients also tends to respect internal stakeholders and therefore enhances engagement. (Respect tops this list of engagement factors – see first section in this chapter.) And, of course, if you're interacting with your customers, the experience is much nicer if they're happy than if they're unhappy, so providing a good service to customers can make your everyday interactions at work more pleasant.

UK businesses come out high on this factor, while Japanese businesses feel that providing good customer service is less important to them in terms of their own engagement and commitment to work.

Base Pay

What a person gets paid comes further down the engagement scale than you might expect. What tends to be more important than pay itself is comparative pay, which helps you gauge how valuable the organisation perceives you to be. Comparative pay is linked to fairness and equity theory (see Chapters 9 and 11), where you consider whether you're being fairly treated by looking at how you're being treated in comparison to how other people are being treated. So if you earn less than I do, but we both do the same job and put in the same amount of effort, you wouldn't feel happy about it.

In terms of base pay, the Japanese come out on top of the engagement table; they see pay as a reflection of their value to the company.

Coworkers

One of the motivating factors at work is the people you work with. When relationships at work are fully functioning and good, people are motivated and happier, feel involved and committed, and perform better to reinforce the camaraderie of the workgroup. Negative relationships at work, such as a lack of support from your colleagues, cause you stress (see Chapter 6), and more extreme relationship problems, such as bullying (see Chapter 11), can cause huge challenges, such as reduced work satisfaction and productivity.

The country that values this dimension the most is Germany.

Benefits

Benefits in this survey refer to the rewards and benefits you get from work on top of your base pay, such as healthcare provision or pension entitlement. For some people, the benefit level enhances the engagement, but this depends on whether the benefit is relevant to you. So, for example, a pension entitlement is of limited value to you if you're only working for an organisation for a limited time, meaning that your pension accrual is negligible.

Benefits are particularly notable as an engagement factor for the Chinese in the Mercer table. Chinese employees tend to look at the benefits they receive and take it as a measure of their value to the organisation; in the same way that their basic salary is felt to reflect perceived value in Japan.

Long-Term Career Potential

You'd perhaps expect this engagement factor to be ranked higher, but it comes near the bottom of the top ten factors. It may be possible that because people are now more accepting of the need to move between organisations to progress their career, the long-term career potential of a current job is seen as less important (although, of course, short-term career potential still matters).

Another explanation of the positioning of this factor is that it reflects the belief that career potential is more important for public sector as opposed to private sector workers. In the private sector, pay and benefits are the main rewards for work, whereas the public sector is traditionally seen to be a more secure place to work, and lower pay is accepted in return for job security.

India leads the other six countries on this factor.

Training and Development

When employers provide training and development for their staff, it can translate into engagement when staff feel that they're valued and that the organisation believes that they're an investment worth supporting. We discuss the importance of training and development to employees in Chapter 19.

As well as making people feel valued, training also equips you with the skills you need to do your job well. If you're asked to do work you haven't been trained to do, you're likely to experience high error levels (at least to begin with) and high stress levels. You also think that you're being put in an unfair position and are likely to be unhappy at work.

India comes top of this list; as a newly industrialised and growing country, training and development are high in corporate and individual terms.

Flexible Working

Linked to improving work–life balance, flexible working is a growing issue for employees with personal family commitments or for employees who want flexible arrangements that reduce the amount of time they spend commuting to and from work. As we see in Chapter 16, with the advent of new technology, flexible working is increasingly possible, and evidence shows that it can reduce absenteeism and increase job satisfaction and productivity.

Most countries value flexible working, but Germany comes out on top of the table on this engagement scale.

Index

• D •

FOR DUMMIES®

Making Everything Easier! ™

UK editions

BUSINESS

Bookkeeping For Dummies
978-0-470-97626-5

Persuasion & Influence For Dummies
978-0-470-74737-7

Starting & Running a Business All-in-One For Dummies
978-1-119-97527-4

REFERENCE

British Politics For Dummies
978-0-470-68637-9

DIY For Dummies
978-0-470-97450-6

Dad's Guide to Pregnancy For Dummies
978-1-119-97660-8

HOBBIES

Growing Your Own Fruit & Veg For Dummies
978-0-470-69960-7

Keeping Chickens For Dummies
978-1-119-99417-6

Beekeeping For Dummies
978-1-119-97250-1

Asperger's Syndrome For Dummies
978-0-470-66087-4

Basic Maths For Dummies
978-1-119-97452-9

Body Language For Dummies,
2nd Edition
978-1-119-95351-7

Boosting Self-Esteem For Dummies
978-0-470-74193-1

British Sign Language For Dummies
978-0-470-69477-0

Cricket For Dummies
978-0-470-03454-5

Diabetes For Dummies, 3rd Edition
978-0-470-97711-8

Electronics For Dummies
978-0-470-68178-7

English Grammar For Dummies
978-0-470-05752-0

Flirting For Dummies
978-0-470-74259-4

IBS For Dummies
978-0-470-51737-6

Improving Your Relationship
For Dummies
978-0-470-68472-6

ITIL For Dummies
978-1-119-95013-4

Management For Dummies,
2nd Edition
978-0-470-97769-9

Neuro-linguistic Programming
For Dummies, 2nd Edition
978-0-470-66543-5

Nutrition For Dummies, 2nd Edition
978-0-470-97276-2

Organic Gardening For Dummies
978-1-119-97706-3

11-37870

UK editions

SELF-HELP

Cognitive Behavioural Therapy For Dummies
978-0-470-66541-1

Creative Visualization For Dummies
978-1-119-99264-6

Mindfulness For Dummies
978-0-470-66086-7

STUDENTS

Philosophy For Dummies
978-0-470-68820-5

Student Cookbook For Dummies
978-0-470-974711-7

Sociology For Dummies
978-1-119-99134-2

HISTORY

The Tudors For Dummies
978-0-470-68792-5

Medieval History For Dummies
978-0-470-74783-4

British History For Dummies
978-0-470-97819-1

Origami Kit For Dummies
978-0-470-75857-1

Overcoming Depression For Dummies
978-0-470-69430-5

Positive Psychology For Dummies
978-0-470-72136-0

PRINCE2 For Dummies, 2009 Edition
978-0-470-71025-8

Project Management For Dummies
978-0-470-71119-4

Psychometric Tests For Dummies
978-0-470-75366-8

Renting Out Your Property For Dummies, 3rd Edition
978-1-119-97640-0

Ruby Union For Dummies, 3rd Edition
978-1-119-99092-5

Sage One For Dummies
978-1-119-95236-7

Self-Hypnosis For Dummies
978-0-470-66073-7

Storing and Preserving Garden Produce For Dummies
978-1-119-95156-8

Study Skills For Dummies
978-0-470-74047-7

Teaching English as a Foreign Language For Dummies
978-0-470-74576-2

Time Management For Dummies
978-0-470-77765-7

Training Your Brain For Dummies
978-0-470-97449-0

Work-Life Balance For Dummies
978-0-470-71380-8

11–37870